Art and Science

Art and Science

The Story of Craig C. Hudson

Craig Cunningham Hudson

AND

Elianne Hudson

RESOURCE *Publications* • Eugene, Oregon

ART AND SCIENCE
The Story of Craig C. Hudson

Resource Publications
An Imprint of Wipf and Stock Publishers
199 W. 8th Ave., Suite 3
Eugene, OR 97401

www.wipfandstock.com

ISBN 13: 978-1-4982-0401-9

Manufactured in the U.S.A.   04/09/2015

Contents

Illustrations

Photographs

Paintings

Preface

Craig Hudson grew up with a mother who had grown up in an age when family connections were very important. There were frequent family gatherings and reunions over the years. As his parents' generation grew into old age, Craig began to work on collecting family stories. Eventually friends and family convinced Craig that since he had lived through interesting times, he should write down his own story.

Craig's notes indicate that he became interested in writing the family genealogy after his retirement in 1973. His writings include *The Palmer Story* and *The Hudson Story* (both unpublished at this writing) as well as his own life story. He worked on-and-off on these genealogy projects, alternating with writing of scientific essays and painting, until health issues completely drained his energy.

For the most part, Craig was able to organize his thoughts, formulate them into intelligent sentences and put them on paper in a continuous flow with little or no editing needed on his part. I might have been inclined to think that he had rewritten his pages, save for the fact that I had on several occasions been at the house and seen him writing in this way. It has been a great pleasure for me to work with his original manuscript where, on many an occasion, six or eight pages of handwritten text would go by without need of any enhancement other than for me to type it.

Elianne Hudson

Acknowledgments

I would like to express my gratitude to my siblings and their spouses who listened and answered all my persistent questions, to family and friends who were patient and supportive, and to Louise for her delightful conversation, wit, and invaluable editing help.

Whether our histories are passed down to us in the form of oral stories or written down for us to read, understanding who we are and what came before us is an important part of our identity as individuals, as a family, as a society, and as humans. I thank both my parents for sharing a wealth of history with us. A special thanks to Mother who spurred me on, and, of course to Dad, who left me such an intriguing project.

E. L. H

PART 1

1

Early Childhood

I was born June 29, 1918 in Portland, Oregon. At this time, Portland was already a small city of about 100,000, largely electrified with many permanent buildings, a public transportation system of street cars, a gas works (producing CO from coal, called "coal gas") and quite a few automobiles as well as horse-drawn vehicles.

"Craig" is a Scottish name derived from "Crag," so it was probably Mother who selected this name; she was proud of her Scottish background. Dad told me my middle name was that of a well-known English athlete; Dad was both English and an athlete, so Dad selected this name.

Harvey and Bertha Hudson had been married on June 27, 1917 in the Palmer[1] house on 41st Street. World War I was in its final, intense stage. Dad was working at the shipyards (in Portland they built mostly small, fast sailing ships of wood, with some coal-fired fast ships also of wood). Later, Dad left the shipyard to take an office with the Artisans Life Insurance Company, of which his father was president at the time. He became the re-insurance agent for the Artisans, working with the Lincoln National Life Insurance Company. There is a very nice photo of Dad in his office at about this time.

I'm unsure of where Bertha and Harvey lived at the time of their marriage. Shortly thereafter, however, they lived on a small farm that Grandpa Hudson had rented for them. It was located in Southeast Portland on the

---

1. [Editor's Note] house of Edwin 'Ed' and Mary Palmer, Bertha's parents.

west side of Mt. Scott near Sunnyside[2]. Dad commuted each day to downtown Portland while Mother kept chickens, a cow, a sow and a garden. She had trouble with the sow which frequently broke out of its fenced area and ran the roads until Dad could bring her back.

How he commuted to town is unsure. There is still a rail right-of-way in the vicinity and I know it operated at the time because we kids used to see it. However, Dad also owned a Model T Flyer and I am certain he used it part of the time.

As the time came for me to be born, they moved into Portland and lived for a while with H S and Neva Hudson[3] at 1183 Laurelhurst Ave., where I was born. In the meantime, a house was being constructed at 1220 Ivon Street SE by Ed Palmer and his brother Tom, into which H S and Neva moved when it was finished. They briefly rented a house near 39th Street and Taggert, which I was shown as a child, but Shirley was born in the Ivon Street house in October 1919, so they must have been moved in by late summer. Dexter and Marilynn[4] were also born in the Ivon Street house, which served until 1928 when they moved to Eastmoreland.

There is a plan of the Ivon Street house which I drew and had checked by Shirley. It was small (less than 1000 ft²) with a partial basement and an unfinished second story. Originally it had two bedrooms, a bath, a living room, dining room and kitchen. When there were four children, Dad finished the second floor into a bedroom for Dexter and me. It was not full-sized, being constrained by the angles of the roof.

My mind is unusually full of memories of this house. We had coal gas piped in. Mother cooked on a gas stove that had a pilot light. I recall even now the image of that little light (flame) in the middle of the black range top and how wonderful it seemed that it should jump out and light whichever of the four plates she wanted it to light. We also had a gas fireplace arrangement in the living room, about four horizontal cylinders, hollow and perforated with holes and made of a white ceramic material. When the gas was lit in the bottom, the flames would jump upward, heating the cylinders until they glowed red and white. A reflector in the back helped the heat to be thrown out into the room. The whole unit was encased in a box about 18"x18"x10," vented to the outside. It could not, of course, heat the whole room but it took the chill off and it was cheerful.

---

2. Once Dad and I were driving in the vicinity and he tried to locate the site of the farm, but in 60 years things had changed too much.

3. [Editor's Note]Harvey Sanford Hudson and Neva Hudson, parents of Harvey E. Hudson.

4. [Editor's Note]Shirley, Dexter, and Marilynn—Craig's siblings.

In the dining room, there was a black heater-stove that operated on wood. It was where I learned what "hot" meant via burned fingers. It was also the source of ashes. Mother told me that when I was 2 years old, in the summer time when the stove was cold, I carried a handful of ashes from the stove to the seats of all the chairs in the room: fun for me, frustrating for her. Wood for this stove was stored in the half-basement. As I recall it, this stove was later replaced by a furnace in the basement which had a register in the hallway. It was still wood fired.

When I was about 5 years old, I wanted to help Dad split kindling in the basement. I was not strong enough to handle the ax safely and I nearly cut off the first finger of my left hand. It bled profusely and Dad rushed me to the bathroom so that the bleeding could take place in the sink, well-washed with tap water. I remember how much the flesh inside looked like a piece of meat. Eventually a doctor came and stitched the wound together with 3 stitches of a curved black steel needle, while I howled in pain. The finger healed nicely, although for years the flesh below the cut was numb; it is no longer and I still (I am now 76) bear that scar. This same index finger also bears another scar, near the tip. It was obtained from a saw-cut while I was "helping" Dad finish the attic into a living space.

That house was not insulated and in the winter it was cold. I remember the beautiful patterns of frost that formed inside the windows. Portland was sometimes subjected to what Dad called a 'silver thaw.' After a good snowfall, the temperature rose and the snow began to melt. Then, during the next night, the east wind blew and the rain turned to sleet. The ice formed in sheets and icicles as water poured out from under the snowfall onto the ground. I remember one severe "silver thaw" with icicles reaching all the way from the eaves to the ground.

On Ivon Street, there were only two families we children became familiar with: the D— family, a Greek family across the street, and the K— family, a family of German stock, next door to the east. There were many other families nearby and many children, but these seemed most important. Mrs. D— was short and roly-poly. She baked heavenly bread, so good that we used to beg for pieces to eat plain. She also made her own pasta and once a week the clothes lines on her back porch were draped with 5-foot long strips of drying pasta. How did she do it? I never found out. In their front yard was a quince tree, the only one I ever knew about until, years later, we had one on the Los Arboles property[5]. The fruit is inedible fresh, but makes wonderful jelly and even a kind of conserve when ground up coarsely and cooked with sugar. Fresh bread with quince conserve spread on it was a real

5. [Editor's Note] Albuquerque, New Mexico.

treat. We all loved Mrs. D— but she spoke English with a strong accent and was hard to understand. I never knew what her husband was like or where he worked. They had five children, all very pleasant. I remember throwing a rock which hit one of the girls in the forehead. I was so ashamed. Mother rushed across the street to help clean and bandage the wound. Mrs. D—, who was at the time nursing a younger child, also began nursing this one. The little girl carried the scar for all time, I was told. Much, much later I talked to the oldest girl on the phone. She was named Georgia and had kept in touch with Marilynn. She wanted me to visit her family while I was visiting Portland but I did not have the time—a missed opportunity.

The K— family was as crude as the D— family had been charming. Their yard was full of junk. Again there were five children but I have no names for any of them. The oldest was a girl and she was pretty and held a job. The second was a boy who wanted to be an electrician. Except for the oldest girl, they all seemed to be in various degrees demented. Mrs. K— was herself poorly endowed with brains. On a number of occasions that I recall, she (a very large, fleshy woman) chased one or another of the children around the outside of the house in a full run, all the time bawling like a cow. The children did not like to stay at home and often visited us, much to Mother's chagrin because they were dirty. It was possible that we all (except for Dad) came down with smallpox and a large sign was posted on the door "Quarantined" because of our contact with this family. But they had the most interesting junk to play with! Once, when explicitly ordered to stay away from them, Mother and Dad circled back from their trip to a function and found us all playing together. Dad was furious and gave me a good thrashing with his belt, the only such punishment I ever received. The siblings only received a severe dressing down. I had been the oldest, of course, and should have been more obedient.

A word about Mr. K—: he worked on the railroad and was gone 10 hours a day 6 days a week. He took the Clinton Streetcar and every other day at dusk came trudging home carrying a gunny sack of old bread for the family. He was the most dejected man I have ever seen, always in dirty clothes, dragging himself along, head down, but unwilling to abandon his family no matter what their condition.

A number of things impressed me while we lived there. On one occasion, during a severe thunder storm, a bolt of lightning hit the street not far from our house. Sure enough, after the storm, we all went out to see the blackened spot with a 1-inch hole in the middle of it in the concrete of the street. On another occasion, a lumber yard on Division Street about 10 blocks from our house caught fire. In spite of every effort, it went up in flames. The glow of the fire lighted the night sky for half an hour.

When I was about 5 years old, Shirley and I were playing with cousin Ruth[6] and some other children on 41st Street near the Palmer house. I started to run across the street and was knocked down by a Model-T Ford. I can still remember the view from under the car as it rolled over me. I was not injured but the driver of the car was panic stricken. At the time, no one realized my eyesight was deficient, so I suppose I misjudged the distance and speed of the car. We all went in to see Grandma Palmer, who ascertained that I was unhurt.

One of the early impressions I recall happened when I was six and just started at Richmond School (1924). I could not see what was on the chalkboard from my seat, so Mother got me corrective glasses. I stood at the window in my upstairs bedroom looking at the cherry tree in the backyard first with my new glasses off and then with them on. With my glasses on, I could actually see the leaves! It was such a revelation. With the glasses off, I could see the tree quite plainly but it was fuzzy. I had thought everyone saw trees like this. But the glasses were a mixed blessing: I was called "four eyes" by all the boys, which was degrading. Under such nagging, I sometimes put the glasses in my pocket which on at least one occasion cost Mother another pair. I wonder why so few boys wore glasses in those days but so many (perhaps more than half) need them today.

I must mention Frank and Peggy d'Arcy in conjunction with the Ivon Street house. In those days (and for many years after), Dad was very popular as a tenor singer in all sorts of operettas and other performances around town. Mother often accompanied him and played small acting roles whenever she could fit in. Vaudeville was on its way out, but there were still many chances for local singers and actors to take minor roles, especially with visiting troops and between movie showings. Mother and Dad were young, talented, good looking and energetic and they had more opportunities than they could handle. Dad had numerous friends among the more professional singers (since he was a trained tenor), and the two of them made friends among the more casual performers. This is where Frank and Peggy came from. They were friends of the household from about 1920 to 1940. Frank was a little heavier than Dad and wore a pencil thin moustache. Peggy was very blonde, beautiful and of voluptuous figure. They were frequent visitors at the house. During those early years, they visited us fairly often both at Ivon Street and at Peach Cove.[7] I do not remember them at 35th Street but they surely were there.

---

6. [Editor's Note] Ruth Messing, daughter of Anna (Palmer) and Claus Messing.

7. I was gone from the house during the latter part of this time so I don't know what happened to them (a vague memory says that Peggy died and Frank moved away).

Two events stand out concerning the d'Arcys; the first, at Ivon Street, was a dinner party in front of the little gas fireplace. We four children were allowed that time to sit with the four adults. Their conversation was lively. In a small voice, Shirley asked "please pass the pickles" but they paid her no attention so she repeated the question 3 or 4 times, always very discreetly because we were in awe of the adults. Frank finally heard her, twitched his moustache and said boldly into one of those silences that occur in conversation "Never mind the pickles, eat your dinner!" It could have been taken as a reprimand but he was so comical that we all burst out laughing. For a long time after that, the phrase "Never mind the pickles, eat your dinner!" was the trigger for gales of laughter whenever a situation became tense.

The other event happened at Peach Cove. At that time, it was largely covered with second growth fir trees about 6–8 inches in diameter. Grandma Palmer always wanted the trees cut down so a garden could be planted, and the idea was to make a cabin out of the logs. Mother and Dad and the d'Arcys and we children, assisted by Catherine and Arthur,[8] cut enough trees (about 50) to form the walls of a small cabin. The men cut the trees and trimmed the trunks; the ladies and we children peeled the bark. The cabin never was built. The logs were used to build a large garage. That was in about 1925; the garage still stands. Of course, when I speak of children, I refer mostly to Shirley and me because Dexter and Marilynn were too young. We have a photo of the d'Arcys with our family at Peach Cove, dressed for swimming as I recall, at about this same time.

Dad had studied voice with a well-known teacher Mme Jeanne Gemelli when he was young, before he and Bertha were married. During the 1920's he was in demand as a singer in operettas, in small parts in visiting opera groups, at churches as a soloist, for weddings and funerals, etc. Some of these activities involved costuming and I remember the two of them in beautiful costumes, going out at night. Once or twice, I was allowed to go along, and that's when I got my first taste of the excitement of backstage at a theatre.

Radio broadcasting stations came into being in 1920. One of the first to be established in Portland was KOIN[9], with a transmitter on Portland Heights and a studio in the Old Heathman Hotel. In those early years, when records and phonographs were yet to be electrified, programming was a

---

8. Catherine and Arthur, sister and brother of Bertha Palmer.

9. [Editor's Note] KOIN (originally KQP, call letters changed in April 1926) was associated with *Portland News*. KOIN Orchestra was founded in June 1926. In 1927 KOIN moved from the basement of the "old" Heathman Hotel to the grand mezzanine of the New Heathman Hotel where it stayed for decades.

Kramer, Ronald, *Pioneer Mikes*,.

problem. The stations usually had singing and talking groups as live programs in their studios. Dad became a member of such a group for KOIN. The size of the group fluctuated but a quartet seemed the most stable. One member was Dolph Thomas, who later left to join one of the moviemaking studios in Hollywood. Mother and Dad continued to see the Thomases into the 1950's. Another member for a while was Arthur Johnson[10], but he had high aspirations and went to New York to make a lifetime of singing on the stage there. Another man from the KOIN days was Joe Sherman, who played banjo, and perhaps cello.[11] Various other members of the studio group were Dad's friends for years.

Back to the Ivon Street house, I must add some memories of what went on outside the house. Mother and Dad always had a garden between us and the K– family, a space perhaps 30' x 100.' Part of it was flowers and part vegetables. In those days, tomatoes were not popular; Grandma Palmer called them "love apples" and because they were a member of the Belladonna family (deadly) she shunned them. By 1936, however, they were widely cultivated. I remember also Dad's large canna bed in which he had about 30 plants for a wonderful summer showing. Mother planted peas, beans, carrots, lettuce, and potatoes (also a member of the Belladonna family!), and various flowers. I remember nasturtiums particularly because Mother taught us how to bite off the little tail and suck out the honey. Earwigs, with sharp pincers on their abdomens, were a garden pest. I always feared that they could bite, but they couldn't. I never have seen them anywhere else other than the Pacific Northwest. There was a large compost pile near the garage and we children liked to climb up to the ridge of the garage (by ladder) and then slide down the roof to land on the compost.

Mother mostly did the shopping, but sometimes I was sent to the bakery on Division Street for bread. Franz Bakery made large fat loaves for sale (nearly as good as the bread of Mrs. D); but then came sliced bread and the quality changed, more like what we have today. Franz Bakery was downtown, but the little bakery near us also made and sold cookies, cakes, etc. However, we seldom bought these because Mother baked frequently. There was a drug store next door. I was very tempted by the licorice bars

10. I met Arthur in Albuquerque in the 1960's, after he had retired and was living with his brother Raymond Jonson (he preferred this spelling of his last name). Raymond was an artist of considerable fame and I had made friends with him.

On one of Mom and Dad's visits to Albuquerque, I arranged a visit between them and Raymond and Arthur. We talked for about an hour but there was no spark between Arthur and Dad. Their careers had diverged too long ago, and Arthur was a little scornful of Dad's singing career since he (Arthur) had become a professional on the New York stage—but not a very well known one.

11. He, too, I met in Albuquerque. He had become a ceramicist of note.

with a metal star on the side to make it look like chewing tobacco; they cost 1 penny, but I seldom had even this tiny sum. The druggist annoyed me constantly by calling me Cunning Ham and making some kind of joke at my expense. Much of our grocery shopping was done at Krupke's store and meat market on Clinton Street at the end of the streetcar line. Mother had an account there and I often went with her to carry things home. Essentially all of our meats were purchased there but we did not eat much meat. A man with a horse-drawn wagon came down 41st Street once or twice a week crying "Fresh Fish, Fresh Fish." The wagon was enclosed, with the back open. It was full of ice and fish; the ice constantly melted, leaving a trail of water on the street. Mother bought from him whenever he came but, of course, he couldn't come in the winter, and sometimes she couldn't run out to 41st Street (about half a block) to catch him. There was a fresh produce (green grocer) peddler who also came down 41st Street in a Model T truck with the back full of produce of various kinds. Mother bought from him also.

As a child, the only career I ever aspired to was that of the street cleaner. He had such an interesting job. Trash (from overhead trees, etc.) accumulated in the gutters of 41st Street. A man with a big stiff broom went down the street sweeping the trash into small piles. The piles were all the same size but were spaced close together or far apart as the situation required. Following him came a truck with another man standing on a small platform at the rear corner. His job was to wield a broad shovel in such a way that he could, in a single stroke, pick up a pile and toss it into the slowly moving truck: scrape, lift, toss; scrape, lift, toss. The speed was, of course, limited by the sweeper, who really worked hard. I admired the man standing on the little platform, wielding his shovel: scrape, lift, toss. He was my first role model; I wanted to do that when I grew up.

Experiences at Richmond Grammar School are mostly a sort of haze. I remember my first day. Dad spoke to me on the driveway as I was playing and he was driving off to work. "You'll have to start school today" he said. "It's the law and it will be a big part of your life." Mother was busy with the younger children, so cousin Ruth took me to the school where she was in her second year. Somehow I was registered and wound up in a classroom with about 15 other students my age. The Messings lived next to the Palmers at that time in a house stained dark brown. Going past our house was on Ruth's way to school, which was about 6 blocks to the north, across Division Street, a rather busy street. I remember having to take a nap in the school room, on a pad laid on the floor. I remember struggling to see the chalkboard on which the characters were very fuzzy. I must have learned how to read rather quickly because I quickly became a bookworm. However, I do not remember using the simple-minded books I have since seen children using nowadays.

I started school in September 1924. The most clear-cut memories of these early times are of games in the school yard at times when classes were not held. There was a softball diamond but only the older boys were allowed to play. Mumbled Peg[12] was a game I could sometimes get into, and I was rather good at it. It consisted of placing a short stick on a wall (usually the school's foundation wall) so that half of it extended out away from the wall. That half was then struck by a longer stick, making the short stick flip end over end to fall some 10 or 12 feet away. Lines were traced in the dirt so that the distance would be judged, and points were given. Larger boys did not necessarily have an advantage because much depended on the shape and weight of the small stick and on how it was struck. There was always a competition to find the best stick, but I do not remember fights or quarrels breaking out. Being Oregon, it rained on our game frequently (which stopped softball but affected mumbled peg very little).

I remember having frequent colds and communicable diseases of which smallpox and measles were the worst because the city tacked large labels on our front door proclaiming "Quarantine" followed by the name of the disease. For me, the measles was the worst because I had to live for 3 days in a darkened room to protect my eyesight. Smallpox was especially hard on Marilynn, hardly more than a baby, because the spots itched. Mother wiped oil of witch-hazel onto them with the tip of a feather, which may have prevented development of pock marks which frequently characterized smallpox. We all were forever afterward immune to smallpox vaccinations, though they were frequently attempted.

The polio epidemic had hardly got started. We were, nevertheless, fortunate not to come down with it. Ruth contracted scarlet fever and I remember that the Messing house was sealed afterward and fumigated. The family had to live elsewhere for several days.

My problem was rheumatic fever (summer 1928). It sometimes enters the body after a severe sore throat and I surely had many of those. The medical profession did not yet know to have the tonsils of children removed[13] (and they did not yet know of antibiotics) and my tonsils were almost always infected. I do not remember the early stages of rheumatic fever, but after a certain point it settled into my hip joints. It is a disease of the heart valves,

12. [Editor's Note] There are several spellings of this game. Originally it was a game of tossing a pocket knife into the ground. The game Craig remembered was probably a safer version of this game.

13. [Editor's Note] Actually tonsillectomy was a well-known surgical procedure at this time. Perhaps this family or the family doctor had negative opinions about it. .

so that the major treatment was associated with my heart. Once a day, for about a week, the doctor came to the house where I was confined to a bed in the dining room. He placed an electric machine on my bare chest and turned on a very weak current. I have no recollection of the electric current, but when it was on, a tiny metal figure on the top of the machine hopped and danced about, to my great amusement. I was strictly forbidden to get out of bed. Once I tried and literally collapsed, so I did not do that again.

For several days I had a very painful ache in my joints especially in my hip joints. The doctor prescribed a concoction of fish liver extract flavored with chocolate. It tasted awful, sorely tested my love of chocolate and seemed to have no effect. Grandma Hudson had a much more direct approach. According to her Christian Science teachings, the pain was not mine. She spent hours telling me over and over to reject it. I wanted to and I tried hard but could not reject it. That was a lesson I never forgot. Real pain can never be rejected by thinking about it, although minor pain can be suppressed by willing it so.

Eventually I got better but I was so very weak. Actually, it took years for my strength to return, and the heart valves show scars to this day. Many patients of rheumatic fever were not so lucky. I have been able to live with myself quite well but vigorous sports of most types have been out of range. This saddened Dad who was always a vigorous and well-coordinated athlete. Nowadays, rheumatic fever is readily treated in this country and its after effects are now rarely seen.

I remember an interesting occurrence while I was sick with rheumatic fever at Ivon Street. Grandma Palmer asked if there was anything I'd like her to bring me from Peach Cove. It was a nice gesture and I asked for a pail of water from the well. I had always enjoyed that well water when it was fresh. But by the time the pail got to me, warm from the long ride, it tasted of minerals, not at all the taste my memory held. I gulped a glassful and poured the rest out, forever after aware of the tricks the emotional memory can play.

During our stay at Ivon Street, it was easy to walk to the Palmer house (2 blocks away) and actually not very far (13 blocks) to the Hudson house on 28th street near Tibbets. In order to get to the Palmer house, I had to walk along 41st Street crossing Clinton Street. The streetcar track on Clinton Street ended just short of 41st Street and I recall as a child being fearful that the 'beast' with its one eye (the light), while stopped at the end of its track, would charge up to eat me. So I ran quickly across its path, knowing that it could not move fast enough to get me. Actually, the rails ended, but I didn't consider that. I soon outgrew this childish notion.

Streets in those days (mid 1920s) were made of a kind of macadam, as they are today, but in places there would be pools of tar. On hot days (always

100° on July 4), the tar softened and could be dug out with a stick. We kids loved to chew gobs of this tar-like gum, even though it didn't taste very good. Of course, this was forbidden. Another gum that was used was cherry tree gum. When borers entered the bark of a cherry tree, a large gob of sap oozed out. Grandpa Palmer showed us how to use this, left over from his childhood experiences. If the cherry gob was not fresh it would not chew; rather it crumbled in the mouth. Chicle gum[14] existed but we seldom had any.

Walking over to the Hudson house was a challenge because to do it one had to go out of sight of familiar landmarks. I knew about the rectilinear layout of streets but it took real willpower to go on pure logic alone. The first time I got lost, but was able to re-orient and find the way. I followed the Clinton Street tracks but cross streets were not always marked.

Staying with Grandma Neva (Hudson) was bitter-sweet. I very much enjoyed the biscuits she made to have either with chipped beef gravy or with butter and jelly. But I also had to sit with her every morning I was there—except Sunday—to read the Christian Science lesson. This consisted in reading aloud alternatively selected passages from the Bible and from Mary Baker Eddy's book[15]. It never made any sense to me; the passages seemed unrelated, and it was a big bore lasting an hour.

On the Sundays I was there, Grandpa Hudson drove us to the First Church of Christ Scientist and we sat on hard benches listening to two other people reading the same lesson over again—but not Grandpa; he ducked out to play golf. Mostly it was a bore, but on one occasion there was a little excitement. About 4 rows ahead of us, a man suddenly vomited and slumped over in a coma. What a mess. He was very well dressed, as was everyone in the church. The ushers quickly rushed down the aisle and carried him out. However, the readers hardly paused in their reading and the church acted as if nothing had happened, even as the ushers were cleaning up the mess. I later learned that the man had suffered a heart attack and died.

The services were always broken by songs sung by a tenor or a soprano. I enjoyed this although the songs were not very inspiring. I often thought about Dad; in fact, I usually day-dreamed through the entire service. But at the end, there was always Grandpa with his cigar and later a delicious dinner.

14. [Editor's Note] Chicle gum was made from the gum from a Manilkara chicle tree native to Mexico and Central America. Natural chicle is not widely used anymore to make chewing gum.
Wikipedia, *Manilkara Chicle.*

15. [Editor's Note] Craig is probably referring to Mary Baker Eddy's book "Science and Health," first published in 1875.

Going to the beach was very popular, often just for the day, usually at a place within easy driving to a golf course. Grandpa (Hudson) and Dad were habitual golfers, enjoying it rain or shine up to the time of their deaths[16]. In these early days, Claus Messing (Mother's brother-in-law) and Dr. Bemis (an optician friend) were frequent partners. Even Maurice Hudson (Dad's brother) and Arthur Palmer (Mother's brother) played occasionally, and Thor Hyslin (Mother's brother-in-law) whenever he could. Mother and Grandma Neva went out a time or two, but were too slow to keep up. Favorite places were Gearhart, Agate Beach[17] and Yachats.

The Gearhart golf course was attractive because it was walking distance from Aunt Emma's[18] cabin on the outskirts of town. On several occasions, the Messing and Hudson families stayed at the cabin, all jammed into this one room house—six kids sleeping on the floor and the four adults using the two beds. At that time, there was still good clamming and crabbing on the beach so we lived on clam chowder and crab au gratin[19], and blueberry cobblers made from berries we picked along the roadsides. Claus and Harvey drove us down to Gearhart in two cars; during the week they stayed in Portland to work. During the weekends when they were there, the two of them played golf.

We were fond of Aunt Emma and her boys and would have enjoyed having them stay with us. But there wasn't room enough, so when one group was there, the other wasn't. This was in about 1925 to 1927.

Some of the beaches were piled high with logs. This was the result of the vigorous logging done in the 1920s and 1930s. Escaped logs floated down the rivers, were caught by the ocean currents and washed up on the sand. Usually they were 1–3 feet in diameter; but once in a while a big one 5–6 feet in diameter washed up. The winter surf piled them like matchsticks into barricades higher than my head. We children, in spite of warnings from our elders, climbed all over the logs. Of course it was dangerous. It was strange how in a pile of logs, there were always a few which were loose, so that if one leaped from log to log—as Ruth and I loved to do—one might be surprised by one which rolled or teetered. That made leaping across the pile an adventure! We were never hurt, except once when I jumped from a large

16. In fact, Dad played golf at least once a week up to the month of his death at 94.

17. In 1987, 10 years after Mother had died, we took Dad on a trip to the beach with us. He wanted to stop at the Agate Beach Golf course and talk about old times but there was no one left there and the young manager couldn't take the time to reminisce. It made Dad feel terribly old.

18. [Editor's Note] Imogene (Emma) Reed Johnson, aunt to Bertha Palmer.

19. The way to prepare clam chowder and crab au gratin was learned and is still practiced by me, as part of our favorite menu.

log to the sand and sprained an ankle. The sand seemed so soft—how could this happen? That was a lesson never forgotten.

Logs could be very dangerous, if being rolled in the surf. Long logs (i.e. 20 ft. or so) were not rolled as unpredictably as short (10 ft.) ones. Waves race in at a speed greater than a child can run, and every 7th wave is especially high. Children loved to play near logs rolling in the surf. Two of my grammar school friends were killed when logs they were playing near rolled over them.

2

Peach Cove Memories

The rural properties at Peach Cove on the Willamette River were obtained separately. Ed Palmer bought his 16 acres in about 1915. At that time there was no road to it; access was by boat. But shortly after, the county put a road through to service the farmers nearby. Grandpa Hudson's piece (2 acres) was obtained in 1924. It lay adjacent to the Palmer property and a gateway was cut through the fence so that, as far as we kids were concerned, the whole place was our playground. The Palmer property had been logged off in the early years and was grown up to second growth forest. The Hudson property had been a peach orchard and some of the trees still bore fruit. There was also a small stand of alder trees.

The Palmer property, where the ground was open, was planted to garden. The Palmer family had a strong attraction to the land for agricultural purposes. The land was loamy and fertile. Corn, beans and potatoes grew readily. With a little more effort, one could grow boysenberries, squash and cantaloupes. Grandpa and Grandma Palmer organized the gardens; Claus and Arthur did much of the work. Various berries grew wild in the woods and along the hedgerows: salmon berries, huckleberries, blackberries, salal berries. We children picked them, a mixture of whatever we could bring in, and from them Mother and Anna would make cobblers.

As small children, we loved to play (on the Palmer side) in a small patch of bracken, a kind of fern that stands like a tree about 3 feet tall with spreading green branches at the top. On our hands and knees, we made paths through this little forest and spent happy hours playing hide and seek.

After I discovered the story of Tarzan[1], we tried running through the trees with no clothes on. Of course the branches and brush and forest floor (in spite of its mat of moss) was very scratchy and these sessions didn't last long. I had to take the Tarzan myth as a highly romanticized picture of reality.

One of our favorite times in late summer was when the potatoes began to form. Pulling the plants out of the ground gave access to potatoes about the size of cherries. The skins were very tender and, after rubbing off the soil, they were sweet and delicious to the taste. Even to this day, I enjoy eating raw potatoes of the white variety.

Near the gate but on the Palmer side was an old rotten stump. When it was finally knocked over, deep inside the roots we could see an eerie light at night that Dad called "phosphorous." It lasted for several nights, slowly fading out, and was for us an awe-inspiring sight.

On the Hudson side there was a giant maple tree whose large branches were just right for climbing. The trunk was covered with moss and tiny ferns. When the roots of the ferns were pulled out and rubbed clean, they tasted like licorice. Ruth, the oldest of us 6 cousins and the more experienced, showed us how to make cigars out of maple leaves and we all tried them. The flavor was rather mild when the leaves were dry; quite strong when the leaves were green.

Near the back porch of the Hudson house, stood a large alder tree with widely spaced limbs up the trunk. Now alder is a smooth barked tree which is just right for boys to climb. One has to be wary of the small branches because alder is a brittle wood, but close to the trunk, the limbs are strong. Remember that I was a weak spindly youth. The Tarzan image was strong in my mind. So I climbed slowly up the tree as far as I could go, then dropped rapidly down slowing my speed just enough hand over hand to arrive safely at the bottom. What a rush! How inspiring! For a few seconds anyway.

One of the summertime pleasures was the dust bath. When the ground dried out, a deep layer of dust formed. We children loved to roll in it, stamp in it, wash in it. Then, when an adult came by and ordered us out of it, we went down to the river and washed off.

The Hudson property was little used for gardening. H S had some fruit trees planted but he had no garden tools, so the grass took over. However, there were good peaches, apricots, and plums. The Hudson property was used most often for picnics for the Artisans[2]. Eventually people came in uninvited for their own private parties, so the entrance had to be closed.

1. [Editor's Note] Craig is referring to Edgar Rice Burroughs' book "Tarzan of the Apes" first published in pulp magazine in 1912 and finally in book form in June 1914. Bill Hillman, History of Tarzan.

2. [Editor's Note] Artisans Life Insurance Company.

Grandpa Hudson had many picnics but I hardly knew any of the people at all. Exceptions were Bert (Smitty) and Mae Smith from Tacoma. They had been friends of Grandpa Hudson and Neva when Grandpa had been with the US Customs Service and Dad and Maurice had been boys. Bert was a very short, stocky Irish man; Mae was a foot taller, slender, and must have been rather pretty as a young woman.

Bert drove an old, large Buick, one of the original models with open sides that had to be covered by snap-on fabric panels with glass windows to keep the rain out. There were also little holders for small vases of flowers on the inside. The headlights were separate cans on the front and the spare tire was stored in a "boot" in the back. The wheels were made of wood spokes like wagon wheels. When he sat in the driver's seat, his eyes barely showed above the windshield bar. The windshield was in two sections: the lower part was fixed; the upper part could be tilted back for circulation. Everything was painted black. For several years, Bert was chided about getting a newer model, but he never gave up the old one.

Bert owned and operated a shoe repair shop in Tacoma that employed about six men. When, during the depression, the shop failed, he killed himself. They had had a son about my age who had died of a fever. I always thought of them as tragic figures. Mae lived until WWII.

One of the favorites at Grandpa Hudson's picnics was homemade ice cream, which he made in quantity (perhaps 10 gallons at a time). Dad and Maurice and Claus turned the cranks on three makers, aided by friends who came early. One thing I remember: H S loved it and ate it by the bowlful[3]. His teeth were all gone so he had no problem with chilling them as the rest of us did. He also smoked cigars constantly. He used to give us children the bands off them and I still remember the feeling of crushing the paper band when I flexed my finger.

We spent much of our summer vacation times at Peach Cove. A distinct memory I have happened when I was 13 or 14 (1931 or 1932). The occasion in mind was in mid-summer and it was dry and hot. There was very little breeze and insects buzzed and birds chirped. Otherwise, it was very quiet. On that particular occasion, the two families of Maurice and Harvey had been left at the Hudson house for the week with plenty of food, nothing to do but to explore, play games and tell stories. In this warm, quiet indolent atmosphere, we children fled like leaves before the wind away from

---

3. He also complained to me about a perpetual thirst. He drank water all the time and, I presumed, also had to urinate frequently. He said his mouth was always dry. In later years he was treated with insulin shots for diabetes, and I understood that thirst was a prominent symptom.

the house (except at meal time). Mother and Lena[4] were left at the home to relax, read, or do whatever came to mind.

We were playing barefoot out under the big maple tree. I left the group to return to the house for something left in the loft where we slept. I silently (but through no intent) on bare feet came up onto the back porch, through the kitchen (all doors were wide open to coax a little air into the hot house) and as I turned to go up the stairs to the left, I was suddenly arrested by a strange sight. There in front of me were Mother and Lena standing in front of a large mirror stripped to the waist looking at their breasts! I had never before seen a mature woman's breasts and it was a shock. After a second or two, I turned and fled. Perhaps they saw me; Mother never mentioned it. Years later, in thinking back, I concluded that Lena, who died of cancer, was perhaps just beginning to be worried about developing lumps in her breasts and was checking with Mother to have a basis for comparison. They had clearly thought they were alone, with the children playing far away.

For me, it left an indelible memory. The spirit of our house had always been the suppression of all things sexual or even very personal. I was never given any sexual guidance, although I suppose the girls were coached by Mother when they began to have periods. Perhaps Dad was supposed to talk to me, but he never did. I often wondered later what happened between Mother and Dad on their wedding night. Years later when I entered Reed, I found that all boys had to submit to a physical exam, including a genital exam. I had never been circumcised and I did not even know that the foreskin could be drawn back. So when the doctor asked that it be done (checking, I am sure, for venereal disease), I could not understand what he meant. I learned more in those ten seconds about my penis than in my previous 20 years.

The happy times on the Hudson property at Peach Cove came to an end in about 1937 when H S had to sell it in order to finance his big house in Portland.

On the Palmer place, picnics were also held. These were to bring together the numerous branches of the Palmer family. Edwin was one of 14 children, of which only 4 were girls. Of the 10 boys, 7 remained in the Portland vicinity. I only remember 5 having come to the picnics and then only in the early days. Most of the clan that attended the picnics over the years was the offspring of the 4 girls. Of all these Palmer offspring, I have kept in touch with only two through the years: Louise (Root) Godfrey[5] and Phoebe

4. [Editor's Note] Lena Marion Lewis, wife of Maurice Hudson.

5. [Editor's Note] Louise (Root) Godfrey is a second cousin to Craig on the Palmer side of the family.

Ann (Bosworth) Hocken[6]. There were lots of Mother's generation (perhaps 20) and quite a few of my generation. Some of the men had died, most had moved away[7].

The picnics began in 1925–30 (no records were kept) and stopped in about 1940 when Ed had a stroke and was no longer interested. That is not to say there have been no picnics since; there have, but only with the close family.

Bathing in the river was always a big event because of the July heat. A few times, Grandpa Palmer donned an old 1900-style bathing suit (with moth holes) and joined us in the water. He always wore a broad brimmed straw hat and did a little dog paddle. Swimming was not important to him; bathing was. Grandma Palmer never ever went into the river. Going into the water near the house was not as nice as going in across on the island where a sand beach had built up. There were snags to watch out for, the water was swift, and the bottom was rocky. So whenever we could, we went to the sandy beach, especially the one called 'the Point,' a short walk up the river to a bend where the beach was quite large. This lasted all through the 1930s but by the end of the war (1945) the property along navigable rivers had been set aside for public use and "the Point" was used by many visitors. Losing privacy took away much of the fun.

On a number of occasions I went to Peach Cove with Grandpa and Grandma Palmer. On one such occasion, I carried a lunch to eat out in the fields while Grandpa and I were working and it contained a piece of cheese. I broke it in half and offered half to him. He declined and said "I used to play with Indians. Do you know what they called cheese? Choke-um-ass because it tends to make one constipated." He enjoyed a little milk in his coffee but otherwise dairy products were off his list. He would not even put butter on his pancakes. On another occasion, in winter, we had gone out to a log he was cutting with his great double-bladed ax. I stood a respectful distance away watching when the blade glanced off the wood with such force that it flew out of his hands directly at me. The handle struck me flat across the forehead which rather dazed me. It must have frightened Grandpa but all he did was shake his head slowly. Neither of us said a word either then or later. His grip had been compromised by the freezing weather, (his leather gloves

6. [Editor's Note] Phoebe Ann (Bosworth) Hocken was a second cousin to Craig on the Palmer side of the family.

7. The picnics left a strong impression on the people who attended. In 1994, I called together the cousins of my generation for a restaurant lunch; there were only 6 of us present (Phoebe Ann couldn't come). The family that used to be so close had blown to far corners.

were stiff and slick) and by the fact that he only had one thumb to grip with (having lost a thumb in an accident when he was a child).

Mother told a story about Grandpa Palmer that always awed me. Poison oak grew everywhere at Peach Cove and we children suffered greatly from it. But Grandpa was immune; whenever we discovered a patch, the call went out "get Grandpa to chop it out." The reason, according to Mother, was that as a young lad playing with his brothers on the farm at Mt. Angel he was the designated horse. They cut (unknowingly, of course) a branch of poison oak to serve as a bridle in Grandpa's mouth. His mouth and throat swelled closed and for a week he was near death. Finally he recovered and was ever after immune to poison oak—the only person I have ever heard of who was so blessed.

In the early days at Peach Cove, when the place was isolated, there were two farms nearby: the Hays farm and a bachelor's farm (I don't remember his name). Grandpa Palmer knew both Mr. Hays and the bachelor and borrowed horses from them for plowing from time to time. I went with Grandpa to the bachelor's place, but I was frightened of him. Mrs. Hays, on the other hand, made me feel very welcome. Mrs. Hays was a great, fat, jolly woman and I loved watching her at chores such as cleaning the cream separator. It was mechanical and had so many parts; but I was never there when the crank was actually turned (at the crack of dawn). Mother taught me how to separate cream by skimming, by the use of a churn, and by use of a jar tilting back and forth; but those methods were so very slow. However you did get butter directly, whereas separated cream was still liquid.

The Hays boy was my age and we had some fun together. He had very little time free from chores, however, and so we never became close. Eventually he was sent off to school some place and I never saw him again.

Grandma Palmer made buckwheat hotcakes every morning and I thought they were delicious. I also enjoyed Grandma Hudson's fresh biscuits with creamed chipped beef. Jeannine and I have tried to make such dishes for our family, but no one likes buckwheat and the chipped beef isn't what it used to be.

Electrification didn't come to Peach Cove until the late 1930s. Until then light was generated by flash lights, kerosene lanterns and a few pressurized "white gas"[8] lamps with mineralized wicks. We were always very careful with fuel lamps and never had an accident. Candles could be used at bedside, but they didn't last very long.

A mechanical crank-wind gramophone with a bell-shaped speaker and steel needles was there, used by us kids to play the old 1920-style record

8. [Editor's Note] i.e. gasoline with no additives.

"I used to think that he was my young man. But mother caught his eye and they got married on the sly—now I have to call him father" or *"yes we got no bananas, no bananas today. . ."* and on and on; and something about a young husband complaining because his wife had a dress *"with 64 buttons up the back"*; and more that I have forgotten.

One ingenious visitor to the Hudson place had even rigged up a small engine with levers and pulleys and belts to the ice cream makers and the pump. It worked after a fashion, in principle one might say, but it was wild and dangerous and had to be abandoned.

There were a couple of gasoline engines: one was a one-cylinder 5-hp engine used to run a wood saw; the other was the old Fordson tractor that replaced the horses. Both these engines are still at Peach Cove, now rusted and useless. The most important uses of the gasoline engine were (1) to power the plow, (2) to power the wood saw, and (3) to power the centrifugal pump that was placed down at the river to lift water up the 50 feet to the fields.

3

Middle Childhood Years

In 1928, Dad began construction of the house on 35th Avenue. It was late summer of that year that I fell ill with rheumatic fever. The house was ready to move into in late fall. Mother must have had her hands full dealing with a sick child and arranging the move at the same time. But we did move and in January of 1929, I was enrolled in Duniway School in the 5th grade. I had missed one semester. I continued to be one semester behind the usual school year all the way through my public school career.

For many months we were getting used to the new house. For the first time, I was required to accept chores. The house was much larger than the old house had been and Mother tried to keep the "new" as long as possible. Many features of this house seemed to us to be quite special: an electric stove (gas before), a refrigerator (an icebox before), forced heat by burning sawdust (heating stoves before), the luxury of large bedrooms, a washing machine and interior lines for drying, two bathrooms, and a wonderful oak staircase connecting the two floors. At the time the house was built (1928), it was very modern and good looking as well. I recall that Dad's mortgage was originally about $5200, but I think that later improvements pushed that up to about $8000. It was a heavy load for Dad at first, and as the Depression settled in, the load worsened.

A large part of the basement was constructed as a sawdust storage bin. Sawdust from the lumber mills in the vicinity accumulated in 2 or 3 large

23

mountains around town. It was delivered to houses by the "unit" in large trucks. A unit was a volume about 6'x6'x12'= 432 cu. ft. which was dumped on the driveway. We (often meaning I) then had to shovel it through a small window into the basement storage which held about 1½ units. It was hard work and fine particles worked their way under one's shirt next to the skin (scratchy). The furnace had a hopper attached which one filled with saw-dust. As it burned out at a constant rate in the firebox, fresh fuel slid down from the hopper, keeping the fire going for hours.

It was Dad's job to start the fire each morning and my job to refill the hopper when I came home from school in the afternoon. At first, the heat was conducted by gravity to each room by means of large pipes. It was a much better system than the old space heaters, but in the winter time the upstairs rooms were not really warm. Of course, there was no insulation in the house and the windows were far from wind-proof when the East wind blew. However, it was quite a comfortable house except for 10 days in the winter when heat did not circulate well enough and 10 days in the summer when the temperature hovered around 100°.

Eventually, the sawdust burner was replaced by an oil burner and a strong circulating fan was installed. Now indeed the heating system was improved: forced air carried heat to every room, the furnace never needed attention 24 hours a day, and a large part of the basement could be con-verted into a shop (which I did with Dad's help and advice).

The house was covered on the outside with 'shakes,' which were extra large rough-cut shingles. They had to be painted every 5 years. And it was roofed by shingles which had to be painted about every 3 years; they were replaced once in the lifetime of the house (60 years). Usually Dad did the work alone until he was 80 years old.

Moving into Eastmoreland had some disadvantages as well as the obvious advantages. We were now in day-to-day contact with people who generally had much more money to spend than we did. This showed itself in the usual ways: poorer clothing (Mother always shopped in the bargain basement), very ordinary food, no new car, no hired help, and quite ordi-nary furniture. I'm sure both Mom and Dad were stung by these depriva-tions compared to other people in the neighborhood. So we found all sorts of ways to compensate.

Here I take an aside to explain about Maurice and his family. Maurice was an attorney and their income was always more than ours and it showed in the way the families dressed. Perhaps his wife Lena made Mother feel socially inferior. Perhaps it was because we lived too far apart to share expe-riences. Lena had moved with her family from Georgia and carried a kind of Southern hauteur about her. She was very pretty with black hair and creamy complexion, about moderate height (shorter than Mother), very voluptuous and of a bright, gay personality. For whatever reasons, I can recall our family visiting their house only 2 or 3 times and they seldom came to see us.

They lived on Willamette Blvd. in North Portland, not far from where Maurice and Dad had grown up. They had a small house with a spectacular view atop a high bluff. Their children were Beverly and Sanford, about the ages of Shirley and Dexter. Our families were never close—nothing like the closeness we had with the Palmer clan. I always wondered why this was so; perhaps it was because Dad and Maurice were not close, although they had been very close as boys. We did meet for Christmas Day dinner at Grandpa Hudson's house every year and it was a joyous occasion. We exchanged gifts, but that was a perfunctory exchange, not the sincere gift giving that took place among the other cousins.[1]

But at the same time, we lived in beautiful surroundings; there were no junky K– family next door—or even close. All houses had nicely kept lawns and gardens. People were generally much better behaved, although some were not. We were quite happy to live there.

At Duniway School, I was in a class of 13 which remained the same the entire time I was there—the same students—because I had entered mid-year. Other regular classes had about 25. In a way we were lucky in that class because we received so much more individual attention than those of the larger classes. That was where I learned the English grammar that was to last the rest of my life, but I have no recollection of the teaching. Miss Hayes was our "Home Room" teacher and she probably taught grammar as well as arithmetic but it is as an arithmetic teacher that I remember her. She was tall and slender and pretty with auburn hair piled up in a school teacher hairdo. In teaching arithmetic, she was a real activist. She put individual problems on the board and demanded that each of us take part. Drill, drill, drill. In the last 5 minutes of each class she would start a cumulative problem on one side of the class (add this, subtract that, multiply by –) for each student to solve moving at a faster and faster pace around and around the class until our heads were spinning. Grammar was taught with the use of the library and there were constant assignments there, as well as weekly tests on the details. Writing was strongly encouraged and aided by turning out endless Lincoln log cabins to practice finger control.

There was a small cafeteria adjoining the kitchen for the girls' cooking class. Mostly it was for seating room for students and teachers who brought their lunches. There were no school buses; about half the students walked

1. After I grew up and went to Reed College, Maurice and I became much closer and Maurice carried my engagement ring to Jeannine in Paris.

home for lunch (we did). The school grounds were quite large (perhaps 10 acres) and little games were played all over. Girls played hopscotch. Boys played marbles ('megs' in the slang of the day) in which each player put his marbles in the center of a large circle so that each player in turn shot from the edge of the circle and kept whatever marbles he could hit and roll out—he kept shooting from within the circle so long as his 'shooter' stayed in and he knocked at least one out. There were always ball games of various sorts and for awhile 'whirlwind' was popular. In this game, the competitors started whirling around on one spot to see who could fall down last. In Oregon it rains a lot so playing outside could be denied either because of rain or muddy ground.

Wet feet and colds were very common. In those days, shoes were not waterproof. On one wintery day after a 1-foot snowstorm, Mother made me wear a pair of her old silk stockings over my shoes to keep the snow off. It worked but I was mortified.

We had one class per day of physical education (called Gym), taught by a diminutive lady called Miss Ryan. She never performed any of the exercises herself; she stood on the side and gave instructions to her class of 40 or 50. We had to use Indian clubs which looked a little like bowling pins with slender handles made of wood. We were asked to swing them around through a series of exercises which were difficult to do. We also had "scaling bars," like ladders affixed to the walls, which we had to climb—easy for us boys, difficult for the girls. We also did stretch exercises mid floor. When the weather permitted, we were allowed to form teams and play games like softball and football outside, or (as happened frequently for girls) stay inside and play gentler games.

In the spring, there were races, high jumps and throwing the discus, the javelin or the shot put. In spite of the potential for injury, there were very few. I was pretty good at the indoor exercises, at baseball (after all, Dad often practiced with me at home, since he had been so fond of the sport), and (surprisingly) at the 12 lb. shot put.

In the spring also, we had spring festival: school-wide games and celebrations. A 12-foot pole with ribbons of various colors was erected in the school yard. Groups of children, 6 boys and 6 girls, were obliged (and I use the word advisedly) to take the ribbons at the ends and, dancing around the pole in opposite directions to music, weave in and out in order to wind the ribbons into a pattern on the May Pole. Then we reversed, unwinding so that the next group could do it. It was amazing, I thought, how easy it was for some students to go astray trying to follow these simple instructions.

There were foot races, broad jumps, high jumps and other competitions. Being tall and skinny, I never could do well at foot races because I couldn't get started fast enough. But I did pretty well in broad jumping and one year was almost winner in the high jump when I somehow slipped and fell. In the fall, my left wrist was broken with a 'snap' that was heard by the whole school of onlookers. I got up with my hand hanging at an odd angle. The principal called Mother and we went to a doctor's office.

I remember the doctor as a kindly man, but even so, it hurt like hell when he put his foot in my arm pit (I was lying on a table), took my hand in his two hands and pulled until the bones were finally aligned. Then the nurse wrapped my hand and wrist in strips of gauze soaked in plaster of Paris. After it had hardened, I was allowed to leave. I remember feeling very embarrassed at having been so un-athletic and hated to go back to school. But to my surprise, everyone was very solicitous of me and wanted to sign my cast. I suddenly became 'big man' on the campus. After the arm had healed and the cast was cut off, my left hand remained weak for a long time.

At about this same time I remember once I was called into the principal's office with a much younger girl who I didn't know at all. The principal said, "Craig, this young lady says you grabbed her blouse and pulled off a button." I had no recollection of being even near the young lady, but I said, "I don't think I did, but I'll be glad to sew it back on." So the principal got out needle and thread and I sewed it back on. Thank goodness Mother had taught me the rudiments of sewing! The little girl thanked me, I left, and there was no reprimand.

On a different occasion, I was playing football during the noon hour. I tried and tried to please Dad by taking part in sports (he had been so good), but to no avail. On this occasion, I had caught the ball, was tackled and piled on. When I tried to get up, my left shoulder hurt and I couldn't move my left arm. Again back to the doctor who put me in a truss, tightened until the broken collar bone was adjusted. Then I was given a lighter truss to wear under my shirt which kept the collar bone in place. There was nothing romantic about this hump-backed thing and I was miserable until it could be taken off.

The two breaks healed very well; the arm become strong and, much later, x-rays taken for other purposes showed no sign of the mended bones. I was always much impressed by this healing process. However, people who break bones in later life have long periods of recuperations and the breaks remain visible in X-rays.

Home Room classes were used to take attendance, to teach arithmetic, reading and grammar and spelling, and—for the first few years—writing. We were taught to have a smooth flowing handwriting. We also had other classes in other rooms. I have mentioned Gym. There was also manual training (or cooking for girls), art and music. I learned how to use tools and glue in manual training which was mostly woodworking. We had a power saw to be used under supervision; at home, I had a small lathe. It was in this class that I made the little footstool with glued mortise and tenon joints[2] that the family still uses today.

It was in Art, however, that I showed some promise. I was 9 years old when we began making little figures by connecting dots on square-marked paper: "go up 3 squares, to the left 3 squares," etc. I soon outgrew such simple assignments and was allowed to make free hand drawings on blank paper. That went well, so the teacher allowed me to draw pictures in chalk on her special blackboard. This blackboard arrangement consisted of three boards on rails so that any two of them could be exposed at a given time. During my last year or so at Duniway, the art teacher gave me colored chalks and asked me to 'paint' pictures on one of her boards. Eagerly I undertook this task. I think I made altogether 4 such 'paintings' on the 4 foot x 8 foot board, spreading the chalk over every square inch so that the black did not show at all. All I can remember now are two: a nativity scene (which stayed up during the holiday season), and a 4-masted square rigger flying before the wind. I was terribly proud of these 'paintings' and hated to see them erased. I had spent afterschool time on them and they took hours.

When I had been confined to bed with rheumatic fever, Grandpa H S bought me a watercolor kit to occupy the time. Later, he introduced me to oil colors in little sample tubes, and finally to real tubes. So by the time I did the colored chalk 'paintings' at school I was already painting in oils at home. I used old window shades as canvas. Of course I showed some of these to my art teacher. She commissioned me to do one for her. I completed it in January of 1933, just before graduating. She took the painting, scarcely dry, and gave me a handful of money—a couple of dollar bills and some coins ($5 in all but I had to count it at home)—as payment, real payment! It was one of the significant moments of my life and made me wish to become an artist. After playing such an important role in my young career, I forgot her name. I never saw her again, though I tried. I still have a similar painting, on window blind material, of an anonymous lake village somewhere in Italy. It is Number 1 of my life's work collection[3].

My days at Duniway came to an end with graduation. In front of the whole school with parents present, the Principal read off the roll of my class, presenting the little graduation certificate in a small roll tied with a ribbon. But my name was not called! I was mortified. Think of Mother sitting

2. [Editor's Note] Mortise and tenon joint is a joint made with a notch, hole or groove made in a piece of wood (mortise) and a piece of wood of the same dimensions as the mortise (tenon) to fit inside.

3. [Editor's Note] see Appendix: Catalog of Paintings.

there hoping that her son would graduate and he wasn't on the list! After the last of the students with their certificates had all been seated and the clapping had abated, the Principal began a little speech. The essence of it was: "Once in a while, not every year, the School Board allows me to present a special award. The recipient is selected by all the teachers partly in the basis of excellence of grades and partly on the basis of character as shown by his behavior in school. This year we are giving the award" pause for effect "to Craig Hudson." So I went up to get two certificates: graduation and the award. Mother could feel pleased after all.

I did not make many friends at Duniway but two of them were important. 'Somebody' Nelson (I can't think of his first name), son of an architect, shared my interest in painting. We used to go out to sketch together. On one of these outings, I painted *Maple Tree*[4] in watercolor. It was in its beautiful fall colors. I lost track of Nelson in high school.

The other friend was Clark Conrad. For awhile, he and his mother and step-father lived near us in Eastmoreland. Then they moved to Milwaukie, a bicycle ride away. His father (his name was also Nelson) operated a lapidary shop and it was through him that I got my interest in rocks, especially agates. I found agates at Peach Cove and had him polish them at 25¢ per square inch. Finally I worked out a deal: I would rough grind sapphires for him (no skill needed—just hard work) for which I was then, in exchange, able to spot polish some of my own agates. He had cutting wheels, etc., all driven by the same powerful motor. Cutting was much more expensive. His principal source of income, however, was faceting precious stones—or at least re-polishing the facets of stones that were dim with wear. I have two items in my rock collection from him that were as distinctive then as they are now: the blue-green agate (very rare) and the black egg agate, polished all around, that my children have all loved to play with. Silicosis is a serious respiratory disease from which Mr. Nelson died. It is also what killed Clark. It is a common hazard of the old fashioned, poorly ventilated lapidary shops. I kept in touch with Clark for many years through Christmas cards, mostly written by his wife. They also had a very pretty daughter. He must have died in about 1970. I never saw Clark again after Duniway, but the influence he had on me by way of agate polishing has stayed with me all my life, slowly broadening into an interest in geophysics.

Aunt Hattie[5] came to live with Grandma and Grandpa Hudson at their house on 28th and Tibbets. Aunt Hattie's husband Orison Garrett died in 1927 or 1928. I remember driving to Little Rock, Washington close to

4. [Editor's Note] see Appendix: Catalog of Paintings.
5. [Editor's Note] Harriette C. Garrett, Harvey S. Hudson's sister.

Olympia, with Grandpa and Grandma Hudson at about that time to see her. The purpose may have been to bring her back to Portland. It may be that they moved from the Laurelhurst house in order to provide the extra room because the Tibbets Street house had three bedrooms plus a sunporch converted to a small bedroom. I know that we kids used to be able to stay overnight at the same time that Aunt Hattie had her room there. There was a bearskin rug on the floor next to her bed—the skin of the bear Grandpa had shot at the beach in 1917 when Mother and Dad were first married. Mother said she and the bear were picking huckleberries from the same bush.

Aunt Hattie was important to me because she did a lot of baby-sitting. With her, the folks could leave, knowing we would be well cared for. She often cooked for us and we were especially pleased with her baking powder biscuits—so delicious they didn't even need butter! She always insisted on letting them cool: "hot biscuits are bad for your digestion." In those times, ladies had strange ideas about food. A balanced diet was never a concern but Grandma Palmer would never let us drink milk and have pickles, cherries or any other tart fruit at the same meal. "It curdles your stomach" she would say, not realizing that the strong stomach acids curdled milk anyway.

Aunt Hattie sometimes took us to the Clinton Theater, a few blocks away, to watch movies. At first they were silent movies and there was a small organ near the screen played by a woman. This lady could see the screen and always managed to keep the extemporaneous music in the tempo of the action. Later, around 1930, sound was installed which was nice, but I missed watching the organist. During the hard times of the 1930s, there were prize drawings for kitchen ware and gifts, so you had to keep your ticket stub. We never won anything. On the way home, we enjoyed an ice cream bar.

Aunt Hattie was afraid of the dark, so we always went to the early show. Also if we saw a black man coming towards us on the sidewalk, we crossed the street rather than pass him close. In the tumultuous times after the assassination of Lincoln I suppose she had had some kind of traumatic experience with Negro men (women were OK). She told us stories about the end of the Civil War[6]. Aunt Hattie had never been a pretty woman and her marriage to Orison had destined her to a deprived and isolated life because he worked in the forests as a timber cruiser[7]. I suppose she had been

---

6. She would have been 5 years old at the end of the Civil War. Also the Hudson Genealogy relates that Harriette's mother Elizabeth Jane Hudson was kidnapped by a negro as a child and always had an aversion to negro men thereafter. This may have contributed to Aunt Hattie's concerns.

7. [Editor's Note] A timber cruiser was "a woodsman who searched the forests for certain kinds of trees or who surveyed stands of trees of commercial value. Orison specialized in searching for 'ship's knees.' In the days of sailing ships, a time on the

reasonably intelligent originally, but by the time I knew her, she was rather dull and childlike except when we children were left in her care. Then she seemed to brighten up, although we teased her a great deal[8].

Another memory that often is revisited in my dreams occurred at the 28th and Tibbets house. Grandpa Hudson had left his car parked on Tibbets, which slowly graded into a hill down to busy Clinton Street. I had baby Marilynn with me as I pretended to drive. Suddenly somehow I released the brake and the car started to roll down, slowly picking up speed. I was petrified, not knowing what to do. As my fear neared panic, Grandpa (who had been watching) ran alongside the car (he had sprinted from the house), opened the door, jumped in and brought the car to a stop. Thinking back, I think it was my feeling of utter helplessness in the face of impending doom that sent me into panic. I'm sure Grandpa was shaken, but he didn't say anything. Little Marilynn had not been aware of danger.

Grandpa Hudson used to pay me $2 to mow his lawn (the going price was 50 cents) but his push-type lawn mower didn't work well, so once I pushed Dad's mower all the way from the 35th Street house, through Eastmoreland, passed Reed College, passed the farmer's market on 28th Street, across Powell Boulevard to the Tibbets Street house, mowed the lawn, and returned the same way, a distance I now reckon was about 4 miles. Whew![9]

The Tibbets Street house had a curbside rose bed all around. In June we helped Grandpa collect all the rose petals into a big sack and when the Rose Festival Parade[10] passed by the Artisans' Building, the men of his office

---

west coast which lasted well into the 20th century, trees that had grown on the side of a steep hill, thus having a "knee" at the base, were much in demand. The "knee" could be shaped in such a way that it fitted onto the keel more firmly than a straight tree could. In the relatively unmapped forests of those days, a man who could locate such a tree and then lead cutters back to it was in considerable demand. I thought such work was very romantic. But the need for timber cruisers soon passed." Excerpt from an unpublished manuscript *The Hudson Story* by Craig C. Hudson.

8. Finally, in summer 1941 while I was out on a camping trip, she died and the funeral service performed without my knowledge.

9. A comment about the Tibbets Street house: many years later in Albuquerque, a friend purchased an old house to renovate. As soon as I walked up to the front porch, I recognized the house—it was the same floor plan and the same interior finishing as the Tibbets Street house. They must have both been made about 1900. The only difference was that the Albuquerque version was on a large lot and had a coach house for horse and buggy in the back.

10. [Editor's Note] The Rose Festival and Portland's first floral parade began as a fiesta put on by the Portland Rose Society in June of 1904 in connection with its annual exhibit of roses. In 1907 the Portland Rose Festival was formally organized as a nonprofit organization. The Rose Festival and the Grand Floral Parade have been enjoyed by Portlanders almost every year since (being cancelled only 3 times in its history) according to The History of the Portland Rose Festival.

rigged up a vacuum cleaner so that it blew a stream of rose petals out the window onto the floats. They fluttered down in a beautiful pink cascade and all the people on the street looked up to see them.

Strawberry picking season in Oregon begins in early June. Grandpa Hudson's birthday was June 11 and he always brought home strawberries on that date with which Grandma made strawberry shortcake. It became a celebration and Jeannine and I continued to observe it in Albuquerque with California berries which are not as good.

I was not able to watch the construction of the 35th Street house. But within a couple of years of our moving in, I was able to watch construction of the house next door (on the corner) and that was interesting on two counts. It had a basement and the excavation for it was dug in part by hand (to square up the corners) but mostly by a man with a team of horses with a digger. The digger was in the form of a large half-clam with a handle on one side and the horses' coupling on the other. The horse-coupling was made so that when the man held down the handle, the leading edge bit into the dirt as it was pulled by the team of horses. When it was full of dirt, the man pushed down harder, the edge came up out of the dirt and—with the horses still pulling—the load skidded across the ground. In dumping, the man let loose the handle, the clam shovel flipped over, dropping its load, and the man then guided the team back for another load. The man was very clever to be able to guide the horses and use his hands on the handle at the same time. It was slow going because, as I realize now, the clam shovel only held about a half a cubic yard and the horses had to be turned around twice on each dig. Also, the dirt dug out had to be deposited on the site. Modern machinery would be much faster and the dirt would be hauled away.

The concrete was mixed on the site. The mixer was a barrel-shaped container very much like present-day mixers only larger: it held perhaps a cubic yard. Sand, gravel, cement and water all had to be brought to the site. Perhaps the water line was installed before any work started; I don't remember. The concrete maker, a powerful man, loaded the mixer with measured shovelfuls of sand and gravel, hoisted the sack of cement up and with a quick motion cracked it open on the mouth of the mixer, emptied it in, and poured in the measured amount of water. Meanwhile, the mixer was rotating, driven by a gasoline engine. When the mix was ready, he tipped it out into waiting wheelbarrows. It was fun to watch, especially as other men rolled the heavy wheelbarrows out along wooden paths to the forms where pouring was done. It was heavy, hard work and, as a skinny string bean, I admired the strong men with big shoulders. Today the use of Ready Mix in big trucks has revolutionized the process of pouring concrete. That was about 1930.

The frame of the house was carpentry. But the finish on the inside was lath and plaster. The 35th Street house had been constructed in the same way. All that plaster on the inside of the house meant that it took weeks for it to dry. Constructing such a house took 4 to 6 months compared to 1 to 2 months today[11].

I have already mentioned the interurban train that served the Sunnyside area. There was also one that served Milwaukie, Oak Grove and Oregon City. These were electrified lines, carried many passengers and were abandoned only about the time of World War II. They also had counterparts in other directions of the Portland suburban region but I was unfamiliar with them. There was also a narrow gauge line that we called the "Toonerville Trolley" after a popular comic strip. Its tracks were located in Knapp Street and extended from 32nd street up the hill to the east. It lasted until the depression times of 1935 and was for the convenience of people who lived up there who wanted to commute into town by way of the Sellwood-Eastmoreland-39th Street electrified train that began as steel tracks, later changed to rubber-wheeled cars with overhead wires and eventually became gasoline buses. We kids used to bait the "Toonerville Trolley" by putting coins and small rocks on the rails to see them squashed. All lines were connected by transfer privileges so that it was possible to go almost anywhere, especially to the Southern Pacific Train Station in downtown Portland.

The 39th Street electrified bus carried us from Eastmoreland across to the Belmont Street trolley. This transfer took us down past Washington High School and on into downtown. We kids made this trip twice a day to school (there were no school buses), a time of about half an hour each way. A few times in heavy snows the electrified bus couldn't make it up the Woodstock hill, so to everyone's delight we had to get out and walk. Also in bad weather, the trolleys jumped off their wires, the bus stopped and the driver hopped out to reposition the trolleys. There was no pollution and the system worked very well. However the ever increasing number of private autos meant that patronage would keep declining. Sometime after WWII, the system was dismantled and replaced by gasoline (actually diesel) buses.

Mother had graduated from Washington High School in 1915. I entered Washington in February 1933 and found some of the same teachers she had left in 1915. I think the school had opened in 1910 and closed in about 1980. Shirley, Dexter and Marilynn also went there.

---

11. As I watch the TV program *This Old House*, I discover that new materials and techniques make even better houses now in a fraction of the time.

[Editor's Note] Craig is referring to a PBS TV series regarding the home-improvement process.

For awhile, the Messings lived in Eastmoreland. Since Uncle Claus had to drive past Washington High School in order to reach Benson where he worked, he kindly picked me up and dropped me and Ruth off at Washington. But it was not a good arrangement because I was always late. That was how I came to use the electrified 39th Street bus. I have no strong memories of the ride to and from the Washington campus except one: we used to have to wait at 39th and Belmont to transfer to the street car in front of a drug store (which is no longer there).On cold winter days with the east wind blowing, it was freezing.

I had to take physical education for the first two years. Most of the boys were big and strong; I was skinny and weak. In good weather, we all went outside for track and field, football and baseball. The coaches were constantly on the lookout for material for the Washington teams. So mostly I sat around watching the bigger boys play. I had friends in the same boat: fat boys, skinny boys, lame boys. From time to time, the PE teacher tried to get us into some kind of exercise group, but the contact sports (which were so popular) dominated the program. The big fellows developed quite a swagger and wore sweaters with letters on them.

One of the things I could do was run and inside the gym there was an elevated track around the periphery, probably about 100 yards in length. I ran around this track as my principal form of exercise. My weak heart did not allow me to compete, but I did get plenty of exercise within that limit. Once, in Eastmoreland, to test myself, I set a course that I judged to be about half a mile and tried to run it. I could not get all the way around. That experience remained a bench mark for the rest of my life. I knew I had some stamina but I could not measure up to other boys. I never told Dad because he always expected so much of me. I had to hide my weakness.

The gym instructor tried to provide exercises for us inside and some of them were tumbling and muscle building. Tumbling didn't work out. One of the first tricks to learn was the rolling summersault. You took a short run, bent over to summersault and then "tuck your head down to your knees, wrap your arms around your legs and keep rolling." On my first try, I punched the lenses out of my glasses with my knees and that was the end of that. The lenses broke but fortunately my eyes were not much cut. For muscle building, we had plenty of equipment but I never was much good at anything but the overhead ladder and the chinning bar. Between those two (running and arm exercises) I managed to have enough exercise.

I was never jealous of the boys in team sports but I was envious of some of the boys (very few) who were dedicated to body building. There were weights to be lifted but that was considered to be dangerous, only to be undertaken under supervision. We did not have a gymnastics coach but there was an instructor who was experienced in the horse, parallel bars, the high bar and the vertical pole. I can still see (in my mind's eye) him grasping the vertical pole with his two hands about 2 feet apart and slowly extending his body out until he was supported in a horizontal position. None of the boys could do that, try as they might. When I was alone, I tried a half-way trick: holding myself close to the pole and extending my legs.

One of his students performed a trick on the stage in the auditorium before all the students which I have never seen repeated. His only prop was a sturdy oak table. He sat on the floor, legs under the table, which was then about shoulder high, and, placing his hands flat on the table, slowly lifted himself off the floor, legs rigidly extended. Then, very slowly, he swung his legs out from under the table and, without touching the table with anything but his palms, he swung himself up, extended his legs and performed a handstand. Then as if that were not enough, he slowly returned to his original position. I was very impressed.

There were two educational tracks at Washington: college-bound and business. I chose college-bound because I wasn't interested in business. However, I had no hopes of going to college because in the 1930s Dad was struggling with the Depression and I could not see a way to find the money. Consequently, my guiding objective in school was to get an exposure to culture and develop my art. The first two years were filled with required courses, mostly math and literature. I dragged myself through two years of math (algebra and Euclidian geometry) but I never quite got the hang of it. It did penetrate my mind what a proof was and I learned to make use of an equation. I was a C student and didn't really care because I consoled myself with the excuse that an artist has little need for mathematics. I could have taken more—up to beginning calculus—but I didn't. However, I took a calculus book out of the library and tried to understand what an integral sign meant, but gave it up.

The first two years of English literature were mostly about sentence structure. The head of the literature department had written a book about sentence structure which we used and I still would like to use that book. Day after day, we analyzed sentences and structured them with a scaffolding device[12] to select the main parts and the parenthetical parts and then put them back together again with punctuation in place of the scaffold. Of course, this brought out many points about grammar that we had not covered at Duniway, and gave names to them which I was not able to remember. Structuring sentences lead directly to structuring paragraphs and I took an extra

12. [Editor's Note] sentence diagram is a pictorial representation of the grammatical structure of a sentence.

course in creative writing to develop those skills. As a homework problem, I wrote a short essay about Grandma Palmer supervising the farming of flower bulbs at Peach Cove (she tried to make a business of selling flower bulbs). Of course, I did not use real names.

I also took two years of Roman and Latin study, which went up to Caesar's Gallic Wars. I didn't learn much Latin, but three things stuck with me: the strict formalism of Latin grammar, a lot of Roman history, and the roots of many English words. That was the time when Mussolini was posturing and orating in news reels and I tried to understand a little; but Italian is not Latin. Ten years later, as a GI I slept in the marvelous hall that he had built for his daughter in Naples. Even though I didn't learn enough Latin to be useful as a language, I consider that course to be one of the most influential of my life because of the introduction to classical civilization it provided.

The second two years of literature treated largely English literature, with one year being devoted almost entirely to Shakespeare. I had more than one teacher, but the one I remember best was Miss Barber. We picked *Julius Caesar* apart line by line to understand the construction, and then read it from the beginning, with students playing the roles, to get a full picture. We did the same thing to *Macbeth*. We went through *King Lear* and the comedies quickly, Miss Barber reading much of the time. Mother was remembered by Miss Barber and I was her favorite pupil.[13] Shirley and Dexter said they had had a hard time with her because they couldn't get interested in the subject. Much of my early interest in English literature was spurred by Grandpa Hudson. His formal education had been rather meager, but he read extensively and used his readings as material for his oratory[14]. He urged me to read, read, read, which was easy for me because I was so poor at sports.

We also had a year of pure English literature: *Mill on the Floss* comes to mind, some of Jane Austen and other English classics (very difficult for teenagers of our time), lots of poetry such as Wordsworth, Byron, Shelley, Keats, and a big dose of Tennyson. We did not study Chaucer (that came at Reed), but we did read *Beowulf* which led me to read *Song of Roland* and *Siegfried* on my own. Those were exciting years for me, not that I anticipated

13. I kept in touch with Miss Barber for many years until she died in about 1970. She did not remember me very well, was only being polite.

14. [Editor's Note] H S Hudson, president of the United Artisan Life Association (1904), Oregon Legislator 1897. "*Grandad H S took pride in his oratory and in his writing, especially poetry. He really was a 19th century man carrying the literary skills of the English Victorian period into the 20th century. I think this may have been his charm for the still rugged West in which he worked.*" From unpublished manuscript *The Hudson Story* by Craig C. Hudson.

a career in literature but rather because I loved culture. It was hard going
in the family, however, because (except for Grandpa Hudson) no one was
interested. I think Maurice would have been interested, but I was not close
to him then. We did not study King Arthur (that was left to individual reading) and we did not study Mark Twain, although again *Tom Sawyer* was
required individual reading. I was very fond of Tarzan stories because I so
much envied his physical prowess, but libraries were not allowed to keep
them (too fanciful) and many bookstores did not sell them (perhaps they
did not consider them good literature). Ruth gave me my first *Tarzan* book
as a birthday present.[15]

We had a two-semester course of history (ancient and US). I took the
US history course taught by Miss Gray, who was small and grey. Her class
was a dream to teach because it was (a) elective and (b) difficult so there
were no discipline problems. Part of the course was reading the *Weekly
Reader*[16] which was mostly a summary of what was going on in the world.
Every week there were stories about Mussolini and Hitler (this was 1936 so
WWII had not started but the preparations were well under way and the
Italians were invading Ethiopia and North Africa). Part of the course was
watching news reels and reporting on events.

I did not take Ancient History because I had already had quite an exposure through the Latin class, and because I became interested in Egyptology, quite by accident. The Portland Public Library (main branch) had a
marvelous collection of books on Egyptian art, even some huge volumes of
stories from the walls of tombs in hieroglyphics which had been translated
into English—many just historic or economic records, but some tender love
stories. I set about learning how to read hieroglyphics, but it proved to be
too hard. That experience (looking at every precious book on Egyptology
they had in the Portland Library, some under lock and key) led me to much
wider interest in the Egyptians and in 1938, while in a Los Angeles used
bookstore, I used all my spending money to buy Petrie's *The Pyramids and
Temples of Gizeh* which I still have and treasure.[17].

We were obliged to take a science course. At that time physics and
chemistry seemed too difficult so I signed up for biology. That was the only

15. [Editor's Note] Craig's son, Marc, is keeper of Craig's copy of *Tarzan of the Apes*,
published 1919.

16. [Editor's Note] Craig is referring to a 6–8 page magazine, *My Weekly Reader*,
designed to make national news available to school age children.

Forman-Brunell, Miriam (Annotated), Children and Youth in History .

17. That opened up the field of archaeology to me and by now I have a small library.
I use the first person singular rather loosely because my wife, Jeannine, has helped
greatly in the years since we have been married.

formal biology training I ever had, but it proved to be seminal. It was one of those classes which, from the teacher's point of view, was a waste of time but from my point of view, it was education personified. I didn't get anything out of the experience of dissecting a worm or a frog, but I learned enough about the system of biota to get me started.

Art was an elective course. I took one or two (the maximum allowed) every semester. Much of the work was just rudimentary like learning the principles of perspective (called foreshortening), but there were three events that warrant notice here: 1) Grandpa Hudson provided me private study with a well-known portrait artist called Sydney Bell,[18] 2) I entered a city-wide competition with a painting of a modernistic French house which won second prize and served as the basis for the design of Grandpa Hudson's house on a hill overlooking the Ross Island Bridge, and 3) as a special extension of the school program, I took Miss Yager's history of art course which included memorizing 100 great works from colored slides she projected. As a result of these three events, I became hooked on art.

The Sydney Bell studio in the old Dekum Building[19] on 3rd Street appeared to me to occupy the entire top floor. It was not one large space however. It was divided into several small private rooms, a large painting studio and a couple of other rooms. There were skylights in each so that every place was well lighted. There were easels everywhere and a large sink area for washing up. He was fastidious about washing up with lots of soap and water until, as he said, you could put the brushes in your mouth and not taste anything. Actually, some of the pigments (such as those of cadmium base) are poisonous, so the precautions made sense.

I had class for 2 hours on Saturday morning. For the first month, I used paper and charcoal—what a bore drawing plaster casts. But he used this as a shakedown period, to see who was going to stick it out. I worked in a cubicle about 6 feet by 10 feet with a skylight. Then I shifted to paint, but only raw umber and white with turpentine as medium, again doing images of plaster casts. And finally, I got to move into the big studio with the advanced students. Some were no better than I; some were nearly as good as Bell himself. Since Sydney Bell always made a first-class portrait of his subject on his canvas with charcoal (fixed) before lifting a brush, he sometimes

18. [Editor's Note] Sydney (Sidney) Bell (1888–1964) was a portrait painter who was born in England and settled in Portland Oregon in 1914. He was one of Oregon's most fashionable portrait artists.

19. [Editor's Note] Dekum Building was completed in 1892 and used exclusively Oregon materials in its construction. Frank Dekum was a prominent Portland businessman who invested in and encouraged the building of large, solid buildings. Prats, *Dekum Building.*

called "time-out!" from painting and had us "go back to basics" with charcoal on paper. His models were usually street people that he picked up on
the way to class. He also used nudes in a private room, where I seldom was
allowed to go. At the end of a class, we were supposed to take a rag soaked in
turpentine and wash the image off so the canvas could be used again.

He always had one of his own paintings in progress, usually of some
political figure or a rancher. We studied these in-process paintings with
great care. His technique was to mix many colors on his palette and then
apply them with small brushes in discrete dabs. "Do not scrub" he used
to say and "do not use a big brush." And it was true; if you looked closely
at his paintings, the individual strokes and colors were really a pointillism
technique in which the colors were very carefully shaded. Each stroke, of
course, was laid on top of the fixed charcoal drawing; shadows were filled
with colors of a darker hue.

Many of Sydney Bell's portraits hung in a gallery at the state capital
building. When the building was consumed by fire (in the early 1940s),
these paintings were destroyed—much of his life's work. But he did other
than political figures and in one of the Portland bank buildings there had
been an exhibit of half a dozen or so, covering the period from the early
1930s to the mid 1940s. I have seen this exhibit and the first one is true to
Sydney Bell's style but by the last one (dated perhaps 1946), gone were the
lovely colors (flesh color shaded with burnt umber appeared), gone were the
delicate brush strokes (scrubbing was evident), and with a big brush at that.
What had happened? I never found out.

Sydney Bell had two daughters. Years later when I met Raymond
Jonson and Arthur Johnson (two brothers, Raymond being a little older)
who had grown up, in part, in Portland, I learned that as young men they
dated the two Bell sisters who at that time lived at the Bell house on Vista
Avenue.[20]

The painting of a modernistic French house, which resulted in the design for Grandpa Hudson's house, I did in 1936 as part of the class work in
Miss Yager's class. At the time, as I remember it now, the painting was given
little recognition in the class because the subject was not considered to be

20. Raymond later became a modern abstract painter of some note in Albuquerque.
Arthur, who had sung with Dad in the radio station in Portland, sought a career on
the New York stage. Arthur never married and when he retired, he came to live with
Raymond, to care for him (whose wife had died) and in particular to organize and
preserve Raymond's many paintings. Arthur died first and the paintings were cared for
by an outsider after all. Raymond died in 1982 at age 91. As one of its most honored
faculty, University of New Mexico built Raymond a house with a large part devoted to
a gallery and workshop, and later added a thermidofied storage area where each of his
1000 works, nicely framed, can be kept standing in its own little compartment.

arty enough but it did win 2nd prize in the city-wide competition. Grandpa gave the picture to his architect and the design of a very nice house was the result. The house was built in 1937 on a large lot on the corner of Abernathy and View Point Terrace. It was in full view of traffic coming across the Ross Island Bridge and became a landmark.[21]

The third event, the course in history of art by Miss Yager, had ramifications difficult to evaluate. It reinforced my interest in art, it broadened my outlook on culture, and it set me on a path of enlightenment and self-education that continues to this day. Our family has been enriched by it.

My friends in high school were few and none has lasted through the years. I knew Eugene Snyder there but he was not a friend; he has become a friend now, some 56 years later, but I lost track of him completely for most of that time. I did become friendly with Deanna Durbin and Bill Chandler (already pledged in marriage to each other) and they played a pivotal role in my life; but they also disappeared after a few years, never to be heard from since. The role they played was to get me interested in science. We met accidentally in home room because we sat near each other in my last year (1936–37). We had many happy hours together but I was always the odd man because I didn't have a partner. They had nothing to talk about except science (especially chemistry where Bill excelled) and I began to be jealous of them for knowing something so completely foreign to me. I finally persuaded Dad to get me started on a correspondence course in electronics (at considerable cost to him, I might add). The course aimed itself at training radio repairmen and as this little by little became evident, I lost interest and never completed the course. But the seed had been planted; my objective then was to catch up. Deanna and Bill and I did have some happy times as when we walked the streets of downtown Portland arm in arm singing "Home on the Range." Passersby were amazed and shook their heads.

Bill's father was general manager at the Willamette Crematorium and in May of 1936, I assisted Bill as guide for the visitors on Memorial Day. The hill overlooking the river was solid rock and had been penetrated by perhaps a couple of miles of passageways hewn into the rock. All along these passageways were crypts, some empty, many containing urns of ashes from the crematorium nearby. There were, of course, numbering systems for the thousands of crypts, differing systems for the successive expansions of the

---

21. Grandpa moved out in 1953; the house was renovated, adding considerably to its first floor, and finally was bought by another architect named Meyer. Meyer contacted me in 1994 through my nephew, David Hudson (Dexter's son), and I gave him the whole story along with pictures. When we visited Portland in 1994, we visited the old house and found it in process of yet another renovation. We were graciously received by the Meyers, took pictures and agreed to keep in touch.

crematorium, which I had to learn in the first hour before visitors came. The visitors came by the hundreds, all carrying flowers. By mid-afternoon the passageways had the lovely smell of a florist's showroom. At that time, no relative that I knew of was interred there.[22] I also was able to see the cremation furnace operating with roaring jets of gas flame engulfing a coffin.

At graduation from high school, Bill went away to a college in the East and I never saw him again. Deanna stayed in Portland and we saw each other for a year at Reed College before she went to marry Bill. I have a portrait of her that she gave me but I have never heard from them again.

As a gawky young man with spectacles, I found it very difficult to obtain dates. It was, naturally, a matter of prestige to have good dates for both boys and girls. I was left out of this social activity and very much felt the loss. However, I did have a girl companion and around her turns a prophetic story. Her name was Marilee M– and she had a pretty face. Even her hands and breasts were pretty, but below that she was thick and unattractive. She could get no dates either. She was very short (not up to my shoulder) and almost surely heavier than I, but her mind was sharp and she had a happy personality, so we got along together rather well. We used to walk from Washington High up to the Jeanne d'Arc statue at 39th and Glisan. There we separated: me to catch the 39th Street bus to Eastmoreland, she to take the Belmont streetcar to her home near Mount Tabor. One spring, I spent the night at her house (we cuddled under a blanket on the davenport) to see Easter Sunday sunrise. Her mother prepared a fine breakfast for sunrise.

But the real story about Marilee had to do with our taking the Belmont streetcar downtown to visit Grandpa Hudson at the Artisans Building. On the way, we had to pass the coffee warehouse down by the river where the aroma of roasting coffee filled the air for blocks around. I remember that with great pleasure even though I did not drink coffee at that time. We got to the office and I tried to introduce Marilee to people I knew there. I could not remember her name! There was a long awkward silence. Finally Marilee whispered to me "I'm Marilee." I must have flushed beet red. Everyone smiled and the spell was broken. But that was the beginning of what was to trouble me all my life: the inability to remember names. It has been a perpetual source of embarrassment. Upon graduation, Marilee and I separated and I never heard from her again.

In the summer of 1936, Dad packed us all into the car (a 1935 Ford) with camping gear and we took a short outing along the Skyline Road from just south of Government Camp down to a camp site near Detroit on the

---

22. By now, however, there are numerous Palmers and Hudsons.

North Santiam River.[23] The road was very primitive and we often found places that were nearly impassable. There were still deep snow banks. None of us children had ever been at that elevation (5000 feet) before and it was a thrill to feel the breathlessness of running up a snow bank. We spent 3 days camping on the ground (our first real such experience) and then we drove down to the Detroit campsite where there were cabins. There we met Grandma and Grandpa Hudson. We stayed there another 3 nights and Dad, Grandpa, Dexter and I fished in the river. We didn't catch anything. Later Grandma Palmer told me that there was a place on the river where the entire flow passed between two rocks close enough together to step across. This was near Lebanon where she and Ed Palmer lived for several years. But I never saw this place.[24]

23. [Editor's note] Detroit, Oregon, east of Salem, Oregon.

24. Much later, in 1993, I learned that Dad's cousin Alton Everest had worked with the Forest Service and in 1935 had helped to build this very road. He wrote a very charming little book called *Tales of High Clackamas Country*. In it he describes the country as it was then and the work that the Civilian Conservation Corps (CCC) was doing to open it up.

[Editor's Note] Everest, F. Alton, 1993, "Tales of High Clackamas Country: An anecdotal history of experiences on the Lakes Ranger District of the Mount Hood National Forest 1930–1935," St. Paul's Press.

4

Young Man, Between High School and College

1937—1939

In the spring of 1937, I had no place to go to school so I stayed on at Washington High as a post graduate. The science bug had bitten me and I took the courses in chemistry and physics that were offered. Of course, I was entering midyear and I found Physics very dull. Chemistry was taught by Miss Geballe and she made it very lively. She had taught Linus Pauling[1] a few years before and one of her nephews was beginning to study solid state physics, so she was inspired. But I was beginning so far behind in both subjects that I did not do well. However, I learned the language of science and some of the important concepts.

The summer of 1937 was my last lazy summer. After finally leaving Washington High School, I spent a few days (less than a week) at Arthur and Mae's[2] house in Albany. At the time Arthur was Manual Arts teacher at Albany High School, where he had come from Oregon State University (OSU). He and Mae met there. Evelyn was a little girl; Jerry was not born yet.

I had bought a very nice piece of myrtle (Oregon's special wood) about 6"x6"x10," perfectly clear with no imperfections. Art had suggested that I

---

1. [Editor's Note] Linus Pauling (February 28, 1901—August 19, 1994), awarded the Nobel Prize in Chemistry 1954.

2. [Editor's Note] Arthur Edwin Palmer (Bertha's brother) and his wife Martha 'Mae' McDougall Palmer.

turn it on the school lathe into a lamp. So I went to Albany on the bus, carrying the block of myrtle. After we looked at the wood together and I said I would like to make something Grecian, he said "but it really would look better if it were fatter in the middle. And I know a trick that would put four nice-looking shields on the sides. And, of course, you need a larger base for stability." So we went to the school and from the scrap box found 4 pieces of dark walnut about 1 inch thick, and 4 pieces of light maple about ½ inch thick and a slab of birch for the base. Then he showed me how to glue the pieces all together into an ungainly block. We then put this block into the school's big lathe and I proceeded to turn out the Grecian-style lamp base which we still have and cherish.[3] And how the students admired my work! I really felt important.

Also, during the summer of 1937, Grandpa Hudson found me a job working as a clerk at the Portland office of the Oregon Motor Vehicle Department. Then, as now, people had to renew their drivers' licenses. It was a perfunctory operation since the license served mostly to make the state know how many drivers were out there. There were few women licensed. At first, things were pretty dull in this 1st floor office arranged in a state building to receive walk-ins from the street. I was the youngest and most naïve of the employees, and the rest of them liked to play jokes on me. Once they sent me up to a 3rd floor office to borrow a 'paper stretcher,' which seemed like a reasonable request. The clerk in the 3rd floor office said he lent it to someone on the 5th floor. By this time I was suspicious that 'paper stretchers' didn't exist, but I went along with the joke. Then back to someone on the 2nd floor, to no avail, of course. And finally, with a straight face, back to my own 1st floor office where there was laughter all around. But they were really nice people and the fun faded when large numbers of people began to come in for renewing before July 1 which was the deadline. Some applicants were huffy and hated to renew. But there were many nice people who couldn't write and I enjoyed filling out their forms for them to sign.

I was invited to join a fraternity at Oregon State and in September went to Corvallis to live at the Frat House for two days to see if they liked me and wished to 'pledge' me. But I saw enough to know that I didn't want to live there so there was no pledge. I returned to Portland and applied to the Oregon Institute of Technology (OIT) for their course as radio operator. That was something I could afford and in addition to teaching me something about radio technology, I would get a practical license.

3. [Editor's Note] Craig's son, Cyril, is keeper of the Grecian-style wood lamp.

OIT was housed in a building at approximately Broadway and Taylor and occupied most of the third floor and the basement.[4] It included a number of courses besides radio, mostly business types. Apparently it was very successful because graduates had little trouble getting placed; but of course, the jobs were not very high paying. President Roosevelt visited Portland and drove by in an open car so that we could look out the window and see him smiling and waving, the only president I ever saw in the flesh. This was either the fall of 1937 or the spring of 1938.

The man who conducted the radio class was a licensed ship's radio operator. We had a very good book on electronics and electricity. Between the two, the practical experience of the teacher and the theoretical-analytical approach of the book, we found the course very good and pitched at about the appropriate level. I say 'we' because I quickly made friends with a man called Meeker and we became inseparable. He had an ugly head poised on a robust body, so in a way we complemented each other.

The math level of the book was held to algebra and trigonometry (which I had to learn) and I discovered that with the aid of diagrams and plots, all I needed to know was accessible. The instructor said, as the course began, that we were being trained to pass the exam for radio-telegrapher which would also satisfy the requirements for radio-telephone. The difference lay in the ability to use Morse code effectively and, to some extent, in the equipment to be used. This was 1937 and most radio equipment was based on vacuum tubes, but there were still some shipboard installations using more primitive equipment so we needed to know about it. Jobs were hard to come by and one took what was available. A ship's radio-telegrapher made $100/month with free room and board while at sea which translated into pretty good pay.

Our textbook included a large section on motors and generators, both AC and DC, single phase and triple phase. In addition, it included a description of the old types of radio transmitters which were based on sparks or arcs feeding a tuned circuit (called a 'tank' coil) attached to an antenna with no amplification. This was essentially the equipment used by Marconi[5] in 1900 and, I understood, some of the older sea captains still called them 'marconis.' The main part of the book, however, was devoted to vacuum tubes and their circuits. One big section was devoted to the principles of tubes of all kinds, another to oscillator and amplifier circuits, a third to modulation and detection, and finally a section to describe modern radio transmitters and

4. OIT is now located in Klamath Falls.

5. [Editor's Note] Guglielmo Marconi (1874–1937) received the Nobel Prize for Physics in 1909 which he shared with Professor Karl Braun.
Nobel Lectures, Physics 1901–1921.

receivers. The course was not academic; there were few problems and only comprehension tests every week. The purpose was to push, push, push so that we would have an understanding of the whole scope of the material. It was really a tremendous course.

The requirement that we know Morse code proved to be the major stumbling block. Our objective was to send and transmit more than 25 words per minute. The best I could do was 20 but Meeker could do more than 25. He got a telegrapher's license; I got a telephone license. You can transmit at 20 words per minute with the conventional telegrapher's key one sees in the movies; to go faster, which is like talking, you need the spring-loaded sideways key. A word was taken to be made of five letters; each letter contained one to four pulses with a short space between and a longer space between words. Thus 25 words per minute translates into about 15 pulses per second, or a monotonous hum. It's quite a feat to be able to read this language. Very few in the class could accomplish it.

The basement was filled with radio equipment, some old and some new. One of the reasons the old spark transmitters remained in use (mostly on tramp freighters) was that they were utterly simple and could be repaired using materials out of ships' stores. They were discouraged because they had short range (a few hundred miles) and they were broadband, meaning that they transmitted at a range of frequencies making cross-talk a nuisance. But it was most interesting to look over this old equipment. Some years later, in 1945 in Paris, I was able to visit the Palais de la Découverte where much of the original electrical machinery in the history of electricity was exhibited. There I found the same feeling of awe at what men did in the beginning. When vacuum tubes and sharply timed circuits came along, it became possible to modulate the signal so that voice could be used. The equipment was more complex but it became much easier to use and more people could become proficient with it. Also, it became possible to transmit over much greater distances and to use an almost unlimited range of frequencies.

At about the time I was learning about vacuum tubes, a modest research effort at Bell Labs was getting started which resulted in the discovery of the transistor in 1948. World War II impelled a great improvement in the vacuum tube, especially in miniaturization and power capacity, but when the transistor came on the scene, the vacuum tube essentially disappeared. Of the broad range of designs originally provided, only three are presently used: the magnetron (every kitchen microwave has one), the klystron and the gas diode, all very powerful devices.

I took my exam and received my radio-telephone license in May 1938; it was in effect my graduation certificate from OIT. I think the license is still in our safe deposit box; it has long since expired. Many of the things I learned about electrical equipment at OIT are still with me, not having been superseded by later experience.[6]

I used my license to get a job in Klamath Falls at the little radio station there. I was to be radio operator officially, but so little was required of the operator that in effect I became announcer and studio technician. And here I learned of a second limitation that dogged me for the rest of my life. There were two studios and several incoming phone lines with programs. Altogether a switch board of a dozen or so hot lines and as many empty lines. It was possible to plug any line into any other line and into the line that modulated the transmitter. With all those cords hanging in front of me, I became hopelessly befuddled. Simple situations I learned to cope with; but when several plug-ins were called for, I was too slow. After about a month, by mutual agreement, we parted company. I was not cut out for that kind of work. However, a couple of nice things happened to me in Klamath Falls. I found a boarding house to live in, the first time I had ever been away from home. The lady who ran it was very sympathetic, a motherly woman who kept very clean rooms and served simple but very nice meals. I also found that the other roomers were pleasant to talk to. The second nice thing happened when, one Sunday morning, while playing the records of an opera for my own amusement, the phone rang. I had supposed no one would be paying attention, but the man's voice said "when you announce the records, please read the libretto." What was a libretto? I guessed that it must be the story line, so I began to read the libretto. It worked out very well.

It was still midsummer, so I telegraphed Mother and Dad and said I was coming home. They decided to pick me up and have a little camp-out on the way home. It was the only time in my conscious life that I had ever had the undivided attention of both of them at the same time and it was wonderful.

There was still a good part of the summer left so I signed up with the Forest Service for fire duty and was sent to the Chetco River[7] fire, then just getting started. First, however, I had to spend 3 days in training. We were given training in the use of a compass and how to use it in conjunction with pacing, to get from one point to another without landmarks for guidance. This is a real trick, especially in rough or steep country, and I had to conclude that much experience is needed unless you can get help from landmarks. In the trackless Chetco wilderness, at that time not even mapped,

6. I lost track of Meeker at that time but accidentally ran into him in Portland in about 1965. He was working for Pacific Telephone at the time and was trying to solve the problem of microwave links across the city. Scintillation was involved so we had something to talk about. But we did not maintain contact.

7. [Editor's Note] Chetco River, wilderness area of southwest Oregon.

only very experienced foresters were allowed to go off alone. Next, we were taught how to use firefighting tools to make an effective fire line. And finally, a fire was set in dense woods and we had to put it out, which took all day of hard, hot work.

We (about 15 young men) were housed in an old CCC barracks somewhere near Estacada. We were up at 4 am, had a huge breakfast of plate-sized hotcakes (called 'flannel cakes'), bacon, eggs, fried potatoes and coffee; then out to the field and back by 6 for a large dinner. It was really more physical labor than I could handle and part of the time I had to rest; but the other fellows kept going all day long. One of the men, not used to using an ax, cut himself rather badly on the instep of one foot, right through the leather of his boot. The crew chief then gave us a lesson in first aid—the use of a butterfly bandage. The wound was washed and the two edges pulled together. Then tape was applied in two diagonal strips across the center of the cut, and finally a bandage applied. The man was sent home; no time to wait for recovery.

I took a bus to Gold Beach after the training class, and then a truck up the old Chetco River Road (rough and unmaintained) to an abandoned farm house at the end of it. By the time we got there, the fire had been raging for more than a week in hilly scrubland. My radio was set up in an open tent near the cook tent. My job was to keep the fire boss and his staff in constant touch with the fire crews. The crews had been working for some days and were dog-tired. As new men arrived, they were sent out to relieve the men 'on the line.' The wind had taken a turn for the worse and the fire moved into heavy timber on Tincup Creek. Backfires were tried without success as the main fire 'crowned' (leaped from treetop to treetop) often over the heads of the men working. Falling blazing limbs (called 'widow makers') fell everywhere, a few times causing wounds so severe that the victims had to be hospitalized. Eventually the fire covered 50,000 acres of mostly old growth trees and was finally put out by a rain.

Activities around the camp were interesting. The men off the line were so tired that they crawled into sleeping bags and discovered in the morning that they shared with rattlesnakes, rather large ones. I did not hear of anyone being bitten, but sometimes we had rattlesnake stew for dinner. Myself, I found an old door on which I could spread my sleeping bag and never had any rattlesnake trouble, but it was hard.

Getting supplies to the line crews was a real problem; they all had to be delivered by pack mule. The stock of supplies at base camp was pretty good—maintained by shipments up the old road by truck. Sometimes, in times of great need, certain supplies (especially eggs) were air dropped from light airplanes. They were wrapped in layers of bread to ease the impact.

There was always some loss, of course, but the airdrops worked reasonably well. Not so the pack mule deliveries. They often were not received by the fast moving fire crews, who then went hungry for days at a time. I was in the middle of messages between the crew chief and the camp boss. At one point, after the crew chief had repeatedly asked for toilet paper, the harried camp boss radioed back: "you haven't had any food; you don't need any toilet paper." I was usually up before sunrise helping the cook prepare breakfast. On one such morning as I sliced the bacon (it arrived the old fashioned way with rind), I noticed that the slices seemed to squirm. Taking it over to where the cook had a light, we found that the bacon was crawling with maggots. The cook said "don't use that slab," but I had a suspicion that later he fried it up anyway, because we were often short of supplies.

The Forest Service had (and still has) men trained especially in firefighting who are able to find their way in the woods. The man who did this at Chetco had a particularly risky job because, as he tried to hike around the fire, it often leaped ahead of him. After two or three days, which took him around the Tincup burn as well as the rest of the burn, he returned dead tired and black from head to foot from smoke and ashes. He had made a map of the area where he went. He said that part of the time a cougar had followed him, probably wanting to be led out of danger.

The firefighting operation took more than a month, after which a heavy rain doused the fire. For the last week of this time, I had been transferred to a newly constructed fire lookout. As the storm moved in, lightning played about the lookout as if in fun. The lookout was protected not only by lightning rods but also by metal fans at the corners of the roof. Strikes were horrendous and the discharges from the fans were nearly as bright as moonlight. It was a frightening night. The rods seemed to attract the lightning, but I wondered if they were big enough to protect the building against all bolts. It was lonely there.

A special bus had been arranged to take us back to Portland from Gold Beach. These were the old days of the Coast Highway when, as they used to say, you could see your own taillights going around a hairpin turn. Fortunately it was late at night so there was no oncoming traffic. The driver was drunk and his lady friend was sitting in the driver's seat with him with the bottle. How he careened around corners at high speed with the ocean just down the bank on the left! But somehow we made it back to Portland about daybreak. I took the city bus back to Eastmoreland, crawled through the milk door,[8] went to bed, and surprised Mother and Dad at breakfast.

8. [Editor's Note] A milk door was a small cupboard built into the thickness of the wall of the house where the milkman would deliver the milk bottles. There was access from inside the house for residents to get the milk bottles without having to go outside.

I wondered what to do with my life. I did not have the resources to go to college. However, I was only 20 and Benson Polytechnic School, where Uncle Claus worked, was tuition-free until age 21 so I decided to spend a year there and signed up in the fall of 1938. Benson had a radio station under the license of the Federal Communications Commission (FCC). Its purpose was to provide experience in the burgeoning field of radio broadcasting. I had a broadcaster's (radio-telephone) license so I became one of two operators. Many students participated in the studio programs, which were pretty amateurish. The station had some pretty good equipment, so students could be trained in all aspects of programming. The station had low power (50 watts, I think) so it had a short range and did not interfere with commercial broadcasting. We also had a library of both classical and popular music, secondhand records that people had given. Long periods of time during the day were set aside for record playing. And, of course, the turntable sat ready to relieve any situation that was coming apart in the studio. The head of the electrical department, who had an operator's license, was in charge of the station and not only had to be responsible to the school which owned the station but also had to insure compliance with all FCC regulations. Language and drama teachers, for the most part, were in charge of programming, but since one of the regulations of the FCC, at that time, was no bad language on the air, the programmers were strictly responsible to the manager.

I discovered that my background in English was much better than that given at Benson. So I fell into a regular program of proper English in which I reviewed all the rules of grammar and syntax, with examples, and descriptions of how to formulate good sentences and paragraphs. I knew that some of the classes were tuned into my programs, but I imagined that they were ignored by the outside world. However, one of the instructors told me that as he walked along the waterfront he could hear my program coming out the open doors of bars occupied by sailors, drifters, working people. I surely felt puffed up after that, thinking that I might be doing some good.

I soon found that Benson was a wonderful place for the technically inclined. I signed up for 3 year-long courses: mathematics, chemistry and electricity, the latter two of which were 2 hours a day each. Math consisted of a formalized study of trigonometry with applications to surveying; and solid geometry (without analysis) with applications to mechanics. Chemistry was a regular course in chemistry theory with laboratory analysis. Electricity was an in-depth study of AC and DC circuits as well as a lab in electrical power machinery. I also took a course in drafting which was

---

Empty milk bottles were set there for the milkman to pick up at the next delivery day.

mostly relaxing, but it did give me an opportunity to learn how to use the fancy equipment they had and to learn how to make usable (unambiguous) drawings with the latest in symbols and dimensioning. This study was helpful many years later when I drafted the plans for our Los Arboles house.[9]

Even though the text books were pretty dull, I did learn much about trigonometry and solid geometry. The theory of surveying that accompanied trigonometry, while rudimentary, nevertheless proved quite adequate for my job on the survey crew in the Yukon. And the solid geometry has proved to be a basis for rational thinking about space ever since.

Except for expanding my knowledge about atoms, chemical bonds, valences and measuring techniques, the chemistry course gave me very little. The lab instructor told us each day what the experiment was about; then he left and the class became chaotic. It was always possible to fill out the lab questionnaire from the book. So about pH, acids, bases, specific reactions, etc. I learned little. But it was preparation for my future studies.

The two things I learned from the class had nothing to do with chemistry. There were no girls in the class and the boys had free run to tell their stories. Mostly dirty ones. But some of the boys (17–18 years old) had been taken by their fathers to downtown whore houses to be 'bred.' What homes they must have come from! They were also husky fellows who played football and had sweaters, and who smoked so much they stunk of it and had yellow fingers. The other thing was the instructor. He said he had never married and refused to marry. He said his family had an inheritable defect which he refused to pass on. It was the first time in my life I had come face to face with these social problems. Things like that had never been discussed in our family. We were so sheltered.

In electricity, all of the theory was developed from trigonometric concepts and it was certainly adequate to describe electric machinery. I rather imagine that the calculus origin for electrical formulas is limited to very advanced concepts. We also had the opportunity to disassemble and reassemble large and small motors and generators, even down to the wiring of fields and armatures, although I did not do this. We learned all about the phase relations for triple- and six-phase machinery. The electric repair shops of Portland were staffed with boys from Benson who had completed this course. In later years, I would go back and forth over this same material in ever greater mathematical rigor, but this exposure to the nuts and bolts of electrical machinery was to last a lifetime.

Benson was a wonder house of the world of technology as it existed then. There was an aircraft department. In it was taught the aerodynamics

9. [Editor's Note] Albuquerque, New Mexico in 1961.

of flight and along with that was a lab in which students constructed models and even a full-sized light airplane. There was an automotive department (very popular) in which students learned the theory of internal combustion engines, how to disassemble them and repair them (rings, piston, timers, drive shafts, etc.); to do body repairs and modifications, to repair carburetors, brakes, etc. And students were encouraged to bring in their own cars for work experience under the supervision of the instructor. There was a print shop with several presses for studying printing. There was a carpenter shop in which construction methods were taught, even to building a small house as a class project. There was a sheet metal shop. Perhaps the shop that was most interesting was the metal casting and forging shop. Students were taught how to form with sand, how to melt metal (not iron,temperature too high), how to pour and forge and to machine the castings. There was also a blacksmithing shop with a dozen or so big anvils for forming iron.

Uncle Claus was in charge of the tool-making shop. In it were row upon row of lathes, drills, boring machines and metal planers. The students were taught the properties of the various steels and the methods of working them. They were taught how to make tools. For a serious student, it was a dream come true. Unhappily there were always a few students who were not serious and who searched to find ways to disable machines. This caused Uncle Claus much grief because he had to spend overtime hours to repair them. Of special interest to me was the dividing machine, a device that could divide a circle into any integral number of subdivisions, which became useful to me at a later time. This shop held a fascination for me. The idea of making the tools with which to make the tools with which to form steel stirred my imagination. Ever since reading the story of Siegfried[10] and learning about the primitive methods of working steel in the Iron Age's dawning days (remember that Siegfried made his own fabulous sword), I have wondered about the men and techniques of making and working steels. Uncle Claus' knowledge of the various steels was limited to what was available on the market; but even here, there were tool steels so hard that they could only be worked on grinding machines. At a later time, I was able to study steels much more extensively; it is a fascinating subject; interest in it was aroused by Uncle Claus.

In addition to the shops at Benson, they had the usual classes in English, math, art, drama, etc., that were familiar from Washington High. But, with the exception of math, they were inferior presumably because of the absence of girls. Benson was a boys' school. In math, they had a very good

10. [Editor's Note] Siegfried: a strong, courageous character in old heroic Norse and Germanic literature.

curriculum even to the teaching of analytical geometry and calculus, which I had for the first time at Reed College.[11]

At Benson, there were two events which must be told here. They both occurred at the winter open house at Christmas time. In one of them, I pushed around a cart loaded with a battery-operated remote radio station the signal of which was rebroadcast from the main radio station. I toured the school with my remote station, moving from one shop to another telling the radio audience what was going on there. That was particularly interesting in the casting and forging shops because the boys were doing things: carrying a molten bucket of brass over to pour into a form, opening another form after a previous pouring. But the most dramatic exhibit occurred at the giant pneumatic hammer. It consisted of an anvil and a hammer with a steel head about a cubic foot which moved regularly up and down about 20 times a minute, the lower level being determined by the operator. It was normally used to forge large pieces of red hot steel and some of this was shown with the resounding thump! thump! thump! which the microphone easily picked up. But its fine control was also demonstrated by means of a pocket watch laid on the anvil. The hammer was smeared with a little paste, a tiny ball of paper laid on the face of the watch, and the operator brought the steel head (moving up and down) slowly down to where it could just touch the paper ball and lift it off the watch. The owner of the watch, a member of the small crowd standing around, breathed a sigh of relief.

The other event occurred in the auditorium. Twelve large anvils had been set up on large blocks of wood on one half of the stage. On the other half stood the Benson chorus. Down in front was the Benson orchestra. The curtain was drawn back and the lights turned up to reveal bare-to-the-waist blacksmiths wielding large hammers. We in the audience were then treated to *The Anvil Chorus* in which the sound of real anvils merged with the voices of chorus and orchestra. It was impressive and sent shivers up my back. *The Anvil Chorus* is from Verdi's *Il Trovatore* (The Troubador) and it forms a very minor part of the plot. The music is inspiring but not very long. In the Benson version, it was played over about three times to get the full benefit of the anvils.

11. I was not aware of these courses at the time, but learned of their existence by way of Leonard Jones. I was acquainted with him in graduate school at U of O. He also went to Reed, but I did not know him there. He was hoping to get a PhD in math, but was thwarted by something I did. One day I took to him a complicated series I had found in regard to a physics problem and asked if he could identify it. After puzzling over it for a while, he took it to his major professor who quickly identified it as a geometric progression. Poor Leonard! He was then told he was not PhD material since he had not been able to recognize one of the elementary forms of mathematics. So he went to Boeing Aircraft, where he carved out a very successful career in quality assurance.

I heard about a young man who played the violin. I invited him to per-
form on the radio, which he did. He was really very accomplished. Sometime later, I asked him to play again. Wordlessly, he held out his hands. They
were badly scratched and red. He said that he was very poor (his clothes
told that) and in order to buy food for them, he had had to work picking
gooseberries, which grow on very thorny bushes. I never got him to play
again because I left Benson and I always wondered if he had been able to
find a career in music. Why indeed was he at Benson? Years later when
I met Frank Franchini[12], who was also a young man planning a career in
violin, I discovered that his hands had been damaged in much the same way,
but from the Bataan Death March.[13] On the other hand, I noticed a man
playing second violin with the June Music Festival Quartet[14] whose fingers
were thick and swollen like those of a dirt farmer, yet he played beautifully.
There's more to this than meets the eye. . .

During this summer, I was saddened by an event in my life that could
not have been changed but nevertheless was for awhile very hopeful. I fell
in love with the girl across the street. This was in the spring and the whole
affair was over by September. Her name was Elaine. She was two years older
than I and by all odds the prettiest girl I had ever been able to attract. Being across the street, I had seen her many times before but she was always
so shy I could never get close to her to speak. Finally that happened—I've
forgotten how—and she smiled and was friendly. One thing led to another
until I was invited into her house. Close up, she was indeed very pretty with
a lovely figure and beautiful auburn hair. But why so shy? She also played
the piano (her mother was a piano teacher) and it was she who introduced
me to Grieg's *Butterflies*.

I soon found out why she was shy. Some time before, she had been
involved in a severe traffic accident that gave her a head injury that left her
in a coma for days. After some brain surgery and a long recuperation, she
was physically back to normal, but her eyes wouldn't track, she couldn't allow even a light touch on her head and her self-confidence was gone. In
time, her beautiful hair grew back—but no touching. Her mouth smiled
at you but her eyes were elsewhere. In some peculiar way, her skill on the
piano was little impaired. Little by little, she allowed me to get close to her
and finally we became quite loving. I enjoyed her music and we sometimes

12. [Editor's Note] In Albuquerque, New Mexico.

13. [Editor's Note] World War II, April 1942, American and Filipino POWs forced
march on the Bataan Peninsula on West Luzon Island in the Philippines.

14. [Editor's Note] now known as Chamber Music Albuquerque (CMA), Albuquerque, New Mexico.

went to houses where groups of musicians gathered. But she would not go out with me.

We had two outings that summer with members of her family. One of them, with her mother, was to a cabin in Washington where we stayed a week. I hoped I would be able to train her to use her eyes better. At one point, we walked across a log spanning a small stream. She made it but the effort was too much and she had to rest for the rest of the day. The other, with an aunt, was to a cabin near Mt. Hood. We took an old logging road up into the forest completely immersed in the solitude. Then a cougar screamed nearby and we had to turn back; but it was a lovely walk.

I made a pencil drawing of her in a broad brimmed hat with the sunlight making pretty patterns on her face. Dad, who at that time was editing *The Artisan*, used the portrait as a cover[15]. We talked amorously of marriage even though I knew I could not support her.

But then tragedy struck. I had invited her to join us for dinner at Grandpa Hudson's house on View Point Terrace. She was to take the bus, transfer in town to the Barbur Blvd. bus and meet me. But she never came. I was soon to discover that the bus had been in an accident—not a big one—but she had been thrown from her seat, striking her head on one of the seat supports. So it was back to the hospital. A couple of weeks later, she died and we all had a cry at the funeral. In a while her family moved away and I forgot about her. The romance had been there but the marriage would have been a sad one. I would have been in no position to support us.

At the end of the summer, I was invited to go on a get-to-know-each-other campout with other Reed students and entering students. We had the choice of individual or communal eating. I chose individual, bought myself a large packsack and loaded it with enough food for a week and some pans and matches and a hunting knife and a sleeping bag. We were driven in a large truck up to the Forest Camp at Breitenbush Lake[16]. I knew no one of the group but many of them knew each other. There were about 20 of us. We piled out of the truck and selected places to sleep. Since there were shelters there, most of us chose places on the ground in the shelters but some chose to sleep in the open; there was one tent for a group of young men and women who knew each other and who I later found out were chaperones. The truck went away, supposed to return in a week.

The night was cold but the next morning opened clear and bright. By this time, the students were making friends and I found some friendly types

15. [Editor's Note] *The Artisan*, official publication of the Artisans Life Association; the cover mentioned here is probably May 1938.

16. [Editor's Note] Breitenbush Lake, located on a high plateau north of Mt. Jefferson, Oregon.

as well. One was a young woman M— with a hare (split) lip, ugly in the face but otherwise well made. She spoke with a lisp and seemed to be rejected by the rest of the group, so I felt sorry for her and became her friend. Getting wood, cooking and camp activities occupied the first day. There was a campfire and songs at night. The second day was warm and pleasant. People drifted off into the woods in small groups to seek the Skyline Trail. I was slow (couldn't keep up with the others) and took off by myself toward the east. Finally getting to the top, I found the trail at the crest and could look over onto the pine forest on the east side. I took the trail to the south and after a mile or so met two huge brown bears stuffed with berries for the winter hibernation. They snuffed and growled at me; I panicked and left the trail, running down into the then deserted camp. The bears, probably wondering at my strange behavior, did not follow; probably they continued lumbering along the trail. Later a large party of students who had walked farther along the trail told the story of meeting three or four bears. They stepped off the trail and the bears moved sedately past them, smelling as bears do, and disappeared.

By this time, discontent was growing in the camp over who was to cook, who to wash up. The chaperones, who were later identified as belonging to the Reed Mountain Club, took a goodly supply of food into their tent and left the rest of the group to fend for itself. After 2 or 3 days of warm, balmy days in which everyone stripped down to briefs for sun bathing, the weather turned suddenly cold during the night and we woke up under a blanket of snow. Those who slept outside found themselves in wet sleeping bags. I was completely dry and being self-sufficient in food managed to adopt a smug attitude towards the rest.

A drizzle set in. Camp morale deteriorated. The plan to have communal meals didn't work well and much of the good food supplies disappeared. One of the most outraged of the group was a tall fellow with blond hair who was not shy about complaining. When he talked to me, I said "Would you like to join me?" to which he agreed. He said his name was Herman Johansen and he was from Astoria. He took a small share of supplies from the communal stores, brought his sleeping bag and we set up a camp in a shelter somewhat farther from the group.

Actually, two girls also joined us. The grumbling continued in the camp and two boys chose to hike out to the little town of Detroit and go home. I cooked for our little group and they washed up. Even my supplies were running low now and we had to eat lots of hot cakes. The last couple of days, I had to stretch the hot cake flour with crumbled bread. But we were a congenial group, swapping stories and laughter.

One day, Herman and M— and I took the trail over into Mt. Jefferson Park, a beautiful area that lay around the foot of Mt. Jefferson. Herman said that he wanted to hike up onto Mt. Jefferson. I knew I couldn't do that, so M— and I turned back. So we went back and Herman returned after dark. I learned then of his great physical endurance.

At the end of the week, the truck came to get us, by now a bedraggled group: no food, dirty clothes, and short tempers. But spirits improved on the way home and songs broke out. On parting, everyone agreed we'd had a good time. But I never felt good about the Mountain Club and never joined.

5

First Two Years at Reed College

1939—MID 1941

I was called a "day dodger" at Reed, to distinguish myself from those living on campus. They always had a camaraderie that I couldn't join, but that cost money I didn't have. Herman lived in the heating plant building with a big fellow called Vernor Anderson. We three were to remain good friends until Vernor died about 1985. He made food his career and established the best delicatessen and catering service in Portland.[1]

Reed consisted of a number of buildings: the women's and men's dormitories; the main lecture hall; the commons, where on-campus students ate (I could get an occasional meal there); the Student Union Building; the Gymnasium; the Library; and a Music Room. I had nothing to do with the dormitories and little to do with the Commons. My life at Reed centered around the main lecture hall and the library although I spent some time in each of the Music Hall and the Student Union. I nearly forgot: there was also an Art Studio building.

The Music Hall was an addition onto the Men's Dorm. It was perhaps 40 feet square, finished in handsome wood paneling, and appointed with a grand table with chairs, overstuffed chairs around the walls, and a record player with a small library of classical music at one end. These were, of course, the old 78 rpm records and the player had a changer which could

---

1. [Editor's Note] Carl Vern Anderson, Anderson's Delicatessen, Portland, Oregon.

accept five records, so that a symphony could be played in its entirety. One of a few designated students was in charge of the player and record collection.

When I went to Reed, I knew very little about classical music. At Grandpa Hudson's house, on the morning music program on the radio, I used to hear the old masters without much comprehension. Some music like Khachaturian's works stirred me deeply. I was fond of *In a Persian Garden*, composer unknown. And I knew the great composers' names but could not associate them with particular works. At Reed, I began to have a real appreciation for music and to receive a rudimentary music education because associating composer with works was very important. Somewhere, perhaps at Reed, I first heard Bizet's *Carmen* and the real power of music hit me. The first record I ever bought for myself was Debussy's *Daphnis and Chloe*. I became hooked on 20th century music. In later years I developed a much deeper appreciation for all music. But at Reed, the seeds were sown.

I only went into the girls' dormitory once on a Sunday afternoon to pick up a girl (name forgotten) to take her to dinner. The room was for two, light and airy, beds and ample desks for studying, not much room for clothing storage. I presume the men's dorm was similar but I never went in.

The Commons was a large cafeteria style building with the kitchen on one end, a main hall with tables and chairs in the middle and a few private rooms on the far end. Professional cooks prepared the food; students served it and cleaned up for which they were paid 25 cents an hour. Once in a great while I bought a lunch here, but since most of the students paid for board and room with their tuition, the Commons was not well set up for cash customers.

The Student Union was planned for informal student meetings, for dances and for lounging around. Students also could buy coffee and soft drinks there and there were tables for day dodgers to eat sack lunches. Since on-campus students had their dorms and the Commons for informal meetings, the Student Union was largely used by day dodgers, with one exception.

On Thursday evenings there was folk dancing. I was not good at ballroom dancing but the idea of dancing was strong, so I joined the folk dance group of about 40 people (10 groups of 4), more women than men. The instructor was Elizabeth Nichols then just out of a dance curriculum at an Eastern school. She was pretty and vivacious and certainly had a head full of dance steps. She also taught a class of modern dance to students, mostly girls, which was apparently very challenging. Occasionally they put on a performance on the stage of the Student Union which always attracted a crowd more because of the dancers' diaphanous costumes than because of their dancing skills. In the folk dancing sessions, Miss Nichols usually stood to one side of the record player and called out the dances. A few of the dances were Western American squares and reels, but most of them were European style dances (actually the forerunners of Western dances) but often with very complicated foot work. Little by little we learned these dances and could have a very exciting evening out of it. Little by little, too, Miss Nichols became Libby to me and we became lifelong friends.

We were obliged to spend part of each week during the first two years at the Gymnasium doing anything that would work up a sweat. There was a separate side for women. I learned that the women's demands were not so great although vigorous exercise was encouraged. There was a large court for basketball and volleyball between the two sides which was time-shared by men and women. One of the sports for women was archery, not available to men. There were three squash courts for the men: one a small hardball court; one a singles squash rackets court (the most popular) and a doubles squash rackets court. In the hardball court, the players could use all six sides of the room; in the squash rackets courts (using tennis rackets and tennis balls) only three sides of the room could be used. These courts were my favorite physical activity. There was also a weight lifting room. Outside there was a swimming pool, well used in spite of the cold water, and a stadium. The stadium contained a football, baseball combination field within a track which was about ¼ mile around. There was also, within the track, space for shot-put, discus, and javelin throws.

Mr. Botsford (called Bots) was in charge of the Gym and he had under his supervision a woman to oversee women's activities. Outside the area of the Gym proper were tennis courts, often used by the faculty. There was no reason at all for a student without handicap not to enjoy sports while putting in his Gym time.

Bots was a most agreeable man always willing to play a game with someone without a partner, full of good spirit and stories and a treasure of information about the human body and sports in general. He was about 60 years old, but I could never beat him at squash rackets. Fortunately for me, he was always there.

One of the parts of the Gym that made a big impression on me was the shower room. There were 6 shower heads widely spaced apart with plenty of hot water. It was a real temptation to stand in one jet and soak for minutes at a time. The next time I saw such an installation was in France, which was even nicer because the floor and walls were covered with white tiles.

Reed did not go in for contact sports very much, but they did have a football team which played in the Oregon intramural organization. One year (1940) they made the pages of *Time Magazine*[2] by not losing a single

2. [Editor's Note] December 4, 1939. Education: Husky Reed. *Time Magazine, Vol.*

game of the series and having only 11 men to play (no substitutes, so the same men had to play the whole game) against teams that could substitute frequently.

The library, as libraries go, was not very large but it was wonderfully equipped with books. Some of the professors gave assignments requiring materials (not always bound volumes) that were kept in multiple copies; but otherwise, books were singles which could be borrowed for 2 to 4 weeks—except by faculty members where the borrowing was indefinite. However, a student could put in a request for a book borrowed by a faculty member and usually get it. There was no light reading in the library, but every academic subject was to some extent covered from ancient to modern. The Physics Department had its own library in Dr. Knowlton's[3] large office, and I understood that other departments had similar branch libraries, actually the private collections of the department heads. It was fun to peruse the physics collection because many of those books had notes written in the margins by Knowlton himself. Most of those books were dated. He did not keep up very well with the contemporary literature in physics, on the argument that students should master the old works first. However, he kept the bound *Physical Review*[4] (then only one section) up to date; also a French journal and some others, up to date. When I had to pass my qualifying language exam, Ellickson[5] had replaced Knowlton. The main library had a very small maintenance fund with which they were able to purchase, each month or so, a few new well-chosen books. Many of the books were donations by professors, alumni or outside agents. There was also a small amount of rebinding to do in order to keep books from deteriorating which also came out of the maintenance fund. But the library's crown jewel was the Tower Room. In it were the really valuable books, books of all ages and sizes, collector's items which could not be checked out. There were huge volumes (2 feet by 3 feet or more) often with hand painted illustrations, bound in leather, really rare items. I loved to peruse these books: but the Tower Room was not very large and the number of readers who could be accommodated was small, so my time up there was limited. Nevertheless, I treasured that time.[6]

XXXIV No. 23 2012·

3. [Editor's Note]Dr. Ansel Alphonse Knowlton, Professor of Physics.

4. [Editor's Note] Craig is probably referring to *Physical Review Letters*.

5. [Editor's Note] Ray Thorwald Ellickson, Associate Professor of Physics.

6. Years later when I visited Mount Angel Abbey to get information about the Palmer family origins, I made friends with Father Pollard, archivist, who let me and Jeannine into the vault where their collection of old books was kept. It was a concrete room, air conditioned and humidity controlled, filled to overflowing with treasures, mostly of the Catholic religion, all donated and many handwritten and illuminated

In the Reed Library, there was also a large card index, not as large as the one in the Portland Public Library, but very complete. One of the first tasks all freshmen had to do at Reed was to take a course (about 3 hours long) having to do with library science and the use of this card catalog.

The whole interior of the library was devoted to tables and chairs for study or reading. It was always busy from opening at 7 AM to closing at 10 PM. Many students prepared their lessons there. Good discipline prevailed most of the time and it was very quiet—except sometimes for the tittering of a boy-girl alliance hidden in the stacks!

Art was one of my primary interests and I signed up for an art course or two each of the first four semesters I was there. The resident artist was Emma Lou Davis[7], not a fine artist perhaps but one very much up to date in what was going on. She was primarily a sculptress, but her ability with line drawing and painting was very good. I thought I had learned a great deal from Sydney Bell; but she showed me a much broader horizon.

The Art Studio was a temporary building in the center of the campus. It had space for a large open studio room, a smaller ceramic studio, a kiln and a couple or three offices. In the ceramic studio were two wheels, one clay preparation table, several individual stands and shelves full of materials. There were plenty of materials at Reed but they were not the expensive sort. We did not have access to canvas, for instance, unless we wished to buy our own. I can't recall anyone doing that. The classes were a motley bunch, some quite serious (I put myself in that class) and some just playing with no expectation even to make progress.

My work at the studio ran along two lines: expanding my painting skills and learning about ceramics. The painting class, as I mentioned, was a very mixed group. No one there had had my level of training, but Emma Lou was nevertheless very critical of both my style and my work: "too old fashioned" she said, and after a bit I began to agree with her. She herself was a master at the simple line technique (like Cassandra[8]); but when she wanted to, she could also paint in the round with feeling. In this sense she was a better teacher than Sydney Bell who was stuck in the 19th century. She ex-

---

manuscripts from early times. I remember one in which the pages were parchment, the skin of goats dried, scraped and smoothed for writing in which the leg holes of the animals still showed! The writing (in Coptic) merely avoided the holes. What a treasure trove for one who loves old books. These books, along with the wonderful large books of Egyptian hieroglyphics I found at the Public Library in Portland, gave me a deep appreciation for books which persists to the present day. .

7. [Editor's Note] Emma Lou Davis, artist in residence 1938—1941.

8. [Editor's Note] Craig's daughter, Cassandra C.H. Shaw, is a talented artist who often employs the pen and ink technique.

tended her simple line technique to planar and space effects, as well. For instance, to sculpt a cat, she used a cat skin to cut out the form, folded the clay over into a body, attached a head, positioned the legs and fired it to produce a cat, unmistakably, but one with an artistic flair. As I continued to paint under her guidance, I developed a more modern style but still retained the brush skill I had learned from Sydney Bell. I still have one of those paintings: *Still Life with a Mushroom.*[9]

Portrait of H S Hudson, painted 1938

9. [Editor's Note] see Appendix: Catalog of Paintings.

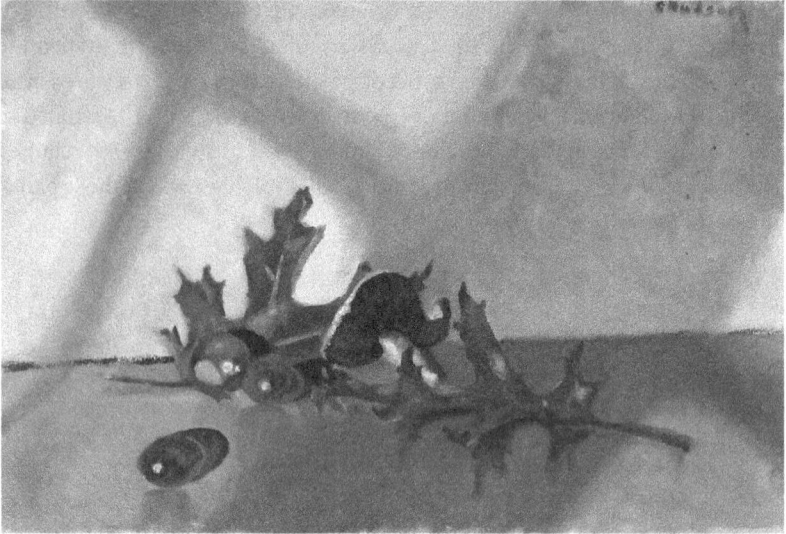

Still Life with a Mushroom, painted 1941

Emma Lou was able to get commissions quite easily. She had one for a large (4'x8') frieze to be completed in white marble for some site in Washington DC. I looked for it later but could not find it. At that time, there was available a kind of insulating material made in 4'x8' sheets of pressed corn shucks. It was easy to cut and by gluing 8 sheets together she had a slab 8"x48"x96" which could be modeled by cutting into it with a knife intaglio-style.[10] The figures were cut in and the whole thing shipped off to the stone cutters. Another commission was to carve out of a slab of walnut some figures to hang in the Student Union building. A third was to paint a series of panels depicting animals of the Tertiary geological period for the Biology Department. She asked me to do one of them, a kind of shrew, and so far as I know it still hangs on the wall there.[11]

Some premed students took the drawing course to develop their skills at representing surgical procedures. We also had live models, even nude models, for part of the course. Some of the class became paralyzed at the sight of a nude model. I did lots of sketching but have very little in the way of finished drawings from these classes.[12]

---

10. [Editor's Note] Intaglio is sculpture or engraving in stone or other hard material so that all lines appear below the surface. It is the opposite of relief sculpture.

11. [Editor's Note] A discussion with the Reed University archivist revealed that a fire in the building destroyed these art works.

12. Later, when I returned to Reed after the war, I conducted a class in painting in which Marge Johansen and Bob Thompson and some others were students. The studio

I was not nearly as experienced in ceramics, but it was fun learning. Work on the wheel was picked up quickly and I still have some of the pieces I did after the war.[13] We only had two kinds of clay to work with: stoneware which was heavy, stiff and hard when fired, and brick clay which was cheap, easy to work but soft and easily chipped after being fired. But it had a decorative advantage: a white slip (thin clay) could be applied over the soft body and then, when dry, scraped off to form rather striking designs. During the summer between the first two years at Reed (1940), Emma Lou had me make mugs for her for sale. I learned how to slip cast and then how to apply slip and carve, making all sorts of geometrical and fanciful designs. It was an opportunity which, in retrospect, I did not treat seriously enough. I talked over with Emma Lou an idea for animating physics experiments, but we could find no money to support it.

Perhaps the most interesting aspect of the ceramics work was that of preparing glazes. There were several facets of it: color, firing temperature, coefficient of expansion, hardness, etc. I made dozens of little two-inch squares of clay and tried all sorts of combinations of fluxes, metal salts and metal powders from the chemistry lab. I could not control the temperature, however. Some crazed, some gave bright colors, and many were unimpressive. I tried to get Uranium salts which, I had read, gave brilliant colors, but it was not available. Lead serves as a very good flux but I did not know at the time that it was a no-no for food vessels. I think the most important result to come from all this was, many years later, to give me material to inspire my son Marc, who later became very proficient in ceramics and glaze preparations.

Emma Lou Davis was quite a personality. She was married to a rather mousey English professor but they were in the process of a divorce. She was so much more energetic and bright than he that I often wondered how they had got together. They both loved to ski; perhaps that had been the initial attraction.

Emma Lou was a small, wiry woman with piercing blue eyes surrounded by thick black eyelashes, under thick black eyebrows. Her hair was jet black, straight and trimmed into a thick boyish bob that she constantly shook. Her complexion was deeply suntanned and she wore a bright red lipstick which set off her even white teeth. She had such a happy tempestuous personality that I do not remember her ever being somber. And she was

---

was open until midnight so we met from 8 to 10.

13. [Editor's Note] Craig's daughter and son, Cassandra and Marc, are keepers of several of Craig's bowls.

constantly active. I suppose she had serene moments sometimes, but I never saw them around the studio.

She had flat breasts and in summer they were scarcely covered. And she wore the briefest of briefs which exposed her lower belly and legs covered with black fur. I must have stared, never having seen such a figure before, but she tolerated my gaze good naturedly. She was one of the most athletic persons I have ever seen. At any free time, she was swimming or in the tennis court; I even played squash with her once. And her love of skiing was notorious. She was always the center of a crowd of skiers. But they told me of her private exploits also. In January when the snow was at its best, she used to climb up the slopes of Mt. Hood as high as she could go, strip down to the waist and come flying down the mountain, all out, in a cloud of snow, singing at the top of her lungs. It was a feat few other skiers attempted. She was sure she exceeded 60 mph and used to tell me about the exhilaration of it the next day.

Needless to say, Emma Lou made a deep impression on me. She was simply too energetic for me to imagine being close to for very long. But I appreciated the opportunity to know that people like her existed. After we moved to Albuquerque, I heard somehow that she lived in Santa Fe, but I never saw her again after I left Reed in 1941. By the time I returned to Reed in 1946, another resident artist had taken her place. Emma Lou is one of the few faces I can remember: very pretty but framed in so much black hair, with a faint black moustache.

My first year at Reed was like opening a window onto a previously unsuspected world. I took five classes: physics, math, ancient history, literature and art. Physics was taught by Dr. Knowlton and was the smallest class, about 12 students. I don't remember who taught math, but it was a big class of about 30 students. Then there was history taught by Dr. Arragon[14], a very large class of at least 100. And Literature taught by Dr. Barry Cerf, also a class of 100.

In each of these classes, I was exposed to ideas that had never before entered my mind. Physics and math went hand in hand, as did history and literature. I had in the past been exposed to the concepts of physics and math. The big change here was that they became quantitative. In Knowlton's class, ideas were discussed and suddenly they were represented by equations! I realized that these were greatly simplified representations—Knowlton said so—but I was struggling to appreciate what equations meant. It was like story problems had been in algebra, but now the stories were from the real world. We used Knowlton's text book and he lectured us over and over again: "Understand the words and then the formulas will fit easily. Do

14. [Editor's Note] Dr. Reginald F. Arragon.

not select formulas in an effort to get the answer!" I still have his book and refer to it from time to time, whenever the material is appropriate. The basic ideas of physics are there, not overlain by a burden of recent developments. Of course, the whole field of particle physics (including molecular physics) came after he wrote that book (in 1935).

The math class was the introduction to calculus, using F.L. Griffin's textbook[15]. Again, it was a wonderful eye-opener, to see how ideas of motion could be quantized into equations. The actual number of students taking math must have been close to 100, but we were divided into about five classes, some (who had calculus in high school) being the more advanced. I was in the slower class and for a long time had difficulty transforming the ideas of movement into equations. And there was a certain amount of algebraic manipulation required, which I was slow at. Little was I to know then—I who was still intent on being an artist—that I would be using equations the rest of my life! It seemed so unreal.

But it was in the area of liberal arts (history and literature) that the greatest shocks were to come. Up to then, I had been guided by the ideas and the spiritual attitudes of my family—my parents and grandparents. In the course of that year, my little world was turned upside down.

My ideas about religion ranged from Grandma Hudson's Christian Science (which I rejected) to the Palmer Protestantism—never very clearly enunciated but always present in the background. Dad, for some years, played around with Hindu mysticism. At Reed, we opened up the whole bucket of worms of religion by studying its historical and literary background in the context of ideas about ethics derived from philosophy. No religious point of view was favored, of course; not even the existence of God was espoused. But the roots of all thinking about religious and ethical concepts were exposed as we read the writings of men from Hammurabi (1000 BC) to Freud (1900). There was close cooperation between Dr. Arragon and Dr. Cerf so that we often touched on the same events and figures in both history and literature. We received from Arragon the essence of human living (not just the wars) and the growth of civilization; and from Cerf the flavor of human thought as represented in literature. We covered the period from the Sumerians to the middle ages with special emphasis on the Greeks and the Romans—especially the Greeks because Reed considered this the classic period which every well-educated person should have as the basis for his thought. Cerf even read Greek and Roman poetry to us in the original tongue, as best as he could determine it.

15. [Editor's Note] Frank Loxley Griffin, *An Introduction to Mathematical Analysis*, Houghton Mifflin 1922.

In these two classes, we had two lectures per week each by the major professors. Then there were three discussion classes each plus term papers. The discussion groups were particularly lively because the students came from diverse backgrounds. We were assigned readings (such as Roman senators' speeches or thoughts of Thomas Aquinas) and we constantly compared the thought of ancient times with that of today. That is where I discovered that the thinking of my Hudson-Palmer ancestors was so out of step with the course of classical thought. One especial piece of literature comes to mind as being unacceptable: Dante's *Inferno*[16] which combined all the myths of the early Christian church. In our discussion groups we hotly debated this work because some of the students came from very religious families.[17] On the other hand, I enjoyed and accepted the writings of Marcus Aurelius, a minor Roman emperor. These experiences led me, years later, to obtain the Durants' *Story of Civilization*[18].

The two instructors of these groups were both graduate students and both were friendly. The history instructor was Elizabeth Wahl and I have forgotten the other name. Elizabeth was a most agreeable woman, perhaps 10 years older than I, who was game to do all sorts of things. For instance, we once made root beer in the kitchen of the 35th Street house and then, after it was ready, we sponsored a party at Peach Cove with some Reed friends. On another occasion, we drove out the Columbia scenic highway and I think I have a picture of her in that context. She was soft spoken, chubby and seemed always to be cold because she constantly wore a wool suit in every kind of weather. She helped me quite a bit. For my term paper, I wrote on the subject of the evolution of the arch in architecture. I think we still have the paper. She was impressed enough to take the paper to Arragon personally (unheard of) and arranged for a conference between the two of us which greatly influenced my thinking about history and contributed to my stature in the school.

The other instructor never seemed so attractive, although she was much prettier. We met a few times in the art studio where I taught her how to carve wood. And on one occasion she and Libby Nichols came to a group I arranged at Grandpa Hudson's then new house for 'tea.' After they arrived, Aunt Hattie, after studying Libby's pert little hat, said "I'll just put this in the closet for you" and tried to lift it off Libby's head! But it was attached to her

16. [Editor's Note] *Inferno*, the first section of *La Divina Comedia*, written by Dante Alighieri (c. 1265–1321).

17. My friend Tom Hall gave me his copy (from his grandfather) which was printed in about 1860 with the original Doré drawings. I cherish it. [Editor's Note] Craig's daughter, Cassandra, is keeper of the volume.

18. [Editor's Note] Durant and Durant, *The Story of Civilization*, vol. I-XI, 1935—1975.

piled-up hair by hat pins. Poor Aunt Hattie! From her background, it was impolite to wear your hat in the house and she was trying to be nice.

The second year at Reed was more somber. I took the advanced calculus class, electricity and electronics (two semesters), psychology, philosophy and, of course, art. The exciting ideas of calculus had been presented in the first year, so the second year was (to me) just dog work—developing technique, solving questions, etc. The electricity semester dealt with 19th century electricity and I chafed to go beyond that. Finally I arrived at electronics, which promised to parallel the work on radio at OIT. And in a way it did but in great mathematical detail. The vacuum tube, which had been at the center of the OIT course, was now relegated to a minor role and I studied the details of the circuits around it.

We had a lab and one night I was working late trying to study the properties of the tetrode. I had it hooked up as a triode. After hours of experimentation, I tried a new trick which gave me a much higher amplification. I was so excited that I called up Dr. Marcus O'Day to tell him about it at 11:30pm. He said "I'll be right over"—he lived next to Knowlton on campus—and five minutes later he came puffing into the lab (he was fat) and looked over my set-up. He was dressed in pajamas, robe and slippers. In about half an hour, he had diagnosed my work and said "you have inadvertently hooked it up as a tetrode. That's why you are getting so much amplification." So much for bright ideas!

We were invited to join a small group of physics students from around the state to give papers at a small conference in the lab at Linfield College in McMinnville. Much later, Herman and Marge[19] would move to McMinnville and Linfield would become a familiar place in the field of art. My paper was about a project I was working on at school with the instrument maker. His work mostly was to keep the various instruments (mostly electrical) in working order for the physics labs. Once in awhile he replaced the scale on an instrument and it was my job to mark out the scale with a caliper and pen and ink. I got the idea that an engine could be built with a large steel disc divided around the periphery in units of ten. Then a blank scale was placed at the center and as the disc rotated, a pen was used to mark the time of the scale. I tried to invent a marking pen that consisted of a small wedge that moved up and down, first to be inked on the edge of the wedge and then to press its line onto the paper. Uncle Claus had his boys at Benson Polytechnic School make the disc (16" diameter) of heavy steel sheet inscribed all around the edge. It worked very well. The Achilles Heel of the machine proved to be the marker, which made a smeared line unsuited to the purpose. The idea originally had

19. Herman Johansen and wife Margaret (Marge).

been to improve the accuracy of the scale; with a smeared line, this was not achieved, although I did not experiment enough with inks and papers. I gave my paper at the conference and it aroused no interest—too classical. John G—, for instance, derived the equations for the magnetron and was the hit of the show—even though he copied most of the derivation from a published paper. I played with the engine for a while but could never solve the marker problem, so it was relegated to storage.

Slowly during this second year in math and physics I developed an appreciation for how science really worked. It was the interplay between mathematics and physical ideas that finally penetrated my thinking and never left. The laws of physics always worked at whatever scale one wished to consider; no amount of wishing or praying could affect their course. This came as a revelation to me because my early training, by way of Grandma Hudson and Christian Science, had been that one's mind and thinking could, in fact, affect the outcome. Even to this day, a subconscious voice tells me sometimes that the physical laws are not immutable in all situations, that they don't really hold in the limits of accuracy. That is wrong and one has to oppose such heresy. Physical laws always hold; mathematics only makes it possible to test them more precisely. Some mathematicians, with unwarranted pride, think that their equations are more fundamental than that. High speed computers, completely unknown when I was at Reed, have demonstrated that mathematics assists physical law, but never replaces it. In recent years, I have become aware of Richard Feynmann[20], who is perhaps the most clear thinker in the field of physical theory who ever lived. He relegates mathematics (and mathematical theory) to the supporting role I have just mentioned.

In this second year, I took courses in psychology and philosophy. Both were very interesting and helpful, since they supplemented the literary and historical studies of the year before. This first course in psychology limited itself to the metrical aspects of the human mind. That is, it discussed at length the idea of intelligence and the attempts to measure it. Whatever it is, people have it in varying amounts and for each individual it rises year by year to about the age of 20 after which it normally remains flat until about the age of 50, after which it slowly declines. However, as we all know, the phrase "use it or lose it" applies to the whole human being and these markers are not immutable. The other important thing I learned in psychology had to do with nerves and their interactions. The famous experiment with dogs (if a bell is rung each time food is presented and the dog salivates, then the dog will salivate when the bell is rung but food is not presented) made a real impression on me and I began to watch for examples in real life. The conclusion I draw is

20. [Editor's Note] Richard P. Feynman, Nobel Prize in Physics 1965.

that free will cannot exist; will is one of the properties of the mind but instead of being free, it is conditioned by past experience and environment. It may be more free for a human being than for an animal but it still is subject to conditioning. The idea of truly free will comes from religious philosophy.

The first course in psychology did not delve into abnormal psychology, but the library was well stocked with books and I read avidly. The distortions of the human mind can be just as grotesque as those of the human body. I sometimes had bad dreams. Looking back over the years that have passed from then to now, psychology has made great strides.

The course in philosophy was much less interesting, partly because of the teacher who was not at all inspirational. We spent hours studying the syllogism and its flaws as well as its strengths. Part of the course carried us through the history of early Greek thought. In subsequent times, I have been aware of the debt I owe to this exposure without being able to single out particulars. But the idea I had when I entered the course of study—that I would learn about the philosophy of science—was ungratified. We never got beyond religious philosophy, which left me with a bad feeling because my newly acquired sense of physical law was completely at odds with questions like "when a tree falls in the forest, does it make a sound?" which derive from the Christian idea that Man is the center of the universe. Actually, the concepts of the philosophy of science were worked out much later; I was expecting too much of the course. Einstein's relativity concept was known but not understood. Relativity was introduced into ethics, where it caused turmoil.

Harvey and Craig, 1919

Ivon Street house, (L to R) Shirley, Craig, Bertha, circa 1921

Harvey in his office, 1925

(L to R, back) Mary Palmer, Edwin Palmer, Elizabeth Rogers Hudson (mother of H S Hudson) holding Craig, Neva Hudson, H S Hudson holding Shirley, circa 1921

(L to R) Shirley, Marilyn, Craig, Dexter (standing), circa 1926

Craig age 12, 1930

6

Need for Money and Adventures in the Yukon

SUMMER 1941—1942

At the end of this school year (May 1941), world events were beginning to stir the United States. The war in Europe was going badly and, of course, the media played up the human interest (mostly terror) aspects predominantly. Shipping to England was being torpedoed at what seemed like a horrendous rate. Japan was marching through SE Asia with seemingly no resistance. The effects of these events on male students were very depressing. We all were subject to the draft, although I was rated 4F which meant that I would not be drafted soon. But this made me feel even more depressed because I feared the prospect of being separated from the main line.

Money was the first concern, however, and by way of a friend of Grandpa Hudson, I was hired by a bill collecting agency. The idea of working at such a job was very distasteful to me, not because of any experiences I had had but because of word-of-mouth innuendo. But I needed the money and I didn't want to disappoint Grandpa. But first I needed a car, so I went to a used car lot with Grandpa and bought (he lent me the money) a 1929 Ford 4-door for $200. It ran very well but the tires were no good and it cost me extra to replace them. It was my first car—in fact, my first major possession—and I felt rather proud, even though I knew it was pretty junky.

The job consisted in taking a handful of cards out with me in the morning. Each card had on it a name, a merchant's name, the amount of indebtedness and 15 or so lines to describe the history of collection. Sometimes that history was rather long and two cards were stapled together. Each time a call was made to the debtor (no matter what the outcome), the collector received 50 cents; so if you made 10 calls a day, you earned $5, less your expenses. Some of the men made 100 calls a day, mostly ineffective. In time, the merchant grew dissatisfied with dead beats and took them to small claims court. But the debtors were not all dead beats; some were people, unable to take money to the merchant, who were pleased that I could pick up the money for their accounts. My area of town was N. Portland, a triangular section mostly north of Burnside and east of the river. It was, of course, the least desirable of the available areas. But I had some interesting experiences; three examples will be sufficient. It was July and about 100° with high humidity, very uncomfortable. I approached a certain house, rang the doorbell several times and finally heard a faint voice call out "come around behind." So I went into the back yard and found the following sight: a large woman naked to the waist with huge breasts. She sat in a big patio chair next to a table with a pitcher of lemonade and glass. She fanned herself with a palm leaf. "Come in, young man," she said as I appeared at the gate, "Excuse my dress; it's too hot to be active." I must have been bug-eyed. But I managed to explain my purpose and she asked me to hand her her purse from the table. She took out a $5 bill, handed it to me and said "Thank you for coming; I just can't get downtown in this weather." A successful contact. On another hot day, I stopped in front of what in its day must have been a mansion, knocked several times on the door. It was finally opened by the most beautiful black girl I had ever seen. In a moment she was joined by three more, all beautiful and dressed in nothing more than night clothes. Being as inexperienced as I was, I finally stammered out that I was trying to see so-and-so about a debt. One of the girls, surprised, said "Oh, I forgot all about that" and ran off to get some money. The other girls, all smiles, invited me in—but I was afraid to go. Soon so-and-so came back with the money and, chattering and laughing with big smiles, they watched me retreat. Another successful contact and my first view of a high-class whorehouse—in fact, my only view. On a third occasion, I stopped at a shop and presented the debt to a dour young man. He blew up, waving his arms, cursing me and finally threatened to beat me up and I thought he was going to do it. I retreated to the car very much upset and wrote the incident up on his card. The next day as I drove down the street, he came rushing out to see me, all smiles, and gave me a handful of bills. I thought that was also a successful contact, but when the boss found out about it next morning, he became quite angry. "My people must not be threatened," he said, "I already started court proceedings against this guy;

now that you have collected, it's all off." Sometimes you can't win. I think I was making perhaps 20 calls a day when a surprise came up.

Late in the summer, in a manner I have now forgotten, I met my friend from Duniway Grammar School, Nelson. Remember that his father was an architect. After high school, Nelson had been training as a draftsman. Now he had a job working at Commercial Iron Works (CIW) (near the west end of the Ross Island Bridge) as a naval draftsman. The company was building mine sweepers, small ships to clear harbors and sea lanes of enemy mines. He said I might be able to get a job there, even though my drafting experience was limited. I applied and did get a job as vault keeper. For security reasons, all principal drawings had to be locked up in a vault at night. It was my job to see that all such drawings (usually quite large) were properly stored in the vault and checked out and in each day as needed. At first it was very confusing; there were so many and the names were so strange. But soon I got the hang of it and it became easy. The pay was much better than I was used to, although not like pay in the Liberty Ship shipyards near Albina. And working at CIW was an easy drive from home and close to Grandpa Hudson's house. After I became familiar with the yards, I was able to spend some time in the loft where specialists made large templates out of ¼" Honduras mahogany from the drawings. And I visited the construction areas and watched ships being launched.

But the big event of my stay at CIW (Commercial Iron Works) was meeting Marley Brown[1] for the first time and renewing my acquaintance with Eugene Snyder[2], whom I had known a little at Washington High School and Reed College. It was a surprise to learn that Marley also attended Reed, but before I went there. He also spent some time working in a mine near Socorro! He hated every day of it.[3] Marley worked in the electrical department, checking electrical drawings; Eugene worked in documentation, but I never knew exactly what he did. All three men, Herman, Marley and Eugene, were draft-classified 1A which meant they could be put in the infantry.

The world situation grew steadily more desperate as 1941 rolled on. Then on Dec 7, 1941 came the electrifying news that Japan had bombed Pearl Harbor. No one knew where they would attack next. In fact, a Japanese submarine did shell the Oregon coast near Astoria[4] but the shells were

1. [Editor's Note] Marley Brown remained a lifelong friend of Craig's.

2. [Editor's Note] Eugene Snyder remained a lifelong friend of Craig's.

3. [Editor's Note] Socorro, New Mexico is approximately 75 miles south of Albuquerque.

4. [Editor's Note] On June 21, 1942 the Japanese I-25 long-range submarine shelled the Oregon coast near Fort Stevens.

small caliber and did no damage. However, the fact that the shelling took place made them appear to be super men and many people in the Portland area acted accordingly. There was a general blackout. Even automobiles had to paint their head and tail lights dark blue with small slits to allow some visibility. Since we came to work at 7:30 am and left at 5:30 pm, with cloudy weather and often rain, driving was very slow. Traffic slowed to 15 mph. Food stamps and gasoline stamps were issued and enforcement was severe. Meat was especially rationed.

In February (1942), I met with Herman, who was still at Reed. He was bitterly discouraged and was looking for any way out. Finally he had heard about a job on the crew of a survey party to push a road through western Canada to Alaska[5]. It sounded like real adventure, supported by the US Public Roads Administration (PRA). Herman was going to sign up. Even though I was relatively satisfied with the present job, the adventure was appealing. I spoke to Marley and Eugene about it. Eugene was definitely not interested. After a little discussion, Marley and I decided to go for it, but actually joining up was slow. I didn't talk to Herman for another month. When I next saw him, he had already signed up and said that the recruiting was almost over. Marley and I went to sign up right away and we were both accepted.

The first step was to get outfitted. We had read books about life in the Yukon, but really had no good information about clothing. We went to the Oregon Outfitting Store on 2nd Street and asked the clerk to suggest some things. We started out with a foot locker and slowly filled it: woolen pants, boots (I chose loggers with nails—a bad choice as it turned out (too cold) while Marley chose composition soles), warm underclothes (full suits of wool), shirts (including a Jantzen[6]), a heavy wool jacket, and (of course) a Yukon hat. I forgot to mention socks, several pairs of heavy wool plus some lighter ones[7]. So, outfitted as we were, it was time to say goodbye to the family. I had the feeling that I might not come back, and so did they, I am sure. But no one said so.

Life on the Home Front .

5. [Editor's Note] The Alaska-Canada Highway is also known as the ALCAN Highway.

6. [Editor's Note] Jantzen is a clothing company. It first began as the Portland Knitting Company in 1910 producing mainly heavy wool sweaters, gloves and socks. The company soon expanded into making swimming suits. The swimwear line became very popular and its signature line. Jantzen continues to produce swimwear and sportswear as part of Perry Ellis International, Inc.

Retrieved from http://vintagefashionguild.org/label-resource/jantzen/ .

7. Everything has by now disappeared except the heavy wool socks, which have been used by the children at Christmas time to hang on the fireplace.

The next step was to get to Seattle; it was my first ride on the train (April 4, 1942). Once there and checked into a hotel, we had a couple of days to look around town since neither Marley nor I had been there before. One of the requirements was a physical. We found ourselves in a group of 12–15 young men all heading out to different places. As part of the physical we had to take shots—3 or 4 types. These were given in both arms—and Marley fell down to the floor! But the doctor said "Think nothing of it. Some people are sensitive to inoculations." Our arms were both sore for days afterward. The next step was to board the Princess liner that was to take us to Skagway [Alaska] by way of the Inland Passage (Japanese submarines, you know). The accommodations were excellent and the food delicious. On the way we passed two glaciers of green-blue ice dropping great icebergs into the water with tremendous splashes. We were, of course, safely distant from the waves. Finally we arrived at Skagway and docked at a shaky-looking pier that extended far out into the water (low tide, of course). Another boat was also docked there, bigger than our Princess but looking pretty rusty. We had to wait two days for passage on the White Pass and Yukon railroad (WP&Y). It was crowded with people and equipment—big bulldozers and graders that extended 2 feet on either side of the flat cars. The WP&Y was a narrow gauge line at that time[8].

Marley and I wandered around Skagway while waiting. At one point, we met Herman, who was very angry. There had been a fire in the hold of his ship and his gear was soaked. Some gear had been burned, but I believe it belonged to the soldiers. A battalion of troops had been sent up, the lead contingent of what was to be thousands, and Herman's group of PRA men had been sent up with them. Mostly Herman was angry at the bad luck that had stolen his chance to come up in the luxury of a Princess boat, as had Marley and I[9].

8. Later, I attended a meeting of the Albuquerque Railroad Club to hear a talk by someone who had taken that ride in the 1980s. It didn't seem that he was talking about the same line, or place. The single narrow gauge line (with turnouts) had been replaced by a double normal gage line with regrading that allowed easy continuous motion. There were also frequent stations. Altogether, the line has been modernized and, of course, modern engines and cars are used.

9. That was the first Herman and Marley had seen of each other and they got off to a bad start. Later they were sent out in the same party and, over the many days of working together, they developed an intense dislike for each other. In good part, this was due to the fact that Herman carried around the socialism chip on his shoulder, which continued to be the case until he became old. To this day (1994) Herman and Marley dislike each other. At that time, however, Herman's group was scheduled on an immediate ride on the train, so Marley and I were free to roam for a while.

Downtown Skagway consisted of a cluster of old buildings on mostly unpaved streets, much as western towns in the movies. Because of the tidal fluctuations, the boats were tied up at long piers perhaps 200 yards from the town. Behind the town was a rocky knoll on which we found set up an open air dentist's office with a treadle-operated drill. Why there? We never found out. Down in town, there was a fairly nice hotel (Skagway had been a small tourist port). On the wall near the fireplace was a huge bear skin, perhaps nine feet across. There were, of course, no tourists now. On the streets were wide-front, rather run-down bars and other businesses needing paint and all pretty empty. The impression on that cold April day in 1942 was one of abandonment and sadness.

Our train left April 10th. After seeing that our footlockers were stored aboard, Marley and I took seats in the passenger car and the train pulled out of the station, which was piled high with boxes and equipment. By means of a series of switch backs, the train quickly gained elevation and moved into ever deeper snow. The line, in places, seemed to cling to the mountain side, so that the view from the window was frightening. Even though the train had gone up the tracks the day before, the engine had a snow plow which was greatly needed. The train came to a shuddering halt, backed up a hundred yards or so and, with all the speed it could muster, rammed the snow pack again. This happened several times until finally we broke through and arrived at Carcross [Canada] on fairly open ground. We paused there for something and finally pulled into Whitehorse in the late afternoon. Herman was lost in the crowd of men there, so Marley and I took a room (with a single double bed) and went out to see our surroundings—and to have dinner on moose steak. The wind outside was bitter cold and the ground was covered with solid ice. It felt good to sit in front of the big fireplace with a roaring fire.

The next morning Marley and I were sent out on separate teams to do minor tasks. My team hiked over to the Yukon narrow gorge (where the river roars through a narrow box canyon mostly choked with ice at that time), a distance of about a mile. I was given a job of putting a "hub" into the ground. A hub is a short fat stake which, when set in the ground, serves as a point over which the instrument man can stand his tripod. The hub is only relatively permanent, lasting a few months, and having a special nail pounded into the top so that the plumb bob of the instrument will be centered. In this case, the ground was frozen so hard even a pickax could hardly penetrate it. I split two hubs before I finally got one halfway in. That was the beginning of my first job in the Yukon—stake-puncher.

In the afternoon, we returned to Whitehorse and I was feeling very well. But later that night, I suddenly got very sick; I vomited and shit in the bed. Poor Marley! I remember spending an hour or so in the toilet room, my bowels flowing freely. The toilet was something to remember: this was the third floor in a land of hard freezing and little plumbing. So the toilet was a seat over the "honey bucket" with a box of sawdust and old newspapers nearby. It was certainly one of my worst nights ever. The next day, Marley was selected to go out with a party (including Herman) and I was supposed to go with them. But I was too weak to get out of bed. I was distraught, but in fact that turned out to be one of the poorly run parties.

The day they left, after the maids at the hotel had cleaned up my room and the toilet room, the city doctor came to see me. He was a kindly man, a Canadian, who diagnosed my trouble as a bad case of the flu, or "moose fever" as they called it. The next day, I tried to move around a little but couldn't eat and felt very weak. I remember walking around town, finally passing behind the hotel. From the third floor window of the toilet room a brown streak went down to the ground—unmistakably the trace of where the "honey bucket" was emptied each day. Why didn't more people get sick? I don't know.

On the 16th, I was selected to go out with Curly Gowan's party. Gowan had already made a reputation for himself as a driver, hard to get along with, intolerant. So, in my weakened condition, it was with great misgivings that I climbed into the truck at 10:00 at night and we all set out for Champagne. Gowan was pretty hard on me and I believe he was really trying to get me to go back to the States; but I would not. I knew nobody in the truck. We drove across frozen streams and across the still frozen Takhini River, although the ice groaned ominously. By early morning we arrived in Champagne. It was the largest settlement west of Whitehorse, but still just a scattering of Indian houses and George Chambers' Trading Post. The rest of the crew was set to work erecting our tents while I was sent down to the river (the Dezadeash) to get water in buckets. The river was frozen but the Indians had chopped a hole in the 2-foot deep ice near the edge. It was hard work in my weakened condition getting the water, but I did. And the men, all strangers just a few hours ago, began to be friendly.

Herman and I kept in touch by letter on occasions throughout the summer. I regret that those letters have been lost. But one letter I received from Herman was in part reprinted in *Crooked Road* by David Remley.[10] I quote part of Herman's letter here because it is such a dramatic episode.

"*We continued to walk the ice [of the Takhini] just for ease of traveling. This was risky indeed. There were open patches of water and the river was full*

10. [Editor's Note] *Crooked Road: The Story of The Alaska Highway.* David A. Remley. McGraw-Hill Book Company 1976. Craig Hudson and Herman Johansen are both quoted by the author.

and fast under the ice. Inevitably it happened: someone went through the ice and disappeared. . .but by luck grasped the downstream edge of the ice with his hands. I'll remember those white fingers desperately clinched on the ice for a good many years more. . .As luck would have it, we were able to get hold of him, crack the ice and drag him out. . ."

The part of the Takhini Herman referred to was between Champagne and Whitehorse, the very part we had driven across on the night of April 16 (close to Herman's camp, but of course I did not know that at the time). Marley and Herman's crew was there only a short time and then moved to the eastern end of the road. When we surveyed east from Champagne, our line tied up with theirs.[11]

This will not be a day-by-day narrative, but some things need to be told. On this, our first day at Champagne, Gowan had already organized us into two parties: the line party to stake out the survey line's direction and distance and the topog party to measure the topography out 100 feet on either side of the line at every stake, 100 feet apart on level ground. I was stake-puncher in the line party and it was my job to put a stake (marked with the measured distance) in the ground, and at about 500 feet to put in a hub so that the instrument man could advance. There was a rear flagman at the last hub, so the line (or tangent, as it was called) was assured of being straight. The instrument man always waved his handkerchief to signal the rear flagman to advance. I learned that 1000 feet was about as far as his handkerchief could be seen against a cluttered background.

In my job as stake-puncher, I had to carry a large packsack of stakes. Eventually the neatly cut stakes we had originally brought ran out and Gowan said "Well that's your job; you'll just have to cut stakes from small trees." I did, but it was extra hard work and twice as heavy as the pre-cut stakes. My hands became sore and the skin cracked. Finally the cook took pity on me and rubbed my hands with bacon grease. Oh the salt in the grease hurt! But my hands got better and I never had that problem again. In about a month, a new supply of stakes arrived.

Our first field line ran east of Champagne. The country was rolling and lightly forested. On some of these days, I took my sketch book with me and made drawings of the country to the west. The Dezadeash River ran in that direction for some miles. One of those sketches, made by climbing to a high point, later became the inspiration for my painting *Dezadeash Valley*[12] in which the St. Elias Mountains stood out in the distance like the tines of a

---

11. Marley never wrote to me. To this day (1994) Marley has never written me a letter, while Herman and I have kept up a lively correspondence.

12. [Editor's Note] see Appendix: Catalog of Paintings.

comb. I painted this picture much later to give Jeannine an idea of the grandeur of the country. It also pointed the way along which our survey line would advance all the way to Kluane Lake.

Dezadeash Valley, painted 1948

At a depth of a couple of feet, the ground was always frozen. As the weather warmed in May, the surface became a quagmire in which it was difficult to walk and nearly impossible to drive our old Dodge truck. On several occasions, George Chambers had to use his "snowmobile" to pull the truck out of the mud. This was a vehicle he had ingeniously fabricated by welding parts together on an old truck of his own. The treads in the back were made by him from a photo he had seen of a tank.

The Chambers Trading Post consisted of a long log house lined with shelves on the inside, shelves that were stocked mostly with Hudson Bay clothing. We PRA men, finding that we had not been properly outfitted for this country, bought clothing from the post stock—especially waterproof boots (mine were useless) and warm undershirts. There were also stocks of canned food, sewing materials, etc., which the Indians traded pelts for. And there was a large warm stove in one end around which we and the Indian men gathered to swap stories. These Indians were of two rather distinct types: one was tall and lean with narrow faces and sharp noses; the other was husky with round faces and flat noses. The first type, I believe, were Athabaskans (at least that was the general thought) while the second seemed to have no formal identity. My friend George John was of the latter type.

Men from England, Scotland and Wales had been in the vicinity long enough to have left progeny that were about my age. Without exception, these young people were taller, stronger and better looking than the parents. It was a most fortuitous mixture. But I have no idea how many people died in plagues of various kinds.

George Chambers also had a garage at the side of the trading post. Here he had tools of all sorts, an electric generator, lathes, etc., for metal working and, of course, welding equipment. He could make or repair nearly anything. While we were there, his whole trading post was open with no locks. Later when the Army came in, he had to lock everything up. The Indian women were unmolested (eventually this too changed); they were lean and athletic, going out with pack dogs to bring in skins they had killed. The older Indian women were good seamstresses—some even had old treadle sewing machines. But the favorite way of making clothing was using moose sinew. Some of us purchased moccasins, coats, etc., some beautifully beaded (beads were a favorite Hudson Bay commodity).[13]

George Chambers also served as banker for the region. He cashed our checks and through him I was able to pay the doctor in Whitehorse who had treated me. Interest was never charged. There was always trust. Everything was in the open. Later when the army and contractor people came in, all this changed.

During this time, my health returned and even improved. I gained weight. I had weighed 140 pounds when I went up there and when in November I left, I weighed about 175 pounds, all muscle. We fellows in the crew used to arm wrestle and I could put down everyone (who tried) except George John and George Criddle. I will relate more about them later.

13. We still have a number of items that I purchased while in Champagne, in our Yukon box.

Axmen at Work, painted 1942

I received $75.00 every two weeks, usually a couple of months behind. I had little use for money up there, so I mostly sent the checks home to Dad who deposited them in an account for me. When I needed money, I could get a money order from George Chambers. Mail was generally slow but mostly reliable. The things I bought up there (from the trading post or from the Indians) were handled on a cash basis. People were entirely trustworthy.

In the early part of that stay at Champagne (we ran line a few miles east of town and then some twenty miles west), the spring thaw came on. It was very cold at night (nearly zero) and the ground froze; but by mid-afternoon it was warm. The snow turned first to slush and then disappeared, leaving mud. The river ice broke up and, with a roar that could be heard quite a ways, rushed down leaving fast cold water.

The cook had real trouble. He slept in the cook tent at night, but couldn't stay awake long enough to maintain a fire in his stove. The bread starter (a bowl of sour yeast) got so cold that the bread wouldn't rise and sometimes we had to take loaves of bread out with us (for lunch) that were small and hard, barely edible. Finally they got a helper for him; the fire was kept going; and the bread improved. But it always had a sour taste and the San Francisco sourdough bread that is so romantically touted today has no appeal for me to this day.

There were some times when the food was not very good, but it was always nutritious. We had fresh beef and pork when a supply truck came by. It was covered with cloth and hung in a cool house (a small portable room with gauze windows which could be sloshed with water in warm weather). There were plenty of potatoes, carrots, onions, fresh vegetables once in a while, and lots of dry beans, prunes, etc. And, of course there were canned goods aplenty. We had some kind of cake or cobbler nearly every night. There was oatmeal or hotcakes for breakfast and always bacon—and eggs once in a while. Coffee was always available, with sugar and canned milk; and we also had available a cold drink made from lemon-flavored crystals like Kool-Aid.[14] On a few occasions, when supplies were delayed, we were rationed, but never seriously deprived. Once one of the men shot a north-flying swan with a rifle! It was large enough so that each man got a piece, but it was tough. On another occasion, one of the Indians brought in a mountain sheep which was gamey but good. And there were often grouse taken from the woods. All in all, we ate well enough. Water was always pure (from fast-running streams) but often was polluted by sediment, which settled out on standing.

We eventually got a cook's helper which greatly eased the burden on the cook. Mind you, the cook and his helper changed from time to time. One of these helpers posed for a photograph later in the summer and from this snapshot I painted my picture *Camp Cook*[15] in 1946, surely one of my best portraits.

From Champagne, we began surveying to the west and we continued this course until we hooked up with the survey near Kluane Lake. On one memorable day, returning to camp from west of Champagne, we heard a growling noise ahead of us. I heard some noise and pretty soon I could see trees just plop, plop, plop, like that. They were just driving the bulldozers right straight through the forest. This was the way we first met the Army which was driving straight ahead without much guidance. In the future months, they would always be ahead of us. Their road was not well-planned but it was a supply road by which we received all our supplies from White-horse. In rainy weather, mud was sometimes axle deep. But it served us well. In time, heavy road equipment (like graders) was brought in and the Army road eventually became quite serviceable. Meanwhile, the PRA survey tied together all the sources of gravel that could be located to build a permanent highway.

14. [Editor's Note] Actually, this powdered drink might have been Kool-Aid because by 1929 Kool-Aid was distributed nationwide.
Hastings Museum, *History of Kool-Aid* .

15. [Editor's Note] see Appendix: Catalog of Paintings.

Camp Cook, painted 1946

Our next main camp site was at Canyon where the Aishihik and Deza-deash Rivers join. This was one of our major (perhaps the major) campsite. The camp consisted of: 4 four-man tents, the cook tent (which was three tents erected end-to-end), and the office tent (which was two tents erected end-to-end). Thus the crew numbered 16 men plus Gowan who slept in the office tent and the two cooks who slept in the cook tent. Each tent had in its center a stove for heat. The four-man tents contained four cots. The cook tent had a long table down its center with benches on the sides. The office tent had a desk and two map tables. None of this furniture was very heavy because it all had to be moved by packhorse after Canyon. The number of men in camp was not always the same. Some left to go back to the States and were, after an interval, replaced. Sometimes there were important visitors. And our Indian guides and axmen (always shifting in number) had their own tents, but ate with us.

I will relate a few of the many events that occurred at Canyon. Because we could now use the army road for travel (walking from it over to our own line), we were able to survey quite a long stretch from this one camp.

We surveyed about 5 miles from Champagne and 15 miles west. Then moved camp to Canyon, where we surveyed 7 miles east (to pick up our old line) and west all the way to Soldiers' Summit just south of Kluane Lake. Much of this latter distance was done by moving camp to several temporary sites which had to be packed in because we were so far from the Army road. Altogether, we surveyed about 90 miles of line, leaving stakes and hubs appropriately. I did not put all the stakes in; after a month or so, I was given the job of rear chainman. Part of the time I served as rear flagman or pole man or tape man on the contour surveys. Work was never dull.

We moved to Canyon about the middle of May and worked out of there most of the summer. By the time we began our temporary site moves, it was mid-August and snow was appearing at the higher elevations. By mid-September, we had to work in snow. And by mid-November, when I left, temperatures at night were 40°F below zero. I was asked to stay on through the winter to help survey the Haines road but the Indians told me that the snow was 10 feet deep there. And besides, I was becoming more eager to take some part in the great war. I wasn't sure that I could do anything, but I had an urge to try.

The rest of this portion of my autobiography will consist not of a narrative but of interesting vignettes about life in the Yukon that summer.

First, I describe some of the men in the camp. The four men in my tent were: near the door, Dick Hardy and Craig Hudson; in the back, Frank Pohle and George Criddle. Hardy was young, energetic and friendly; Pohle was not very bright but he kept us entertained with his guitar, playing mournful songs of the South. All three were from Montana. George Criddle was lamed by some accident that damaged his left leg. But that did not slow him down at all; he was a powerful man with some college education.

Vince Brown was about 40 years old, tall and spare but strong. In spite of his being the most religious one in camp (very hard on swearing and dirty talk), he and I got along very well. He was responsible and Gowan always sent Vince out to do a special job.

Elmer (Spike) Murdock joined our crew at Canyon to serve as a surveyor. Gowan sent him out with a crew to survey a closed line—that is, one that returns to its origin. Spike couldn't close it, meaning that when he came back to the origin, he was many feet off. We found out that Spike was a drunkard and storyteller—a stretcher of the truth. He never became a surveyor on our crew but instead served all sorts of other positions.

We had two surveyors, Nelson and someone else. Nelson was needed to head another party; this was the reason for hiring Murdock. Since Murdock didn't work out, Nelson had to stay. He was quiet, a gentle man, well educated in civil engineering, trusted by Gowan. The other surveyor (instrument man) was the one I worked for and I cannot remember his name.

Then there was the ex-marine, a giant of a man but not to be trusted. In our camp, he worked as axman; but he had been cook in Herman's camp. He used all the sugar, flavorings, fruit, etc, to make a kind of liquor which he drank. At last they caught on to his trick and he was discharged, only to come to our camp. I lent (actually gave) him $10 on our trip together in November; but of course I never heard from him. Actually I was glad of that because I was sure he could become a real leech.

From time to time, there were a number of Indians who served as ax-men and guides, but the only one I remember was George John. He was as tall as I and much heavier. He had a round face, lots of straight black hair which he kept pulled back in a knot, and twinkling eyes. He never said much but he always saw the happy side of things. He and I became close friends. George was the cleanest man in camp. Every afternoon before dinner, rain or shine and even in freezing weather, he stripped to the waist and washed thoroughly in cold water. When he was naked, one could see the huge scars on his left shoulder and back. He had been mauled by a grizzly bear and left for dead. His friends carried him out of the bush and into Whitehorse (several days). The doctor patched him up, but it was George's great vitality that pulled him through. That was some 5 years before I knew him. While he was working for the crew as an axman, using a double-bitted ax which he always kept sharp, the ax bounced out of a branch and before he could stop it, impaled itself in his head. The heavy hair somewhat moderated the blow but he bled profusely. So he hiked back to camp (with the other axman) and Gowan closed the wound; and within two days he was back at work.

But the best George John story relates to a trek in the woods. Our camp was about 4 miles from the army road with swamp and forest between. An arrangement had been made by Gowan for some of us to hike over and pick up some mail from a truck which would go by in the afternoon. There were five of us, including George John, and hiking over was just a good outing. But the truck was late and we started back as night was falling. After penetrating the woods, all guiding landmarks were lost and we began to drift apart. I stayed with George because he seemed to know where he was going. Finally I called to the others and we finally lined up behind George. By this time it was quite dark and I gave George my flashlight. "How do you know where you are going?" I asked. Laconically, he pointed the beam of the flashlight toward a branch that had been bent over, pointing in the direction we had gone earlier. Out of all the broken branches around, he was able to identify the ones he had broken on the way over! In due time, we marched directly up to the camp, where they were worried about us and had a large fire blazing. Never fear; George is here![16]

Two other crew members we picked up about this time were Alec Davis (from Wales) and Bill Lawson. Alec was much older than I; Bill was my age. Alec[17] had married an Indian woman and was very comfortable with the culture. I never met his family, except for his stepson. Once, out on line, Alec was carrying a heavy pack of stakes, got out of breath and sat down panting. His stepson, about 18 years old, came trotting up behind us, carrying his own heavy pack. Seeing his stepfather's predicament, he stooped and picked up Alec's pack, threw it over his shoulder and continued running out of sight up the trail hardly missing a stride! This is the same youth who ran down and captured one of our pack horses that had shaken loose its hobble in an open meadow.

Bill Lawson had been working in a gold mining operation in British Columbia when he heard about our project. This region had all been glaciated down to bare rock and later filled in with sand and gravel. The typical method of gold mining in such a place is to dig down to the bare rock glacial valley, then tunnel along what used to be the old stream bed. The gold, being heavy, tended to settle down to the bare rock surface. By tunneling along this old channel, the yield of gold dust and nuggets was greatly enhanced over sluicing the surface streams. But the tunneling was hard work, with some risk of cave-ins, and hot, because they were working 100'-200' below the surface.

We were at Canyon camp during the summer and the weather was often clear. This gave me the opportunity to make some water-color drawings of the countryside. These are also in the Yukon sketch collection. The drawing materials as well as a camera, film and dark room equipment were sent me by my loving family. I eventually made oil paintings of five of them: *Portrait of the Cook's Helper*; *Portrait of Ada*, a girl up there (which has been lost); *Dezadeash Valley*; *Yukon Landmark* (owned by Libby Nichols Carter); and *St. Elias Mountains*.[18] During late summer, one of my favorites of the party, Ted something-or-other (a student from Stanford) and I packed a lunch and one Sunday took a day-long walk up a trail near the river up to Pine Lake. I took 2 rolls of film on this walk and later developed them. They are granular because the water from the river was silty even after sitting for

16. The last I heard about George John was in about 1985 when we had a visit from a friend coming from Haines Junction. The woman told me that George was alive and well, and I sent back to her some photos. I never got a reply.

17. I made a very nice pencil sketch of Alec which is among the sketches I made in the Yukon. This collection is not part of my documented paintings.

18. [Editor's Note] see Appendix: Catalog of Paintings.

a while. We still have these old negatives, most of which have never been printed.[19] At one point on the trail, we found a tree with its branches broken off on one side and with tufts of coarse hair stuck here and there up to about as high as I could reach—nearly 8 feet! Imagine that! It was supposed to be a bear-scratching tree—some bear! I never saw a bear in the Yukon but one day we went through a bear's wallow; it smelled strong. The shrubs were all smashed down; and our dogs went wild, yipping and skulking around with tails between their legs.

Speaking of dogs, I saw very few sled dogs, or malamutes, up there. The Indians always kept dogs that looked like oversized coyotes. They were only half tame, not well-nourished and did not come up to you tail-wagging in the typical dog fashion. I'm sure they were used as sled teams in the winter, but the ones I saw being used were fixed up with harnesses to be pack dogs and were used by women.

At widely spaced locations along the road, which followed the centuries-old Indian trail, were road houses. They were about 12'x 16' in size, made of large logs with a sod roof, and fitted with a door and one or two windows which were open when I saw them. The Indians said they were erected as safe havens in blizzards. They had no amenities and were only for protection. I made sketches for my collection.

At Canyon and near Champagne, there were houses erected on stilts. Some of them were caches for food to avoid the depredations of wolves and other animals; and some of them were burial biers for the dead. I made a sketch of one of them with a US airplane flying overhead. Planes were being flown to Russia for use against German tanks.

One of the activities at the Canyon Camp was the construction of the Canyon Bridge. Prior to its construction, vehicles had to use a ford, which was very chancy on days of runoff, which was determined by conditions far upstream and could not be predicted on the basis of local weather. I made two sketches showing its construction by Army engineers. We had surveyed a bridge site at the location of large rock outcrops. But the Army bridge was located farther upstream where the approaches were more gentle. It was made of logs and I was attracted by the clever construction. Later a steel bridge was constructed still farther upstream. Remley photographed the old bridge through the struts of the new one and used my drawings to confirm that it was indeed the original one built in 1942[20]. My three drawings of the bridge are in the Yukon collection. The Canadian Department of Highways

19. [Editor's Note] Jeannine reported (2010) that the negatives became too degraded and were discarded.

20. [Editor's Note] Craig's sketch is included in the photograph section of David Remley's book.

believed the bridge to be one constructed by the early 1900 prospectors and had put up a sign to that effect. My drawing, therefore, changed their view of history!

Our last permanent campsite was at Pine Creek, which does not even show on maps. For much of the time at this site, we were away. The PRA line following the gravel barrows[21] in order to achieve a better roadbed drifted far east of the Army road. We were obliged to go by way of temporary camps (2 or 3 days at a time) through virgin country. Pack horses were hired and a pack master. While we were surveying the line, the packers gathered up the camp, strapped it to the pack horses and moved to the next site. Life was rather primitive; food was not tasty and sleeping on the ground was a far cry from sleeping on our army cots.

One of the packers was Mickey Blackmore. Mickey had fled the US after some sort of fracas upon which he was pursued as a wanted man. He refused to discuss the details except to say that he fled in the 1920s and disappeared into the Canadian wilderness. Mickey was short, wiry, and swarthy of complexion, with a mass of black hair which was only partly controlled by a dirty hat. He shaved occasionally and usually went around with a surly attitude, but he did his work well. However, sitting around the campfire, he opened up and proved to be a wonderful storyteller.

Many of his stories were about himself. After he came into the Yukon country, he took an Indian wife, but she died. His second Indian wife bore him two children, both girls about a year apart. She died, giving birth to the second one. So he was left, with winter coming on, with a baby still needing milk and a newborn quite unable to be left alone. Mickey was a hunter, caring for a trapline, so he had to go out to service the trapline on snowshoes. He left the year-old baby with a lady who lived near his house and took the tiny one with him in a packsack. Somehow he kept the little girl alive, wrapped in moss and furs, fed on canned milk, throughout the winter while servicing the trapline on snowshoes. In the spring, he searched for another solution, and managed to have both children cared for. By the time the little girls were running about, he had located a Catholic charity willing to care for them. By the time he was telling the story, the girls were in their early teens. He visited them once a year and still operated his trapline.

The interaction of Mickey Blackmore and Spike Murdock around the campfire was a real treat. Spike was a liar and a braggart and at first, when he told one of his outrageous stories, Mickey was nonplussed. But when Spike began invading Mickey's territory with his stories, Mickey (not to be outdone) invented stories of his own. Each campfire gathering became a

21. [Editor's Note] mounds.

vaudeville session at which they entertained us for an hour or so. One of their routines, which they fell into quite by chance, was the baseball game. Each man took a side and, with sound effects, invented the course of the game in a most entertaining way. For me, both Spike and Mickey are only memories; I never heard about either of them again after leaving the Yukon.

On one occasion, Vince and I had some reason (to search for a lost tool, I think) to return to one of these campfire sites. Everything was found exactly as we had left it. A blue jay was hopping around trying to find some dropped morsel of food. The afternoon sun was warm but I'm sure Vince felt the same oppressive melancholy as we watched the ghosts of Spike and Mickey and all the others around the campfire that was now cold.

About halfway between Canyon and Pine Creek, near what is now known as Haines Junction, we found Mrs. MacIntosh. She had come into the Yukon Territory with her husband, a mining engineer from Scotland. By that time, Mrs. MacIntosh was about 60 years old and had been a widow for 20 years. He had built a nice log cabin of considerable size. When she found herself alone and having already made friends with the Indians, she elected to make a small trading post out of the house. She served the Indians who lived in the area with small things (we used to buy candy bars there); for large items, they still had to go to Champagne. She also stocked ammunition and fishing gear for the occasional tourists who came through. She maintained a small school for children and kept a good garden nearby. Her cabbages were bigger than one's head and cucumbers were 2 feet long. The long summer was great for all sorts of things, especially carrots, potatoes and turnips which could hide from the early frosts. Even flowers grew.

In some parts of the country, in sheltered places, the ice never melted. But usually by mid-summer the upper 1–2 feet of soil was melted. Of course, since the ground was then saturated with water, roads became a mire of mud, often impassable. The state of the ground was really quite remarkable. One day, we had driven our old Dodge truck off the road a ways to be nearer our survey line. It was parked under the protection of some trees. The day was hot and after lunch we lay around half asleep. The truck was parked on a bed of pine needles. I woke up to notice that the wheels had sunk 4 inches into the duff[22] just while we had been there! Obviously we had to move it every half hour or so if it was off the road.

This was country full of geological structures. In places, I could trace large faults in the distant hills. In others, outcroppings of rocks were found, but it was glacial country and by and large the hills were smoothed off and

22. [Editor's Note] organic matter in various stages of decomposition on the floor of the forest.

the valleys scoured. However, the gravel in the river beds presented a museum of rock and mineral types. I brought about 30 pounds of these home with me and they are still in the family rock collection. I even brought back samples of the local clay. At one place, high in a rocky saddle smoothed off by a glacier, I found some pebbles—clearly the result of being carried down by ice and then left there upon melting.

As fall, September, changed into winter—October until I left in November—the beautiful colors faded, the leaves dropped and it became cold. By 'cold' I mean below zero. Our thermometer was calibrated down to -30°F and it was much colder than that on some nights. We had a special mission one day to survey in a landing strip 1000' long near Pine Lake. I wore my logger boots with the nails in the soles because we were going to be working in the trees. The air was bitter cold and there was not a breath of wind. After a while, I began to notice my feet getting cold. Heat was draining out through the nails. The utter stillness (no sound of any kind except our own) and the extreme coldness cast a depression over me that I could not shake off. I began to fear that my feet were freezing. Eventually the work was completed, we got back to the truck and I warmed up.

Freezing feet in that country is serious. Once, Vince and I were out doing a short piece of surveying in the vicinity of Soldiers' Summit. The sky was dark; it was very cold. We were about a mile away from the rest of the party. Ice and snow were everywhere and the ground looked to be frozen solid. But in one place it was not. Vince plunged his foot down to the knee into water before he could stop himself. His boot, of course, filled up with water. We immediately stopped working and headed over to the truck. That was one of the longest miles I have ever seen. Hardly had we set out before it began snowing. Vince clumped along on this wet foot getting closer to freezing all the time; by the time we were halfway there, visibility through the snow was half what it had been and the truck became a dim shadow. By the time we reached it, visibility was virtually zero. Vince took off his boot and warmed his foot in a blanket. The drive back to camp was very slow but otherwise uneventful. Vince was quite grateful that the snow had held off long enough that we not be lost in it. And we learned about freezing water.

An amusing event also occurred there. The Pine Creek crapper (outhouse) had been constructed of boards in a way that was a little bit more elegant than usual; a 'splash plate' made of a flattened tin can was placed under the front of the seat—for no good reason, just cleverness. In time it happened: at 40 below zero, with a little moisture, body parts freeze instantly to cold metal. One of the men's penis tip froze to the splash plate, and to get it off a tiny bit of skin had to be sacrificed.

One of the notable events of our stay at Pine Creek was the following mysterious episode. As I mentioned, we four men (Hardy, Pohle, Criddle and Hudson) shared the same tent, with Pohle and Criddle in the back. The little sheet metal space heater sat in the middle of the tent, venting through the ceiling and on these cold nights it was stoked up until it turned red. On this particular night, we turned off the lamp and went to bed as usual. The red heater cast a ruddy glow around the inside of the tent. I fell asleep. Later I woke up and the tent was filled with a dim, soft orange glow but the stove was black, so it must have been in the early hours of the morning. Bending over my bed, and silhouetted against the orange glow, was Aunt Hattie. She seemed to try to speak but I heard no words. Seeing her there, however, had a pleasant peaceful effect; she had cared for me so many times in the past; and it did not occur to me that she had been dead for more than a year. I went back to sleep. But the next morning while we were all sitting around the breakfast table, Dick Hardy said "Craig, who was that who visited you during the night?" Recall that Hardy's bed was next to the door of the tent on the other side. He had also been aroused from sleep by someone or something coming into the tent, which of course, was not fastened shut. How to account for the orange glow? It seemed to be the same orange glow that would fill my room as a child when I awoke to find snakes crawling all over the bed. In that case, the light switch was close at hand; I turned on the light and the snakes disappeared. Somehow the glow is associated with the hallucination; in fact, without the glow, there would be no hallucination. I never found out who, or what, entered the tent at Pine Creek that night; but it wasn't a bear. Bears smell strong.

Before we left Pine Creek, some of us took a ride up to Burwash Landing at the western end of Kluane Lake. The country there is awe-inspiring because the mountains are so close. Unfortunately I did not take as many pictures as I wish I now had. There is a sportsman's hotel (few comforts) at Burwash Landing. The sportsmen fly in by plane and climb out onto the Landing without any long hiking. Because of the war, the place was deserted when we were there, but we looked around. I had my picture taken there holding a large fish. And nearby was a large reel on which a fish net of great length could be wound. Boats were tied up at the Landing. Eventually the lake would freeze over, but this was only November, fishing was a major industry there both to satisfy the human population and to provide frozen fish for the dogsled teams in the winter. The fish looked like salmon but I was told they were whitefish (a kind of trout).

In the last few days at camp, there was little to do. Our line and levels had all been run. One morning, we four tent fellows, stripped down to the buff, broke the ice in Pine Creek and went in to wash in a deep pool. Brrr!

That was cold! Soap would hardly lather. Gowan was trying to organize his party to survey the Haines road. I did not want to go and a few days later hitched a ride to Whitehorse. On the way, we stopped at Champagne. What a change from the open community it had been. Now everything was secured. There were new houses made of boards instead of logs. The trading post was now more like a country store. There were large displays of Indian-made beadwork—jackets and moccasins. Before, I had bought things directly from the woman who made them, often to my specifications. Then we drove on to Whitehorse, this time over bridges instead of frozen rivers.

In Whitehorse, the PRA office helped me plan my trip back to Seattle. O'Neil, the big marine, followed me around wherever I went. We purchased tickets back on the White Pass and Yukon, which seemed to be very much as before except that there was no freight. In Skagway, we were able to get passage to Seattle on a yacht that was under contract to the government. It carried about 20 people. After we got out into open water, a storm which had been threatening finally reached us. The captain aimed for the lee side of an island, but before we could get there, we were hit by some pretty big waves. I was in the cabin at the time, talking to the captain, when one washed over the deck—even over the cabin, and I could look out through the windshield and see green for several seconds. But we weathered the storm and arrived in Seattle. From there, I took a bus to Portland, arriving late at night. Another bus took me to Eastmoreland; I crawled through the milk door and up to bed. In the morning, I surprised the folks by coming down to breakfast. The Yukon Adventure was over.

In a few days, both Herman and Marley showed up (separately, of course) and we began to plan what to do with the rest of our lives.

Craig in the Yukon, 1942

Yukon Kitchen, 1942

7

The Army, Being Sent to Europe, and Meeting Jeannine

1942—1946

Herman had heard about the Mountain Troops and signed up with them. In a short time, he reported to duty in the Colorado Rockies training center. I was not to see him again until the war was over. Arthur told me about a Signal Corps program to prepare for radar—a very romantic idea in those days. I talked it over with Marley. He was interested, so we signed up for the Enlisted Reserve Corps (ERC). The conditions of the enrollment were that we would receive a small stipend to attend army sponsored, privately operated electronics schools for six months to a year after which we would enter the army as privates and go to a radar school.

It worked out pretty much as planned. In late November 1942, Marley and I reported to the school in Eugene. We settled in a boarding house, having twin beds in one room. We had breakfast there and sometimes dinner. The lady who ran the place with about six boarders was very motherly and helpful to us. We had to get to school, a small vocational school on Eugene's south side, at 7:00 AM. It was still dark. The class was elementary in which we were supposed to learn the basic radio circuits and build an amplifier. Marley was not very good with the soldering iron because his hands shook from too many cigarettes, and he often burned his fingers. He would not admit to nervousness, saying that he was only quick. As did everyone else, we received a monthly quota of meat and gasoline stamps. The gasoline stamps we gave to our parents; the meat stamps we had to give out every time we had a meat meal or bought meat (not often). We spent 8 hours at the school and then had time on our hands. We studied a little, read a little and bowled. But bowling cost 25 cents a line and our money didn't go very far. The pins were set up by boys and sometimes they were lazy, so an evening could go by easily. We sometimes ate at a cafeteria where I was introduced to baked beef heart served in plenty of thick meat sauce. I grew very fond of that; in spite of trying, we have never been able to prepare baked heart in brown sauce like that.

In January (1943), the students were sent to other schools, Marley and I to Santa Barbara. We stayed at the old California Hotel, somewhat rundown; but from there it was only a short walk through a beautiful park full of eucalyptus trees over to the Junior College where our ERA classes were held. There we had some pretty good instruction, our first contact with microwaves and waveguides. We had hoped for some social life, but our resources were too limited. We did walk around and saw the giant fig tree in the yard of the RR station. Many years later, Jeannine and I visited it and we have pictures to prove it.

In March, we moved to the school in LA. In the hope that we could live in an exotic place, we looked for an apartment near Sunset and Vine, famous for its movie stars. We found a comfortable apartment only 2 blocks away. But there were no movie stars. The best we could do was to spend some meat stamps to get into the Brown Derby, where we saw Victor Mc-Glaughlin[1]—not very impressive. He was a film star when I was a teen-ager. But perhaps the most interesting experience occurred when we were walking to the apartment building one afternoon. Ahead of us was a short man from whom came Donald Duck conversations. We overtook him and discovered that he was the man who made all the animal conversations in the cartoons. It was fun talking about how he did it. We tried to obtain some kind of social life there but without success. However, Marley visited one of his relatives and I visited the family of one of Grandpa Palmer's nieces. That was a pleasant Sunday. We also went out to various jazz places; Marley was a jazz devotee and knew many of the performers by name. Quite a few of them held forth in small clubs. I found this to be rather boring. Work at the LA school seemed to be better and more advanced than either of the other two; we had labs with real waveguide apparatus. But in truth, the pace was much slower than we could have tolerated.

In May we were moved to a school in Sacramento. Here we were set back to the rudiments again and we felt bored with what was going on. So after a month, Marley said "Let's quit; we are going to be inducted anyway so

1. [Editor's Note] Craig is probably referring to Victor McLaglen.

let's do it on our own initiative." I agreed and we went back to Portland and reported to the ERC office. They said we should report to Ft. Lewis (WA) in July; until then, we had time for a vacation.

At Ft. Lewis we went through all of the physical and mental tests that the Army has for inductees. We got our first taste of marching in formation and walking "guard duty," although there was nothing to guard. The medics found my irregular heartbeat and held me up a week for tests. So Marley and I were separated finally; our paths crossed from time to time but never coincided again.

I was sent with about 20 men I did not know to Camp Murphy in Florida—but first with a stop at the Air Force boot camp at Miami Beach. There we stayed in hotels on the shore front, but the living was anything but easy. There were numerous experiences there, but I remained friendly with no one, so I will pass over this episode with the observation that the humidity was often a larger number than the temperature in this crazy land.

After basic training at Miami Beach, I was sent to Camp Murphy in West Palm Beach. It was a nice camp, quite new and well-run. Here was the Signal Corp's main radar school, except for Lincoln Labs at MIT which served more as a research center than as a radar school. By the time I got there (winter of 1943), the field of radar had expanded from the original search and detect (low frequency) radars used in the Battle of Britain (and later modified for shipboard use) into the high frequency regime of "gun laying" radars—that is, radars that can both track the target and give instructions to guns to shoot at it. One of the first four of these was the SCR-268 and I was assigned to study it. This was a whole new world of technology for which the ERC training was poor preparation. But the science of the SCR-268 was fundamental to all the more advanced radars (even those on night fighter aircraft) and I was happy at this school.

At Camp Murphy I met many of the people Jeannine has heard me talk about later: Marley was there, Elmer Gauche, Harold Kerns, Cliff Anet, Virgil Edwards, Joseph Roper, Earl Isaacson, and others. Other than Marley, the only one of these to remain a friend was Elmer Gauche, who was a frequent visitor at the Amazon Apartments in Eugene after Marc was born. The others are just names now.

Vern Garratt was also one of the ones in that Camp Murphy group. He has been in and out of our lives for 50 years. He deserves special mention. Vern lived with his mother, a widow, in a small house near Eastmoreland. He was abnormally bright, but was rather ugly in the face. I first met him at Ft. Lewis, but did not know him well until we wound up in Camp Murphy. Later he was sent to the Pacific, and I to Europe. He called me up in the fall of 1946 after I had enrolled at Reed. He wanted to use his GI Bill rights to enhance his learning. He was, of course, a very shy person. After he was enrolled in Lewis and Clark College, he came to see me at the 35th Street house for coaching in math; but there was something amiss for him. Little by little I lost track of him.

We sometimes went into Palm Beach where the elegant mansions were. On one occasion, we found the grounds of a mansion open and walked in, out of curiosity. After a little while, the groundskeeper found us. We were friendly and inquisitive, so he said that if we stayed out of the main house, we were free to look around, one of the outer rooms was light and airy, contained an easel standing on one side, clearly a private studio. So I asked if I might be permitted to paint (using pastels), and was given permission provided we return the following Sunday. We did return on the next Sunday, and I made portraits of Cliff Anet, Isaacson's wife (a pretty girl) and someone else (but I've forgotten who). I still have the portraits of Anet and Mrs. Isaacson. Thinking about it, I believe the other portrait was of Elmer Gauche, which I gave to him. I also made a drawing (painting) of the drab Florida landscape, which I still have. After the painting session, the groundskeeper gave us some ice tea and cookies and let us look through the private museum there. In it were many beautiful things, but the one that interested me most was a large display of carved jade, both green and pink. I have seldom seen the equal of that exhibit even in art museums.

Cliff Anet, painted 1943

Mrs. Isaacson, painted 1943

After some months at Camp Murphy, our class at school was broken up and I was sent to Camp Davis in North Carolina where I prepared for assignment to the European theater. Meanwhile, Marley had elected to go to Officer's Training School in engineering, and Herman was still in training in the Mountain Troops in Colorado. Herman and Marge were married there.

Camp Davis was intended to expose us to relatively realistic battlefield training. We experienced crossing a field of fire with live ammunition overhead (keep your head down!) accompanied by frequent explosions near at hand. We had to find out about gas warfare and long tough marches. We also spent two weeks living in the bush with no protection against chiggers. We saw very grizzly battlefield movies and movies about the horrors of sexually transmitted diseases. Now we were prepared to be assigned to European combat zones.

I was assigned to a radar team: five men, one of whom was an officer, who were to have a certain amount of autonomy and be assigned wherever we were needed. One of the men was to be "company sergeant," that is to take care of the team paperwork; that was GI Taylor from North Carolina, a school teacher; we got on very well. One was a mechanic to keep our machines running: that was McGee B. Mantooth from Tennessee. One was the scientific person: that was I. And one was the flunky, whose name I forget. The lieutenant may have been Erwin Tomash, a graduate of MIT. Tomash did us a great service by being very aggressive and getting us the most interesting assignments. What happened to us on this team was very interesting, but I never heard from any of the men after the war. In due time, the flunky was transferred out (we couldn't stand him) and was replaced.

Our first task as a team was to assemble the gear we were to take with us. I was in charge of the test equipment, tools, electronic spare parts, etc. Mantooth was in charge of the two vehicles (a weapons carrier—a sort of large jeep –and the repair van) and an electric power generator. Taylor was in charge of setting up the company records—not much of a job at first so he helped me. The flunky got in the way. And Tomash was dealing with the officer staff, trying to get us the best possible arrangement. Finally we were ready to embark. Our equipment was loaded onto a military freighter; we all piled onto an overloaded troop ship. We were assigned berths below decks that were stacked 20 inches apart, floor to ceiling. Officers and females had spaces above decks that were only a little less crowded. The ship zig-zagged all the way across the Atlantic and every morning and evening we could hear (actually feel) the six-inch guns booming in practice. So far as I could tell, no shot was ever aimed at a U-boat. We finally arrived off the coast of North Africa near Tunis, where we waited for a day for some off-loading; and then we sailed to Naples.

The harbor at Naples was a wreck. We tied up at a pier that extended out into the water on floating pontoons. We walked up through the rubble on a sort of trail, were picked up by trucks and were taken to a sort of gymnasium, where we were fed, and then spent the night sleeping on the most beautiful terrazzo floor[2] I had ever seen—but it was cold and hard. Next day, we were taken by truck through Naples to the town of Santa Maria, which had been an Italian barracks, then a German barracks, and finally, much expanded, an American Signal Corps camp. We were assigned a four-man tent, much like the one I stayed in during the Yukon time. The weather was beastly hot: 80° at night and up to 110° in the afternoon. We were located near a field of SCR-268 units which had been retired when the SCR-584s became available. We were to repair these radars in order to turn them over to the French Army, which had none. Spare parts were a problem so some of the damaged units were scavenged to put others in working order.

The main differences between the 268 and 584 were frequency and automation. The operating frequency of the 584 was five times that of the 268

2. [Editor's Note] terrazzo is made by putting together remnants of marble, then smoothed and flattened, to produce a smooth surface. Arcadian Flooring, http://arcadianflooring.com/history.html.

which allowed much better resolution and some simplification in antenna design. Automation allowed the 584 to be operated by one man while the 268 needed three. But in many ways, the two units were simpler; but the 584 was better.

Our stay in Naples was wonderful in one sense; we were able to see the gardens and building of both Roman and Modern southern Italy. Some mental images: the Appian way with huge sycamores lining each side, with piles of artillery shells between trees; the church at New Pompei covered on the inside with gold leaf; the streets of Old Pompeii with all their magnificent buildings as well as the simple structures of everyday life[3]; the mother sitting nearby on the train to Pompei, asleep, nursing her baby with flies crawling into the baby's mouth; poverty and dirt and flies everywhere except in rich districts where houses were clean and magnificent; a young farmer walking out to his field at sun-up, hoe over his shoulder, singing like Caruso; the theater at Santa Maria with four balconies looking down on a troupe of American actors.

The local Red Cross arranged to have a party to which young women from Santa Maria were invited. Great effort was made to obtain a nice hall, obtain refreshments and put up decorations. The big night came. The pretty young Italian girls arrived, with chaperones, and mixing and dancing had just begun. Suddenly a truck-load of whores was driven up by some GIs who thought this would be a good joke. The chaperones gathered together the nice girls within minutes and they were returned home as quickly as possible. The party was over.

A few of us went over to visit a man (and his family) who had lived in New York for a while. He spoke with an accent but was readily understandable. As a young man he had emigrated to the US and worked as a street sweeper in the Bronx. He lived frugally and saved his money. After some years, he returned to Santa Maria, his home, and took up his real skill as a stone mason. He bought a piece of rocky land, married and began to raise a family. He mined the soft volcanic tuff of his land and built the walls of a nice house. Little by little, the house was finished in terrazzo—floors, even sinks and bathtub and kitchen counters—with a red tile roof and gardens all around. We could hardly believe that all this had been started with what he had saved from a street sweeper's job.

We did not sample much of the local Italian food because we were specifically asked not to add to the burden of the Italians feeding themselves. But our kitchen had hired a few Italian cooks who tried to prepare

---

3. I was able to buy in Pompei, from a boy guide, a small volume which we still have showing the excavated building.

native foods with GI supplies. Even though it was simple fare, I enjoyed it: pizza with tomato sauce and herbs and ordinary cheese was pleasant but was no great treat. However, most of the men scorned Italian food, just as they scorned most things Italian because they had the idea that the Italians were inferior; after all, poverty was everywhere. Even southern France, when we got there, received the same treatment. One thing I noticed that was interesting: porch roofs were covered with tomato halves left to dry in the hot sun. I suppose this served as a basis for sauces during winter. We were able to get Italian beer, bottled in reusable containers. I did not like beer very well and usually did not accept my ration of Army beer. But this Italian beer was quite good—very flavorful and with no added CO_2 so I was happy to buy it. Drink was a real problem in Santa Maria. The water supply was not usable by the Army because of the fear of disease. So great plastic bags of water, with spigots around the bottom which made them look like giant udders, were mounted in the compound; but the water tasted so strong of disinfectant that we used it as little as possible.

In the streets of Santa Maria, Naples and other Italian towns, we could buy pieces of pink coral from the Bay of Naples that had been carved into brooches, pins, etc, often in the shape of women or fish. I bought some of these and cherished them for years until they, along with other semi-precious stones, were stolen from our house at Los Arboles. That was a tragic loss. The price of cut coral has since skyrocketed.

Some of us occasionally hitched a ride into Naples to visit the Red Cross compound there. Mostly such visits were not very pleasant for me. The girls were always surrounded by 10 or so GIs and the food served was strictly commonplace American. However on one occasion I met Buddy Hudson![4] We were just wandering through the crowd and saw each other. Buddy was greatly changed since I last saw him. He was taller but emaciated. His face twitched and his hands trembled. His eyes kept roving from side to side. This was not the Buddy I had known. He was on R and R leave (Rest and Recreation) from a bomber squadron based in England where he had been continuously flying as tail gunner on flights over Germany. He also told me sadly of Lena's death, she who had been so close to him. Later, after the war, Buddy tried unsuccessfully to work at a variety of jobs, and sponged quite a bit off Grandpa Hudson. He married and eventually drifted away. But as fate would have it, on the morning our whole family was gathered at Dad's house in preparation to go to Mother's funeral, Buddy called (actually had his wife call) wanting to talk to Dad. Buddy was in the hospital, gravely

4. [Editor's Note] William (Buddy) Sanford Hudson (Maurice and Lena Hudson's son) Craig's cousin younger by five years.

ill. Dad refused to take the time to talk, and that was the last I ever heard about Buddy.

The Naples Red Cross was important in ways I was not to know until much later. That was where Libby Nichols (later Carter) worked as a Red Cross hostess. And that was where Marley Brown met Ruth, and probably was where they were married. Perhaps, even, Herman visited there on his way to (or from) the front in Northern Italy.

There has always been a grand boulevard around the bay, with the fancy houses rising tier upon tier inland. I walked along that boulevard but with all the rubble of war, it was hardly a romantic place.

We were not very pleased with the job of renovating the 268s, but we worked at it anyway. However, before the job was done, Tomash had us transferred to a tiny town west of Pozzuoli where the Signal Corps had set up a school in the SCR-584. All this time, we had been awaiting our vehicles, so we were obliged to bum rides from others. At the 584 school, we were at the end of a railroad operating trains into Naples on a fairly regular daily basis. So, with a little walking, we could catch the interurban and go to town frequently, and some men did. I preferred to visit the nearby country-side. This was farming country and fields were cultivated between Roman ruins (temples, houses, amphitheaters, etc). The weather was hot and dry, so people dressed lightly; but it was farming country so clothing was utili-tarian. However, the poverty of Naples was not evident. Fields were full of beans and melons (Oh, what melons!). There were hillsides of grapes—large black grapes in some fields, hanging in bunches a foot long. Here and there were small volcano-like hills; I hiked to the top of one—and behold!—in the crater was a field of grapes. This must have been, at one time, a very beauti-ful country, lovely to live in, quiet and gentle, never very cold.

Word finally came that our trucks and equipment had been off-loaded and were being stored at Livorno (Leghorn), a small seaport near Pisa. So we hitched rides (after the 584 school was over, so that it could be put on our records) up through Rome to Livorno. There, at night in the quiet, we could sometimes hear the big guns booming on the front a few miles north. We stayed in a building the Germans had used, cold and damp, with Ger-man graffiti on the walls. But those German soldiers were not obsessed by sex as were the American soldiers (who drew obscene pictures); this graffiti seemed to be about homesickness, with names of towns here and there. It took awhile to get our vehicles out of storage and to check everything out. Meanwhile, we were free to visit Pisa and nearby Florence. So close to the front, MP (Military Police) security was especially tight and we sometimes had to wait but were never stopped. Florence is a city of great art treasures; I was only able to see some of the famous building; all museums were closed.

But small shops were open and I bought a few cut stones here, among them the two aquamarines and a large smoky topaz. We loved these mementos for years, but they eventually disappeared in the great Los Arboles robbery.

The 584 school had occupied all of September. But the experience had been eye-opening. Nothing new in the basic measurement technology showed up, but the change to a higher frequency allowed the use of a parabola which could be turned in any direction to follow a moving target (but not moving too fast) and some tricks allowed automatic tracking. The 268 antenna had weighed about a ton with a large moment of inertia; the dish of the 584 weighed a few hundred pounds with a small moment of inertia. Thus the latter was much more steerable in addition to being remotely operated. And with the change in frequency came a whole new technology in electronics with everything scaled down in size by a factor of five. And the whole 584 unit was enclosed in a van which meant that the operators were protected from the elements and that the unit was ready to operate in much less time. All the armies in the European theater had, by this time, been given the 584s.

So, in early October, we were ready, with our trucks and equipment, to sally forth to work on the 584s. The first stop was Corsica. We were loaded onto an LST (Landing Ship Tank) which was a rather large (100 ft) open vessel designed for carrying tanks on short ocean voyages. Just outside Livorno, we ran into heavy weather and, standing in the "cabin" in the rear looking forward, I could see the ship twist frighteningly. It had no lateral strengthening, of course, because the hull was open at the top. It was not even braced at the bow, because the bow had to plop down to allow the tanks to move off onto the beach. But we made it (I had a new respect for the people who designed these vessels) around the southern tip of Corsica to Ajaccio, the capitol and important port of Corsica.

We were housed in a public building that had been perhaps a courthouse, although one end was bombed out. Everything inside was a shambles and exposed to the rain. We had cots and tiny tarps to keep out the rain; fortunately, the weather was quite good while we were there. A kitchen and some bath quarters were set up in the other end. Most of the time, we had little to do. Our activities (i.e. my memories) included the following: seeing Napoleon's birth place (empty rooms); watching a tall waterspout off the coast (I have never seen another); watching ladies in town pump water out of a well fitted with an Archimedes screw operated by a small hand crank; trying to meet young ladies in an apartment house across the plaza by means of signs in fractured French on wrapping paper, using binoculars (it didn't work); going to the public bath (my first) in which there were two tubs (very large) to a room—with real hot water (one of the men was matched up with an elderly woman); looking at a bombed cemetery (apparently bombed by the Germans) which greatly offended the local people.[5]

In the early part of November, we took our trucks out for their first real drive—the mountain road from Ajaccio to Bastia. Much of this drive was through a forest of chestnuts. When we stopped for lunch, to heat up our C-rations, we also gathered some chestnuts. Raw chestnuts are not a taste delight and it proved difficult to roast them over our little burners. Later, in Marseilles, we learned how nice they could be. At Bastia, we boarded a freighter and set sail for Marseilles.

The port of Marseilles was almost untouched by the war except for the lack of fuel and manpower. We were housed in a bomb-damaged school for girls. Of course, we got the damaged end, but it was possible to set up a relatively comfortable area. By this time, the weather was turning decidedly cool. It seemed very much like November in Oregon to me. By "we" I mean more than our five-man radar team. There were other loosely assigned people quartered there. One of them and I became good friends and often took walks around town to admire the boulevards and buildings of Marseilles. On one of these occasions, while walking along a small street called Rue Pierre Dupres, a pretty young woman ran out of a doorway and stopped us. She spoke halting English with a very strong accent. Her problem was a drunken GI who had gone to sleep in the entryway. She feared he was injured. The problem was cleared up by finding the MPs who took him off to dry out. Meanwhile I had struck up an acquaintance with the girl, who turned out to be Genevieve Icard. She lived there with her mother Mme Icard and her (unmarried) aunt Marcelle Lemer. In due time, I became a regular at the Icard house. Mme Icard had a small business selling laces and such and a small pension from her husband who had been killed in WWI. Marcelle had been a cook in England and spoke a little English. I return to their story presently.

My friend, whose name I have forgotten (I shall call him Robert for convenience), explored the area of the Vieux Port, where we were housed, with delight. Even though Marseilles had been the port of entry for the US invasion of southern France in August, the city had been little affected—a few bombs here and there, some street fighting, etc, but the famous buildings were untouched and the beautiful trees were not marred. So the city quickly got back to normal—all except the shipyards with their tall cranes and the docks, which were empty except for the American off-loading.

5. Out of the rubble, I dug a law book. After cleaning it of dust and dirt, I gave it to Uncle Maurice, who was an attorney. When he died, we got the book back and gave it to one of our friends who is also an attorney.

Several ships had been sunk in the harbor. But the street cars were mostly operating and we could go places.

Robert and I found a nice bar. On a shelf was a line of bottles of aperitif that we had never heard of before, perhaps 20 in all. So we set out to taste them all, one each visit. We never really finished, but I found one—Cap Corse—which I had to sample again and again: deep red, sweet with strong wine flavor. I could never find it again, although I have seen it listed in books as exceptional. One of the places I found was the Ecole des Beaux Arts. I went in to inquire if I could take classes. My communications with the professor (there were probably several but I spoke to only one who seemed to be teaching an intermediate class) was very sketchy, but I got the idea that I could join. I also cleared it with the Lieutenant because I had to be there in daylight. So I joined the class about twice a week, with supplies I purchased at a nearby store. Of course, I received no instruction—couldn't speak the language—but I managed to put in two hours twice a week. I made no friends and was not able to carry away any of my drawings. Eventually, I was transferred away, but the memory of my time at the school is a very warm one. The school itself was very old and rather rundown. The studio suffered from having no heat and no artificial light. Nearly all the students smoked so the air had a sort of romantic haze about it. Had I been able to stay longer, I am sure some of the students would have become friendly.

Meanwhile, Robert (who was from NY and married) had been out on his own too and had somehow met a pretty young woman who spoke English. She was married to an officer in the French navy, but she had not heard from him in many months and feared he was dead. They got together and consoled each other (!). One night when it was cold and foggy outside, Robert and I went to see her and she served us roasted chestnuts and a deli-cious sweet white wine (reminiscent of haut sauterne but of local origin). The stove was small, of glazed cast iron and had a small shelf in the front of the grate, apparently for roasting chestnuts and other such delicacies. So we sat around the stove, roasting and eating chestnuts for 2 hours. Robert saw her much more than I did, and upon leaving Marseilles, she gave him a lovely cut glass decanter in the shape of a duck. He did not want to have to explain it to his wife, so he gave it to me and to this day it stands among our glass treasures[6]. The story of it has been told a hundred times.

I visited the Icard family as often as I could. Little by little, I discovered that Genevieve was a devout Catholic. My religious feelings were so con-trary to that that we could never have a peaceful discussion in which this topic might arise, so we agreed to be friends and discuss other things. Later,

---

6. [Editor's Note] Craig's son, Cyril, is the keeper of the duck-shaped decanter.

I learned that she had already met a US medic who was equally dedicated to Catholicism. That relationship eventually ripened into marriage, they moved to South Carolina, followed in due time by Mme Icard and Marcelle Lemer. They had eight children, all of whom (from Genevieve's accounts on Christmas cards) became successful in various fields. Eventually Mme Icard died, and then Marcelle, and finally they were hit by a disastrous hurricane. After that we heard no more from Genevieve.

But while I was in Marseilles, we had fine Sunday dinners together. I was able to bring them occasionally something from our GI mess. Marcelle prepared soups and potatoes that delighted me. I was always careful not to eat very much, especially of meat which was, for them, hard to get. One day, Marcelle met me with the exclamation "I have an egg! How would you like it?" So I said "Make it into a mayonnaise; then we can share it." So she did; the first homemade mayonnaise I can remember, and it was delicious. She had trouble with her kitchen stove which had been hit by a bullet that came through the window as the US Army swept the Germans out of town. The cast iron stove had shattered on one corner of the firebox. Repair was impossible but I was able to wire the pieces together so that it worked better.

Mme Icard was a tiny, shy person who may have exerted considerable influence over the household (after all, she had the income) but certainly did not seem to have much to say when I was there. Marcelle (who spoke some English) and Genevieve (whose English improved quickly) often arranged outings for us, typically to places at the ends of the rail lines. The two that I remember now were: to the Notre Dame on a hill overlooking the bay; and to the west of Marseilles at a lovely picnic area near the water. Notre Dame was a striking place, more a church than a cathedral. In the nave, especially at the altar end, hung models of ships and airplanes dangling at the ends of strings so as to give the impression of a false ceiling, hundreds of them—some surely in memory of family members who didn't come back. And far out in the bay was Chateau d'If, the prison where the Count of Monte Cristo[7] had been incarcerated. They were very proud of being so close to such a famous, though fictional, event. The ride to the picnic area took us through some older parts of Marseilles and Genevieve delighted in telling me about the historical buildings. We had a simple lunch on a grassy sward near where boats were tied up in a tiny fishing village. There were discussions of the prewar days when all sorts of seafood could be got in the markets (it was still there but at too high a price) for making various types of bouillabaisse. Then the trip home in the now cold air.

---

7. [Editor's Note] Alexandre Dumas. *The Count of Monte Cristo*, 1844.

We had turkey dinners at both Thanksgiving and Christmas. But that Christmas we were also invited to the home of Louis and Suzanne N— for a second Christmas dinner. The people had been friends of Robert's girl-friend. Their apartment was much larger than that of the Icard's and much better furnished in a modern Art Deco style. Robert and I felt rather special at being invited to such a personal occasion. There were eight people there and English was the language used. Robert and I once tried to use Army slang to express a private idea only to discover that one of the guests was employed at the Army PX and knew Army slang! The dinner was far afield from what we imagined a Christmas feast to be. Suzanne N— was a good cook but things had an Italian flavor. There were several courses, all more or less good, but the one that most surprised me was a kind of pie-casserole in which were layered, between crusts, sliced ham, tomato sauce, spinach and scrambled eggs. It made a beautiful mixture and was very tasty.[8] I enjoyed the N— family very much but never saw them again.

In the old quarter of Marseilles, there were a number of antique shops. I used to window-shop there a great deal, but mostly prices were beyond my means (or the items were too bulky to carry). I found some little cameos and selected one in the form of Socrates head, white agate carved on a black background; and there were two little boy heads set in small dishes of brown glass-like material—a matched set. These I bought. And I found two lovely carved darning eggs of walnut burl, each divided so that the two halves could be screwed together. The cameos were lost in the evil Los Arboles robbery. The carved darning eggs we still have on display in our vitrine.

In January we moved to a Signal Corps base in the Miramas region west of Marseilles. It was a rather desolate region, first a French army base, then occupied by the Germans, and finally by the US Signal Corps with a German prison camp in one sector. It is close to the mouth of the Rhone River, in the flood plain.

The Battle of the Bulge had begun on December 15 with very bad weather. The Germans brought up every tank they could get their hands on and broke through the Allied line where the British and American forces joined. It was the same kind of attack that had been so successful before against the French, the Poles and the Russians. But this time it did not work. Nevertheless, the people in Marseilles were terrified. Again and again, in spite of my feelings of confidence, they said we didn't know the German Army, how strong it was. To me, the German Army was already beaten, trying desperately to reach the port of Antwerp so they could have leverage

8. Now that I have had the experience in Santa Fe at a French restaurant, it seems rather like the Torte Milannaise that we enjoy there.

for a separate peace. Then they could turn full force against the Russians. They knew the Russian build-up was tremendous. At any rate, every German reconnaissance plane that flew over Marseilles resulted in a panic. In the middle of this, the damaged 584s began accumulating at our new depot in Miramas. By then the weather began to get very cold. The poor German POWs were captured wearing summer uniforms and they had to stand the cold any way they could.

Mostly the 584s merely suffered from broken or worn out parts and were easily repaired. Some had damage and could be salvaged to repair others. The weather remained cold for weeks on end but it snowed very little. I measured 10 inches of ice in a ditch. Once, at the beginning of the deep cold, we went out to work at night. In order that the electric generator (for lights and power in the van) operate, the truck engine had to be running. At the end of a couple of hours, when we were ready to leave, Mantooth turned the switch to cut off the engine; but it kept on going. He lifted the hood and the engine block was a dull red! It was dieseling; that is, the cylinders fired without spark. So Mantooth disconnected the fuel line and it stopped. After the engine cooled somewhat, he reconnected the fuel line and operated it in a normal manner to prevent "freezing." We later learned that someone from the base motor pool had drained all the engines of coolant to prevent freezing in the cold. The remarkable part of this story is that the engine continued to operate normally when the coolant was replaced.

The stay at the Miramas depot was interesting in the sense that I learned a great deal about radar and electronics. We had books and plenty of time. but in March Lt. Tomash had had enough so he finagled a place for us in Paris and the orders took us up the spectacular Durance Valley to Grenoble, over to Lyon, then Dijon and Paris. We spent two nights in small towns along the way; Tomash had military credit cards which allowed us to stay where we chose—for a dollar limit. The small town accommodations offered more for less. In one place, we had great fluffy goose-down quilts on the bed. In the other, a wonderful white tiled (floor to ceiling) shower to accommodate six at one time. We began to think "These French really know how to live."

Grenoble was, at that time, a very quiet town. We did not stay, but saw people sweeping the gutters and sidewalks. The houses were old and picturesque, and everything was very clean. It was an attractive place to stay, but our orders had us reporting to quarters in Paris by a certain date. Then we skirted Lyon and Dijon and rolled into Paris late one afternoon. The streets were a maze until finally we came out on the Boulevard Rivoli, then the Champs Élysées and finally to the Parc Monceau. There we received our orders for quarters and messing. The place where we received the orders was a house on Avenue Hoche that was owned by an American woman who had turned it over to the Signal Corps for use during the war. All furniture had been removed and it was converted into laboratories and offices. This was April 1, 1945.

We were quartered in what I was told was the Mal Maison, the palace that Napoleon had built for his mistress. My recollection of it is a rather large building of dark stone and sloping roof containing a number of rooms, one of which was a bedroom in which stood a magnificent 4-poster bed with elegantly carved posts. This was the officers' quarters. The men's quarters may have been cold in winter, but this was spring and the air was warm. While we were living there, I bought a 3"x4" used camera that held glass plate negatives. To test it out, I took some pictures of Byron Sasser walking down a curved roadway fenced on each side by an 8-foot wrought iron fence, with tall elm trees on either side. But years later, when Jeannine and I were taken to Mal Maison, it was not at all the same place I remembered. The house was much larger and flat-roofed, the color of stone (red) was wrong and there were few trees. After looking all around, I had to conclude that the "Mal Maison" I remembered was at best the grounds' keeper's house (hidden in the trees and private), and possibly had been misidentified.

We were given food cards which could be used in restaurants in the vicinity of Avenue Hoch. And so I got my first taste of Parisian cooking. The dinners I had eaten at the Icard house in Marseilles had a Provencal flavor, but were mostly limited to potatoes and cabbage because of the poverty of the household. Nevertheless, Marcelle Lemer's cooking had been very good compared to Army chow. But here in Paris, money was no object and the food was correspondingly delicious.

I used to walk behind French couples trying to pick up French expressions I was familiar with from *The Three Musketeers*[9]: I did hear a few "n'est-ce pas," but listened in vain for "Sacré Bleu!" At the restaurant, I found posters on the walls labeled "patatras!" showing a waitress dropping dishes. But my French remained abysmal and is poor to this day.

Being in Paris as a soldier on a fulltime basis was a dream come true. The Métro[10], all trains and all museums were free. My first day there, I walked the circumference (about 20 miles) just to get the feel of the city. People were friendly to the extent my limited French permitted. I was interested in seeing how the workmen dressed, how the young women dressed for work (even though times were tough, they were neat and trim) and how

9. [Editor's Note] Alexandre Dumas. *The Three Musketeers, 1844.*

10. [Editor's Note] Métro, short for le métropolitain, is the subway system of Paris. The first line was completed and in use in 1900.

the older people looked. I compared them with similar people in Naples (there was a much wider spread in Italy—so much poverty there). Also the city seemed so much better constructed than Naples: utilities were out of sight or located better. I had to conclude that Italy was not as up-to-date as France in spite of the ravages of war. Mussolini, just as Stalin, took over a country that was economically destitute and used his power to build up the military rather than the social infrastructure.

Our lab was located close to the Arc de Triomphe on one end and Parc Monceau on the other, closer to the Parc. Often during lunch hour, Byron Sasser and I took seats in the Parc to watch the world go by: lots of young women pushing baby buggies; a few well-dressed old ladies and men "taking the air," seemingly with little else to do; and some men dressed in black business suits, apparently using their lunch hour. However, I found that lunch hour for office workers in Paris was 1–2 pm, so we must have missed most of them. It was March and the Parc was coming alive with flowering bulbs and green shoots on all the trees. Actually we remained there well into July and were able eventually to see the shrubs and trees bloom, too.

What I most liked about Paris were the museums. Of course, I had heard about the Louvre and visited there as soon as I could do so. Many of the paintings were still in hiding from the occupation (the Germans did steal thousands of art works from private collections, but the big museum collections were safe), but the *Mona Lisa* was on display, behind a security barricade and watched by two guards. There was always a large crowd around it but I once worked my way to the barricade, at which point I could lean forward until my eyes were only about 6 feet from the painting and I looked as intently as I could. Actually there is very little about the painting technique that is unusual so that coming close doesn't add much to its charm. For the paintings of Van Gogh, to the contrary, seeing it close up gives a very different impression than seeing it from a distance—due to the bold brush strokes, of course. The same distance effect is also true for Monet's paintings, too; but this is not due to bold strokes, but rather to gradations of color.

Perhaps the most memorable piece at the Louvre is the sculpture *Winged Victory of Samothrace, Nike* which is roughly twice lifesize and stood then on a large landing of a beautiful marble staircase, well lighted by both window and spotlights. I understand that it is not considered to be a great work of art; but its spectacular exhibition makes it a very impressive piece.

I did walk through as many of the halls of the Louvre as I had time for. Most of the impressionists' paintings, my favorites, were not there. But I saw many others including David's huge canvases (he must have used a dozen apprentices to help) and I was pleased to be able to see some of Salvador

Dali's paintings—he of the melted clock fame. Of course I saw many other works there but those memories have dimmed; I confuse things between the Louvre, the Metropolitan and the National Gallery in Washington D.C. also, at that time my knowledge of archaeology was much less than now, so I was less discriminating concerning the antique collections. In time, the fine paintings were returned, but many of them went to the new Orsay Museum.

There are other museums in Paris; in fact, there are so many small ones that the list is long. I enjoyed the following four very much.

Palais de la Découverte was filled with the artifacts of scientific discovery, mostly from the period 1890 to 1930. In it, I found the original transformers, etc, that had been used to establish the principles of electricity and of mechanics and chemistry (I was most interested in electricity at the time). Everything was dusty and uncared for, as musty as a museum was supposed to be! When I returned in 1987, I could hardly recognize the place: clean, new exhibits, my old friends in storage someplace.

Musée des Arts et Métiers occupied me for hours. It included exhibits on all the industrial and agricultural activities of France since the Industrial Revolution. I found scale models of iron and coal mines, of open hearth steelmaking operations, of rolling and steel fabrication mills; I found exhibits of agricultural products: many kinds of grains, wax models of fruits like apples and pears showing the evolution from very early varieties to modern ones (in nice color, full size); and exhibits of tools of all sorts, including the malformations of the workmen who used these tools.[11]

The Musée de l'Homme proved to be a most fascinating place. Some of the earliest artifacts in the history of Man were there. But the place was dusty and run-down and quite out of date.[12]

There was also another museum at the Trocadéro which caught my eye. I have forgotten the name but it illustrated the artifacts of the Middle Ages, including carvings in stone on the sarcophagi of the kings and queens, etc, contained therein. The men were all military in armor and swords, while the women were all shown pregnant.

---

11. I add here a curious sequel (Feb 1995): prehistoric women showed deformation of the knee and big toes from spending so much time kneeling at a grinding stone to make flour out of wheat and barley seeds. Do SW Indian women show the same deformity? Not that I have heard about.

12. In 1987, Jeannine and I visited both the Museum of Man in Vienna (which happened to include at the time a wonderful up-to-date traveling exhibit on the rise of Man) and the Musee de l'Homme; the latter suffered greatly in the comparison; but I am sure a new exhibit was being prepared. .

Certainly one of the most impressive museums to me was the one at the Jardin des Plants[13]. The main purpose was to exhibit plants from all over the world, both modern and prehistoric. And this was very exciting, but also shown, in a much more limited exhibit, were the remains of deformed animals, possible mutants and other aberrations of reproduction, all preserved in jars. It was a grizzly exhibit, quite morbid but interesting. If one needed proof that there was no God, this would work.[14]

I visited other smaller museums, too, but can no longer remember their names. Paris is a storehouse of human artifacts as well as natural ones.

The work at our little laboratory in Paris was not at all demanding. For some of our team, it was not work at all. It was a Signal Corps office and it did have a project: to build four models of a mortar-finding radar. Mortars are and can be crudely aimed. A shell is dropped into it from the top; a small charge propels the shell out on a high trajectory and it eventually falls and explodes on the ground. The shell diameters are varied from about two inches to six inches. They burst releasing shrapnel. For front line troops, mortars are devastating because even though they cannot be aimed very accurately, they cause many casualties and counter measures are ineffective because the mortars can be fired and then be moved quickly. What was needed was radar that could locate the shell shortly after it left the mortar and thus permit fire to be aimed at that point. The problem was that most radar could not "see" mortar shells: their operating frequency was too low. Or, conversely, their wavelength was too long. When we were there in 1945, the aircraft night fighters were being outfitted with very short wave nose radars for tracking other night fighters. To give good radar resolution, the wavelength should be of the order of (or smaller than) the small dimension of the target. These radars had a wavelength of about a centimeter, just capable of seeing a mortar shell.

The project, then, was to convert the aircraft radar into one which was rugged, could be mounted on a jeep trailer and which had the displays needed to spot mortar shells. The men who were already there had accomplished most of the design work. We merely helped to assemble. Of the four units that were made, one failed to work in the field, one was blown up

13. [Editor's Note] The Jardin des Plantes, the oldest garden in Paris, is a botanical garden. The Natural History Museum is located in the Jardin des Plantes.

14. Jeannine and I revisited this museum in 1987. The exhibits were cleaned up and modernized and the grizzly exhibits were in storage. We had been sent there by Ann Marie Decroix to visit a friend of hers who worked in a lab there. He was the scientist in charge of the French undersea explorations in the South Atlantic. We spent some marvelous times together. His name was Francois Frohlich and we parted good friends, tho we never saw him again. He showed us a number of drill cores (hundred in total) that explored the ocean bottom and a long silica filament from a sponge which we have.

by a mine, one was unfinished when I left and the fourth was taken into Germany (near Ulm) by our team and was tested against real mortar fire. It worked but not very well. However, its problems were not fundamental. It could be made to work, but I did not stay with the project.

While I was there, I was asked to examine captured German electronic apparatus, to identify its purpose and to evaluate its quality—to the extent I was able. It was an interesting assignment and allowed me to see what kind of equipment was being made for field use by the German army at the end of the war. It seemed to be cheaper than ours but of good enough quality to serve, and made use of plastics in places where the US would have used metal. It was a good experience.

And now I come to the episode that was due to change my life; but of course that did not occur to me at the time. I met Jeannine. It happened like this.

I was unable to make social connections—nothing new: I had always been like this. The other fellows went out in town and found female companions. Not I; I was too shy.

One day in April, I'm sure it was a Sunday, I walked around in the area of the Trocadéro[15] and found a lovely grassy bank on which I lay down to bask in the sun to watch the people go by. There was a sign saying "Keep off the Grass" but I couldn't read French. Quite a few people gave me dirty looks. Finally a man spoke to me and pointed to the sign, and I finally understood and moved away. The grassy bank, as it turned out, was part of the landscaping of the Paris Aquarium which was out of sight, buried in the ground. So I found the entrance and went in. It was quite dark; only the fish tanks were lighted (some from skylights). I had never been very fond of fish in tanks, but out of boredom I looked. Then a rather amazing sight appeared: a man taking pictures of the fish using the natural light. At his side was a young girl holding his arm. She appeared to be 12–14 years old, modestly dressed with thick wooly hair twisted into curls all around the sides and with a bow on top. Her legs were very slender, her face was round with adolescent fat, and she had a happy shy smile showing small, even, pearly teeth. Her father was short, baldish with a moustache, wearing a black suit and tie. He had a Mediterranean look.

What caused me to speak to him was related to taking photographs in the dark (I was interested in photography and was curious about his camera and film). I remember being prepared for nothing because we probably could not converse. He did speak, with a smile, and sure enough I could

---

15. [Editor's Note] The Trocadéro gardens are laid out on either side of the Trocadéro Fountain.

not understand. But then to my surprise, Jeannine answered me in English, school girl English to be sure, but quite understandable. We conversed briefly and then M. Dumas invited me to have coffee with them at a nearby shop (quite a distance actually, because there is nothing like that on the museum grounds). We talked, with Jeannine translating, for perhaps half an hour. Then they had to leave to have the dinner that Mme Dumas had prepared. But before going (after a short conference in French) M. Dumas gave me a slip of paper with their address on it and an invitation to dinner the next Sunday. Quite an encounter, wouldn't you say? I was delighted to be brought into a real French family.

Waiting for the week to pass was worrisome. I had no idea whether or not the address was real. After all, I had spent hardly an hour with these people. How could one expect such a chance encounter to be serious? I spent the days in my usual routine (but I cannot remember what it was!) and finally Sunday came. I knew how to take the Métro and finally found myself at 118 Rue Vielle du Temple, in front of a narrow, tall building. I walked up four flights to confront a door bearing the small brass plaque "Jean Dumas, "Ebéniste", so I knew I was in the right place. I knocked on the door and it was promptly opened by Jeannine with the shy smile, pearly teeth and fuzzy hair with dangling ringlets. I could see M. Dumas behind her and in a moment Mme Dumas appeared, a lovely woman with dark auburn hair—not beautiful but pretty enough and nicely proportioned. She had a nice smile, although a misplaced front tooth was at first difficult to ignore.

I soon learned that Jeannine was called Ninette or just Nin, and so I also addressed her in this way. She was very obviously much loved by her parents and, on her part, did nothing to displease them. I learned this from the beginning and was much touched by it. As I was to learn later, this trait of character—to be cooperative rather than combative—was one of her finest points. I greatly admired her for it throughout the marriage which was to come.

The Dumas apartment was small, literally a living room and sleeping room with a tiny kitchen off to the side and an under-the-rafters storage room adjacent to the sleeping room. The bathroom (literally a toilet) was outside on the stairway landing. The apartment was scrupulously clean and furnished with fine pieces of furniture, quality bric-a-brac and excellent tableware. Of course, I did not appreciate all this on my first visit, but in time I grew to love it all. The area of the apartment was perhaps only 300 square feet but it was so tastefully arranged that it seemed much larger. There was no bath; I learned later that ablutions were conducted by means of a sponge and basin of water, as was typical of much of Paris.

The meal that I had with the Dumas family that first time consisted of soup (always and forever soup for the first course) followed by a fine piece of beef served with green beans, followed by a salad with vinaigrette and finally cheese and wonderful coffee. The entire meal was accompanied by one of those skinny French breads called *baguettes*. There were none of the fatty, sugary dishes I had become accustomed to, and I remember going away feeling that the new cuisine was wonderful. And I wondered how Mme Dumas had been able to prepare it in the tiny kitchen.

I left the apartment rather late in the evening and immediately sought the *pisserie* (where men urinated) on the way to the Métro. This habit was to continue all the visits I made to the Dumas apartment. I didn't find out where the toilet was until much later. Always I made a run for the *pisserie*. I was too shy to ask for the toilet. As I was growing up, this was a matter one did not discuss, especially in the presence of women. So I suffered in silence. Meanwhile, as I learned much later, the Dumas' wondered, just as silently, how this strange American did not have the same urges as did French people—he surely did have!

I had discovered *pisseries* in the countryside of Italy. There they were individual, standing by the side of the roads, quite in the open. In Paris, the *pisseries* were round to accommodate 6 or 8 men at a time and were screened. The screen covered the body from below the knee to above the shoulder and had a wrap-around entrance so that from the outside one could not see who was inside—you could only see feet and hats. They smelled bad even though they were washed out from time to time. There were not very many of them; the only ones I ever saw were in the older parts of Paris and by 1987, they had all been removed. It was a male-dominated society that installed them in the first place. Where did the women go? I suppose they did not go out as much and perhaps found WCs (toilets) where men were not welcome.

In the spring of 1945, I went to see the *Folies Bergère* with my friend Byron Sasser. The entrance fee was considerable and seats were limited. Ours were behind a column which limited our view somewhat. But the show was all that we had expected it to be: bright lights, beautiful semi-nude women in various costumes with lots of feathers, exciting music, and some comedians who told jokes sometimes in English. We also went to the Moulin Rouge but the glitter had worn off. I remember talking to the Dumases about the experience. M. Dumas had seen the show and was favorably impressed by it; but Jeannine and her mother had not and were somewhat scornful.[16]

While quartered at Mal Maison, our repair van, filled with all sorts of electronic test gear, was parked in front of the lab. It attracted quite a bit of

16. Later, I saw essentially the same show in Las Vegas when I was at the Test Site.

interest since radar was still unfamiliar to most people. A young French boy stopped by and tried to strike up conversations with us. The other GI would not talk to him, even though the boy spoke quite good English; but I was more cooperative and soon found him to be an interesting fellow of about 16 years. He was enrolled at the Sorbonne in mainly mathematics. I asked him how come he was at the Sorbonne at such an early age. He answered with a shrug, as if it were no big deal, that he had passed the tests and there was no problem. His name was Eddie Faussion and to show appreciation for our friendship, he gave me a book of Dubout[17], a French cartoonist popular at the time. He also showed me his quarters, a very run-down apartment which he shared with three other students in a rather slummy part of the neighborhood near the Sorbonne. They were all very boisterous and I deduced that they did not all stay in the apartment at the same time. I think the only clothes he had were the ones he wore, and the others were equally poor. Eddie took me onto the campus where I was much impressed by some of the lecture amphitheaters which reminded me of pictures I had seen. I last saw Eddie just before leaving for Germany. We have the Dubout book[18] to this day, and Jeannine still chuckles over some of the outrageous pictures of very small husbands and very fat, big wives. For me, they were interesting commentary but never funny. I learned that French and American humor are quite different and do not cross the cultural line well at all.

In those early days in Paris, I went to the movies (Cinema) a few times. I remember seeing a French movie in not very good color called *Arc du Ciel*.[19] It described life in a prison camp for women and was rather brutal. One image I cannot forget was of the heroine, by now immensely pregnant, struggling in the mud alone and unloved. I could not understand the dialog, but the thrust of the plot was pretty clear. All Germans were beasts. I know this to be false, but it was emphasized in French drama after the war.

I also saw my favorite Laurel and Hardy comedy *Fra Diavolo*.[20] I laughed and laughed at it, as I had the first time I saw it years before. But I soon discovered that the rest of the audience was not laughing at all. Humor is certainly culturally biased.

17. [Editor's Note] Albert Dubout was a French painter, sculptor, book illustrator, and a cartoonist.

18. [Editor's Note] Craig's daughter, Cassandra Shaw, is the keeper of the Dubout book.

19. [Editor's Note] *Arc du Ciel*. Fiction film, USSR, circa 1943, Mark Donskoi. http://iconotheque-russe.ehess.fr/film/470/ .

20. [Editor's Note] *Fra Diavolo* (aka *The Devil's Brother*). Circa 1933 http://www.laurel-and-hardy.com/ .

At about this time, although it could have been earlier, I signed up for University of Chicago extension courses in math (three of them) which were offered to GIs either free or for a nominal sum. Remembering my earlier disappointment with an extension course about radio repairing, I was worried. But it all worked out well and, as I recall it, I got the credit.

As long as I worked at the Signal Corps Lab (April-June), I had to catch the truck back to the barracks at Mal Maison at about 10 pm. There were no dining facilities at Mal Maison, so everyone stayed in town long enough to get dinner. My visits to the Dumas apartment continued at about the once-a-week schedule (typically on Sunday) and fortunately I was able to get a late ride back to the barracks. The dinners were always wonderful: a soup, a meat dish (typically chicken or rabbit) with *frits* (delicious French fried potatoes) and a vegetable, salad and coffee. There was also always red wine and *baguettes*. On some occasions, the chicken came in a bowl of sauce and mushrooms with the feet and head swimming in it. Mme Dumas later swore she never served the heads, but I have a clear memory of M. Dumas opening the head with a sharp knife to get at the brain. He also chewed the chicken legs with gusto, down to the inedible part. It was a wonderful experience for me to see—and to hear—someone eat the whole animal, crunching the gristle off the bones. Mme Dumas obviously thought he was crude in this habit; but, while I never saw her, Jeannine tended to pick up her father's habits and to this day happily chews bones when guests are not present.

On my evenings at the Dumas apartment, Jeannine and I were often left to ourselves. M. Dumas sometimes went out; Mme Dumas cleaned up and did sewing. So Jeannine and I played games I invented; or I drew pictures for her; or I taught her some algebra and electronics; or I showed her a trick my brother Dexter and I used to play. I lay on my back; she put her hands on my knees; I took her shoulders in my hands; and she did a handstand. At first she was very shaky but in time was able to do a good handstand and was quite steady. Of course, she had to fasten her skirt up; sometimes she wore trousers. On some occasions, M. Dumas joined in the fun and showed off some tricks of his own; one was to stand with his heels against the wall and twist forward to touch his toes. It was easy for him but I could never do it. I think it was because he was short, had big feet and was very strong.

In early June, our radar unit was ready to be tested. By then the war was over in the European Theater (May 8 VE Day). But for reasons I never knew, the tests were to take place in Germany. So preparations were made and in early June our radar group headed out to the east. A few days before, I had visited the Dumas for a fine dinner and a walk in Butte Chaumont, a lovely park with the butte in the center. Jeannine and I felt this was an especially tender and critical moment. We had grown very fond of each other; but the duration of our relationship had been only three months—and she was so young! We could both see the trip into Germany being only the first step in a permanent separation. It was well-known that units were being shipped to the Pacific Theater. So we said a very tearful goodbye. I thought it was probably the end of our little affair.

The actual situation was that we returned to Paris in mid-summer. This time, however, we were quartered at the Signal Corps Depot just outside Paris, in the vicinity of Montrouge. It had been an old warehouse taken over by the German army and finally by the US Signal Corps. It was the major Signal Corps Depot in the European Theater. I never really learned the full extent of it. Our vehicles were absorbed by the depot car pool. From then on, we had to rely on public transportation. We still did not have to pay, so the problems were minimal. A Métro line could be boarded nearby which gave us access to the whole of downtown Paris with only a change or two.

I had just returned to Paris in time for the 14th of July celebration. The streets were massed with people. In the evening, perhaps 9 pm, I entered a subway station and we stood shoulder to shoulder. The crowd slowly moved downward as trains moved them off the platform; but I was still near the entrance when—in the heat and stuffiness—a young woman in front of me collapsed unconscious. I helped to hold her upright and looked around for someone to take charge. No one did. I heaved her like a sack of potatoes over one shoulder and several people showed me an exit. I struggled through the crowd, made it to the exit and once outside in the cool air, she revived. She was about 20, slender, not pretty but good looking enough. She spoke halting English so we were able to converse. I said I would see her home, which I did—not really home, but as far as she would let me take her. By this time, the streets were nearly empty. A jeep came whizzing by. "Stop him!" she cried, "I want to ride in one." No such luck; it was full. I knew her name at one time. She had a minimal education and no aspirations for any more. She was a seamstress and her clothes always showed off her nice figure. We met a few times—always at a prearranged place—and once she took me to a beach on the Marne River, a very popular place where she swam but I watched. Inevitably she finally did not show up at a rendezvous and it was all over.

While I was still trying to work out the Métro route, I wasn't very confident and asked information of a passing woman. She spoke fluent English (!) and was very helpful. After a little while, she invited me to her apartment for an *aperitif*. I accepted and was taken to a very handsome building, up to the 3rd floor by elevator and into a large (about 2000 sq ft) apartment very richly furnished. Inside were her two children Bernard and Monique. An older daughter was married and lived elsewhere. Mme Philbert was perhaps 50 years old at that time and was very handsome and charming. Bernard was about 14 years and Monique perhaps 20. They both were fluent in English. Monique was very shy (she had the oriental eye fold which embarrassed her) but Bernard was lively, outgoing and very self-assured. He was interested in my mathematical and electrical background since his educational goal was a PhD in math. Monique was interested in ophthalmology.

I visited the Philbert's apartment on several occasions for lunches and dinners. The food was always very good. On one occasion, I was served calf brains in a sauce, which obviously was considered a great delicacy. But I choked on it (a psychological hang-up that I hugely regret) and only barely managed to get through the meal. It still bothers me. On another occasion, I announced myself at the door and heard noises from the inside suggesting the unlocking of massive bars and locks. Sure enough, the inside of the door was secured by four locks including a steel bar that spanned the door frame. The explanation was that several nearby apartments had been robbed. And so was the Philbert apartment, but by way of the service entrance in the kitchen, which was not protected at all!

One afternoon when I came for lunch I was sent into the sitting room while Mme Philbert finished preparations. There, a lovely old lady was waiting, M. Philbert's mother, and we tried conversation in French. Progress was very slow. I tried English; slower still. Then I committed a great error: I invited her to speak in German, thinking I was only chattering. But my word what a rush of German came forth! She was from Alsace and this was her native tongue. My knowledge of German was utterly limited. Mme Philbert came in and rescued the situation. She explained that M. Philbert operated a steel mill in Alsace, had family there and came to Paris only monthly; I never met him. Jeannine and I sent Mme Philbert an invitation to our wedding and she came, bearing as a gift a lovely crystal vase which we still have. For a long time we corresponded with Mme Philbert by mail; but eventually her letters stopped coming.

That summer (possibly in early August) Dexter got some leave time and we met in Paris. He stayed at the Depot and during the day we walked around the city. We took each other's pictures in front of Notre Dame. We went to the Sacré-Coeur and actually climbed up onto the roof. There were lightning rods at a number of points with copper cables to the ground. There was an intricate system of gutters to carry off rainwater. We still have some of those pictures of Dexter and me, a nice remembrance since his life ended so tragically. We talked about our experiences: he had had a dreadful time at the Omaha Beach landing; only a few of his company were spared. I took him twice to the Dumas apartment, but it was summer vacation for the family and there was no one there. Jeannine did get to meet him later after we were married and found him to be a happy-go-lucky man.

In September I went to see the Dumas family again. They were as happy to see me as I was to see them and the visits began again, making it difficult for Jeannine to keep up with her studies and still have time for me. But keep up she did. In the fall of that year, the rumors started that I was to be sent home. And indeed the date was set: March. So we could see the end. I walked a tight rope, wanting to love her but knowing that a crisis to that love was in sight. Our relationship took on a more sober aspect, always aware of the impending separation. We did discuss marriage but in vague terms.

My work at the depot was not very exciting. It was a depot, so parts by the thousands had to be received, counted, catalogued and shelved. Parts were from radars, radios and telephones (switch boards, etc), as well as electric motors and generators—anything electrical. I had about 20 German POWs working for me, headed by a colonel who spoke excellent English. Some of the POWs were horribly scarred from fires in the tanks and other vehicles in which they were trapped. They were all cooperative and of good spirit—glad to be where they were. The colonel was fun to talk to since he had been a professor and was well trained in art. He had one trait I didn't like: when the men went to the toilet, they wiped with sawdust. He had a square of cloth which he washed and hung to dry on our radiator. After a while, it began to smell.

We had come on a shipment of classified electronic devices, mostly radar magnetrons and klystrons, with orders to destroy them. It was very sad to see all this wonderful technology—the best in the world at that time—registered and then smashed to smithereens by the POWs using heavy mallets, under my supervision, of course.

There were about 100 French men working at the Depot. They could be paid either in dollars or bread. Can you imagine choosing those big soft loaves of white bread in preference to the French baguettes? But they did, often.

Quite often, during break times, it was possible to see the Frenchmen and the Germans swapping stories together, apparently in good humor. The war was over and the world could become normal again.

As the winter season wore on, M. Dumas arranged many outings. One of them was to a sports park where, I understood, he used to engage in all sorts of sports. It was interesting to watch. While soccer was very popular, there was no baseball, football, or basketball. A great emphasis was placed on gymnastics where I understood M. Dumas had excelled.

But this did not appeal to Mme Dumas. What she liked was to dress up and go to the theater, so we did some of that, too. Once we went to the Opera to see *The Magic Flute*. It was my first big opera in the grand style and my first exposure to this opera. Jeannine and her mother were beautifully dressed and the evening went very well but I didn't care much for the opera—still don't as a matter of fact. The music is very fine Mozart; I guess I just can't get interested in the story.

On another occasion, we went to see *l'Eglon* (The Eagle), a story full of pathos for the days of Napoleon, about his son and his abortive attempt to return to power. This play was at the Châtelet Theater[21], which is quite spectacular. I was also taken to two other productions that I can remember: a story about the Resistance with Germans torturing captured French people (I can still hear in my mind the off-stage screams of a woman), and a wonderful musical featuring a wonderful cancan[22].

Some Sundays we went for walks around the city and Mme Dumas sometimes went with us. In this way, I was able to see parts of Paris I never could have found on my own. Jeannine was always shy, but her father was full of exuberant spirit. If Mme Dumas influenced the course of the walks, I never knew about it. She was so quiet. M. Dumas often took Jeannine to the flea markets where he bought for her books and bric-a-brac which she cherishes to this day. M. and Mme Dumas had never had much education, but they both had great feeling for refinement and nice things. It was one of the things that made a great impression on me, especially after I returned to Oregon and began to think about marriage.

What began as a benign friendship to understand a different culture ripened in the end to a deep affection not only for Jeannine but for her parents as well. My father had showed me the rudiments of woodworking, so it was with great interest that M. Dumas showed me his shop. He had worked as a master ébéniste before the war and had built many fine pieces of furniture. Now, after the war, he assembled the machines and the workmen to build his own business, and I was fascinated. And Mme Dumas was of great interest as well. She was so calm and efficient and such a good cook that I was entranced. My own mother was a good cook in the American way, but Mme Dumas' cooking opened up a new vista in the culinary field. I was accustomed to chicken boiled and fried, but Mme Dumas added a new dimension with her sauces and vegetables. I could count on one hand the

21. [Editor's Note] Théâtre du Châtelet is located on one side of the Place du Châtelet in the heart of Paris.

22. [Editor's Note] The cancan is a lively dance involving high kicks in unison usually performed by a row of women with full skirts with petticoats.
Encyclopedia Britannica. *Cancan* .

number of time I had eaten rabbit—always fried—but at the Dumas house it was served often and with an elegant sauce. Once or twice in that time, we had beef—but not the American cut, sliced off on a saw. These were the most tasty parts cooked to perfection. And always the vegetables! Never were they just boiled; always cooked specially. So I was very much attracted to M. and Mme Dumas.

At first, I felt like a big brother to Jeannine. And I am sure I was admitted into the family on this basis. I could entertain them endlessly being able to draw pictures and by stories of the Yukon and backwoods of Oregon. But as the months went by, things changed. She now wanted to be kissed on the mouth, lover style. And she agreed to being held close. At first, I was uneasy about this. She was only 14; I was 28. But the situation developed so smoothly and seemingly with the approval of her parents that I made no effort to break it off. But where could such a relationship go? I asked myself this over and over; but Jeannine was always steadfast, so I gained confidence. The future is always uncertain; let us be led.

I understood that Jeannine still had a great deal of school to attend. She had already completed two years of Latin, three years of English, some French history and literature, and the rudiments of mathematics. (When I married her she had added two years of Greek, another year of Latin, two more years of English, along with much more mathematics.) But she was ignorant of world history, social studies and the practical aspects of life—she couldn't even shop for food or cook. Her mother had protected her from all these things in order for her to excel at her classical studies—which she did, winning prize after prize at her Lycée for girls. When she and I went shopping with her mother in the market streets—a very interesting experience—she was as naïve as I about how to buy things. Mme Dumas had certain preferred stalls and was treated well there. To us they all looked alike. Incidentally, this very old method of vending has in many places been replaced by the supermarket approach, although the markets are not yet as huge as the ones in the US.

But Jeannine could sew! How deftly her slender fingers sewed fine things, how deftly they knitted and crocheted. What she lacked in experience, she more than made up for in patience and skill, learned from her mother of course. And she loved art and literature (French, to be sure) and her father (of little education) indulged her by buying things in the bookstalls and flea markets—things always in good taste. They went to museums of art (Paris is full of technology museums and they never went there; that was for me to initiate). They went to operas and fine plays and listened to opera and concerts on the radio until Jeannine knew the names, the music, and the composers by heart.

I continued the visits, the walks along the Seine River with Jeannine in the brisk air of winter, and many more wonderful meals with Mme Dumas. But eventually it had to end. My orders to return to the States finally came. By this time, the attachment between Jeannine and me had developed into a real affection. But I was always conscious of the age difference: she was not yet fourteen and immature. What could we do about this situation? The days of Romeo and Juliette were gone. And I could sense the worry of M. and Mme Dumas. So, with tears, we had to settle for the only practical course: we would write to each other. As time proved, this was a very satisfactory solution.

Finally I did leave Paris by truck for Le Havre with about 20 other men. It was cold and wet and when we finally arrived at the camp, all we found were leaky tents and a mess kitchen. I wrote Jeannine a very sad letter about that. I was able to write her once more before we left. Then I was put aboard a luxury-liner troop ship—nothing like the cramped quarters of the first trip. The food was good. The men were all comfortable and happy. And in due time we landed in New Jersey. Carrying our gear, we were lodged in a very nice barracks, offered some wonderful showers, and finally sat down to dinner of beefsteak and cake! There were movies and free beer.

After a few days I boarded a train for Ft. Lewis, Washington. The discharge formalities were smooth and I was soon picked up by Grandpa and Grandma Hudson (Dad was working). The homecoming was very warm; Dexter had arrived sometime earlier and we talked and talked and told stories to all the stay-at-homes.

This was early April (discharge was 4 April 1946) and for a while we could be lazy. But within a few days, decisions had to be made concerning the directions of the rest of our lives. After looking into it, I decided to go back to Reed College and finish my degree.

8

Reed College and Jeannine

Here I begin the record of the most important period of my life: 1946–1948. It was important for two reasons: I learned more physics in these two years than in any other two year period; and I took the steps to arrange for my marriage to Jeannine, which has meant so much to me.

Jeannine and I exchanged weekly letters during the period March 1946 when I left France to June 1948 when we were married. We still have those letters and they bear not only the developing love affair but some hints of my life and hers during those years.

In many of these letters, I described what my life was like; in some of them, I tried to teach her mathematics, electricity, etc, to compensate for the lack of these subjects in her classical curriculum. In each letter, I shamelessly declared my love for her and she responded in kind. Although she was not socially developed at all, Jeannine had already a far deeper knowledge of classical studies than anyone I had ever known except professionals. My own classical studies (in high school, at Reed College and on my own initiative) were the joy of my life, and so I decided Jeannine was for me if I could have her.

Finally in July we were able to talk of marriage and actually begin to make plans. They were, of course, very tentative. We knew they would depend on M. and Mme Dumas' decision to let Jeannine go. The first rough date was summer of 1947. This was hardly a serious plan because Jeannine would have been only fifteen and I would not have graduated from Reed. Eventually, we began to plan more sensibly for the summer of 1948.

During the summer of 1946, I signed up for a refresher course in calculus with Bob Rosenbaum, whom I had known before. In fact, I had communicated with him from the Yukon. At the Canyon Creek camp, the stove pipe entered the tent in such a way that the morning sun reflected off the pipe, the light figure appeared to me to be a conic section, perhaps an hyperbole. So I wrote Bob about it and we exchanged ideas. He was always a friendly fellow. Actually, I had taken two correspondence courses from the University of Chicago in algebra. So, you see, I was trying to improve my weak standing in math.

In September, I signed up for the fall semester at Reed. That first year, I took Knowlton's advanced general physics (4), Scott's freshman chemistry (6), advanced calculus (4), French (4), and Art (1) for a total of 19 hours, a pretty heavy schedule. I really worked hard that winter, but it was exciting. The advanced calculus was from F.L. Griffin's second book, which I already knew somewhat. The real essence of it was integration technique—a skill which served all the rest of my life.

Knowlton's course was a repeat of his first year general physics course, this time with all mathematical derivations. The fields of fluid mechanics and particle physics were given brief coverage; otherwise the physics I learned there was basic to my career.

I did not do well in the chemistry lab, but the concepts dealing with reacting molecules formed the basis of my understanding, essential to the comprehension of the physical world. We had a smattering of thermodynamics and reaction rate theory, later to be developed in other courses. So even though I did not do well in this class, it proved to be very influential in my career.

The French class was essential to my marriage plans. I knew that. But my brain does not deal well with name identifications. The class was *hard*. So I struggled with it manfully but never really felt good about it. The following year, I took the language qualifying exam in French and failed it. The material had been literary. Dr. Ellickson was furious and got permission for me to qualify in scientific French, which I did. But I have always been conscious of my verbal weakness, in English as well as in French.

Art turned out to be a very interesting course. There was, of course, drawing and painting, which I felt comfortable at. But there was also ceramics. I became interested in glazes, clay bodies, firing techniques and high temperature chemistry in general. In my chemistry course, everything transpired at room temperature. In ceramics the action was all at 1000°F or more. I read all the books in our library on the ceramics industry and they helped. But in my experimental efforts, there were many chances for strange things to happen.

I had access to two varieties of clay: ordinary red clay and stoneware. The Reed kiln had to be fired at a prescribed temperature because many students had work in it. Small variations in any of the several factors were quite noticeable in the final product, in my case tiles. I had made several dozen 2"x2"x¼" tiles of both red clay and stoneware, fired them at various temperatures, and then applied glazes of my own making and fired again. The glazes were made of two different fluxes (transparent, low melting) and a variety of different metal oxides. The results were interesting and I kept a record of each. In general, each metal had its own characteristic color when fired: cobalt=blue, iron=red, etc., but temperature had an effect, too. Most significantly, however, were the physical, rather than the chemical, effects. Some combinations proved to be not-wetting (that is, the glaze formed glass droplets on the ceramic base). In other cases, the coefficient of expansion was wrong and the glaze cracked (crazed).[1]

I can no longer remember any day-by-day occurrences of this year's studies, but I know that the work was hard in all the classes, except art. Nothing came easily, in part because I was not prepared well, but also in large part because I was not intelligent enough. And I suppose I could blame my poor showing on lack of discipline. I decided, however, that I would do the best I could and quit only when I was told to. Meanwhile, I could try to improve my study habits. Thus it came as a surprise at the end of my senior year that my grades put me in the top 10% of the school. This was required information on applications for graduate school. At this time, in 1946–47, I had no plans for graduate school. I was determined to get the best training in science that I could while being paid by the GI Bill.

During the summer of 1946, I drove Grandpa and Grandma Hudson with Mr. Thompson, president of the Maccabees and his family (in his car) first to Vancouver and then into Yosemite, Kings Canyon and San Francisco. The purpose of the trip was half business, half pleasure. The Artisans, because of hard times, had merged with the Maccabees and the business part of the trip was to let Mr. Thompson meet the various officers of the Artisans up and down the coast. The pleasure part of the trip was to allow the Thompson family (Mr. and Mrs. Thompson and two daughters: Mary, about 30, and Jean, about 25) to see the west. Mary had a bad heart condition (what my condition would eventually become years later) and she did not even walk around very much. Jean, on the other hand was quite lively

---

1. These effects were unwanted in my experiments; but contemporary potters are pleased to get them for decorative effect. Much later, I was able to communicate the ideas of these experiments to my son Marc and he became a very good potter.

and she and I explored all around. After they left, I never saw or heard about any of them again.

On March 11, I wrote a letter to M. Dumas asking for Jeannine's "hand in marriage." It was in the best French I could muster but still must have been pretty crude. He answered on the 18th and Jeannine was so excited she could not do even simple things and had to have her mother's help. "*While he was writing*," she wrote in her letter to me, "*I was in the bedroom trying to make a multiplication. . .*" which she was unable to do. And, according to this letter, M. and Mme Dumas were also very moved. They all realized that this was a turning point in their lives. This letter of hers dated 17 March 1947 is one of the most important I ever received. It began the series of events that changed my life.

I purchased an engagement ring and put it in the mail for her in March 1947. She never received it and was very unhappy. It must have been stolen. But in the summer, Uncle Maurice visited Paris and carried a second ring with him. Jeannine has a curious memory about that one. She had to ask for it because he had forgotten he had it. Finally he found it in a coat pocket—in a box stuck with chewing gum—and finally Jeannine felt that our plans were real. She was so proud to wear it, but felt she could not tell any of her friends of its purpose.

The visit of Uncle Maurice in early June was spoiled for the Dumas family by the presence of M. Guindollet, Uncle Maurice's French friend who was very possessive. Almost against his will, Uncle Maurice was housed at M. Guindollet's apartment and taken everywhere by him. The Dumas spotted Mr. Guindollet as an insincere money-loving man and, of course, Uncle Maurice could not tell. At any rate, Jeannine was able to go alone with Uncle Maurice to the American Embassy and find out what was required for her admission into the United States.

On May 20, I wrote suggesting that we plan our wedding for June 29, 1948—about one year away. On June 7, she wrote back that this date was acceptable. From that time on, we were able to make plans in detail. There were a number of formal papers that had to be exchanged both for the marriage and for the emigration. This exchange took place over the space of the next year.

I took the graduate record exam in May 1947, and passed it nicely. This was considered to be the admission to senior studies at Reed. In my 20 May letter, I was not planning to go to graduate school and wrote to Jeannine about several possibilities of towns in Oregon in which to live. I was really very naïve about finding a job! But I was determined to finish at Reed. After hearing about my descriptions of towns, Jeannine chose Salem. At that time, it seemed quite possible that we would live our little lives out in Salem, possibly with me teaching.

Also in May I received the chance of working with Ellickson's induced fluorescence project. It was something he had been working on for some years before coming to Reed and consisted of a phosphor (actually a family of phosphors) which, after being excited by UV and kept cold, could then be induced to fluoresce by irradiation with IR. The military had developed them to use in night vision devices. After becoming familiar with the apparatus, I was to base my thesis project on such an experiment.

Another opportunity to work for money came in the form of an offer to work with the instrument maker. Instruments (mostly electrical) were constantly breaking down and I helped to repair them. A third opportunity came in the form of a request from Dr. Scott to make crystal models for his classes. I wrote to Jeannine about this, but actually I have no recollection of doing it.

During May and June, Mme Dumas was very sick. It was reported to be a heart attack and she was sent to bed. During this time, Jeannine's letters were very worried as she nursed her mother and cooked for her father (she did not come to me with no culinary experience!). She actually quit school for awhile. Mme Dumas was somewhat ill during the time in early June when Uncle Maurice was there, but she did not let him know about it. For many years afterwards, we considered Mme Dumas to have a weak heart; but here she is at 90 years and her heart still works. M. Dumas' heart, on the other hand, gave out when he was 65 years old.

I tried to make up for Jeannine's youth and lack of a practical background by filling my letters with lessons of all sorts. Sometimes it was math: I explained many aspects of algebra, geometry and even the underlying ideas of differential calculus. I sent her problems to solve, which she did but the three weeks lapse between the problem and its solution was in itself a problem. Sometimes it was physics: mechanics of balls, electric circuits, atomic theory, etc. Except for Ohm's law, there were few problems, mostly description, but the ideas of acceleration and gravity were developed in some detail. Then there was geology (about which Jeannine already had some knowledge) and biology—especially growth and reproduction. And finally the letters often contained sketches and descriptions of outings, camping gear, etc. Jeannine said that she often saw French boys and girls leaving town with camping equipment and she felt pangs of jealousy. As it turned out, she had more experiences in the wilds than they did. One of the reasons for marrying me and leaving her family, she confided much later, was her spirit of adventure. In her letter to me dated 7 March 1947, she writes:

"My darling: March 7. Do you remember? The last evening at home. Only one year since the emotion of you leaving. I see these last hours again. They are written in my mind and I know it will be like this till your return.

I often think of the life which awaits for us, of the life which you make me see in the Nature. I feel sure you are afraid I am too much citified. Don't fear. On the contrary, I dream to ride a horse, to walk near you."

And indeed she did this and much more.

Jeannine asked me to explain the American method of counting money, which I did. And I also sent her a few prices of 1947:

> Hotel room—$3/night
> Beef steak, 1 lb—$0.60
> A shirt—$5.00
> Electricity, 1 kwh—$0.004
> Typical automobile—$2000

What a difference from now (1995)!

During the summer of 1947, I took two classes (E&M and mechanics) and continued to work with the infra-red phosphors. These summer courses were very intense and I learned much of what I know from them. I wrote to Jeannine giving a much simplified version. She probably got more physics than she wanted but never complained.

Since the wedding was scarcely nine months away, Jeannine asked her mother and father to take her to as many famous French places—especially in Paris—as possible so she would be able to carry with her the French culture. This they did and Jeannine has retained an enormous amount of French culture memory.

This was also (August 1947) the time of the famous bouillabaisse. Dexter and I, using Jeannine's recipe, made a huge pot of it and Herman and Marge, Dex and Rosie,[2] Mom and Dad and I ate the whole thing! Herman was a real clown. It was a delicious dish, of course, but he insisted on sucking every crab leg and clam shell until it was tasteless.

This was the time, too, of the trip with Grandpa and Grandma Hudson to the Snake River Canyon. What a grand vista! But the air was hazy, as it always is in September, and the pictures I took were not very good. This is a view that I always wanted Jeannine to see—but she never did. However, many years later, she and I were able to see the canyon from the bottom.

I took a one-semester course in differential equations, but I can't remember whether it was in the summer or in the regular school year. It gave

2. [Editor's Note] Dexter Hudson and wife Roseanna (Rosie).

me the fundamentals of the subject that has been basic to all my studies and practice of physics.

By the middle of September, I had laid out my final year's work: theoretical physics, physical chemistry, modern (nuclear) physics, ceramics and, of course, the thesis on IR-phosphors. In addition, I taught a laboratory session in freshman physics once a week. It was a very full schedule and a mind-expanding one. In graduate school, I went over much of the same material, but these courses were very important, more so than the later ones.

During this time, I wrote little lectures to Jeannine on a variety of subjects in science, simplified to be easy to understand. At the very least, she became conversant with the area of thought that would surround us for the rest of our lives. In later years, she chose to move away from science into dance, music, art and literature—with my approval because I liked her to be specialist in an area different from mine. Many years later, I wrote my "Essay on Temperature[3]" which coordinated all of my thoughts on science and related them to religion. On this subject, religion, Jeannine and I have always been together.

In one of these letters of fall 1947, I gave Jeannine a lengthy account of the vacuum tube and its operation. Imagine! At almost this same time, Bell Labs' semiconductor was being prepared to push the vacuum tube off market. But the transition would take a decade.

From about October 1947 on, plans of the marriage became more and more a topic of the letters. I tried to make no demands. I had wanted a simple marriage, but that was not to be—and for good reason. I had been selfish, not considering the fact that for the Dumas this was the end of an era. One of the most troublesome parts of the preparations was obtaining the necessary official papers. There were so many and new ones kept appearing. In at least one case, the French required one that was unknown in the states: the certificate of domicile. Most of the official papers were required by the French bureaucracy and had to be obtained by Jeannine herself.

Of course we talked in our letters about a little house—what couple of fiancées has not? I drew pictures and plans; how romantic. None of them came true; fate is not nearly so simple. When we finally made serious plans for a house, it was a much bigger one than that of our first dreams. Our whole world was so different then. As this story progresses, I will happily tell about the maturing of Jeannine, a remarkable transformation. But in those days of fall 1947, Jeannine gave me a count-down in each letter of the days to wedding.

---

3. [Editor's Note] unpublished manuscript *Essay on Temperature* by Craig C. Hudson, 1994.

Sometime in the winter of 1947–48, my idea of our future changed. Until then, I had imagined myself as a high school teacher—or if that did not work, having a job in some field not directly related to my education; perhaps a civil service job, perhaps even a job in France. We talked quite a bit about that. However, two things occurred to change this outlook. First, a law was effected by Congress which allowed free entry of foreign brides of servicemen into the US until December 1948. This meant that I had to bring Jeannine here during 1948 or wait indefinitely. Second, pressure was put on me to decide about graduate school. When I graduated from Reed, I would still have GI Bill time left.

My record at Reed had been good but not tops, so I had no illusions about making a fine advanced student. I did not have that kind of confidence in myself. I was sure I could enter some of the eastern graduate schools, but what I needed was an assistantship to supplement the GI Bill. These were of limited number and hard to get. In December I began writing to various schools around the country applying for graduate school in physics. Dr. Knowlton even pressured me to go to a big eastern school. Then Dr. Ellickson said that he was transferring to University of Oregon (U of O) and I might like to try there. So I also applied there.

Also in December, I tried to get passage on a ship for France. All of the big lines were already booked full. Finally I found one, the United States Line that was operating WWII troopships to accommodate young people and students on trips to Europe for low fare and limited accommodations. The catch was that France-to-US reservations had to be made from France. When M. Dumas learned that Jeannine and I would have to occupy different cabins, he obtained reservations on the Holland-America Line for the return trip, second class. I took the troopship from New York to Le Havre.

By this time, our lives were beginning to be quite hectic. Both of us were studying hard. Both of us had official papers to obtain. And both of us were becoming involved in rather complex travel plans. But one thing became very clear: I was probably going to graduate school in physics and my—our—future would take a completely new course, determined by my success there. The possibilities now opening up were: work in an industrial lab or teaching at the university level. In any event, the die was cast: Jeannine and I would be living in the US, the Spartan existence of graduate students at some as yet unnamed location. My future was at last determined and with mine, Jeannine's also.

The spring of 1948 was taken up with all sorts of preparations for the coming marriage, by both Jeannine and myself. The details are in the letters. Meanwhile at Reed, I had to finish my course work. The heavy load had begun to tell on me: I wasn't doing as well as I had hoped and my health—especially my eyesight—began to show the strain. The IR-phosphor experiment for my thesis took a great deal of time but at least it went well[4]. When I started this thesis, I felt good about it and rather scorned Dick Stavseth's project—building a Cavendish balance to test the strength of the constant of gravitation G, but as time went on, my feelings about his G-measurement increased and for my phosphor project decreased. Now, years later, I can remember his apparatus very well, but the phosphor project has dropped from memory.

All the final exams and final notebooks had to be completed. I was assured to graduate. I received a very nice offer from Case Institute and one from Lehigh. But I was worried about living conditions for Jeannine. I wrote out an acceptance letter for Case, stamped the envelope and at the last minute held it back for a day. In that day, I received an offer from University of Oregon (U of O) of $780/year and a guaranteed place to live. I knew U of O was not a great physics department—but I was not a very hotshot candidate either. I also knew that Ellickson was going to take over the department soon. What to do? I asked Knowlton what he thought (he had personally interceded on my behalf to get the Case offer) and he said I would probably be happier at U of O. I also had a conversation with Uncle Arthur.

The U of O was the least prestigious of the three physics departments and offered the smallest assistantship ($900). But Arthur pointed out something the U of O had that the others didn't: proximity to family and friends which could be of value to Jeannine. Then he asked the big question, "Do you have a goal? Are you driven to get a PhD?" and I had to admit that while a PhD was a long range goal, what I really wanted was the striving for it and the education that came with that. So I decided I would pursue it as a goal but only to the point where the sacrifice became too great. "Go as far as you can" I told myself secretly. And so the choice was University of Oregon.[5]

Little by little, all the details of graduating were worked out. But the graduation ceremony was to be at the time I was to leave for France. Nothing could be done about that. I had been keeping up a correspondence of two letters a week and in the last few days there were extra letters, embarrassingly passionate letters as I now view them. Jeannine must have wondered what she was getting. My last letter from home was dated June 11, 1948. I flew to New York—my first flight on a commercial plane—and stayed

4. [Editor's Note] Hudson, C. C., & Reed College (Portland, Or.). *The measurement of infra-red phosphor light sums by an ac method*, 1948.

5. I have never regretted it although there have been times when I regretted not having the degree. When I have known other PhDs in physics, I have often felt unworthy. On the other hand, life with Jeannine flourished and I have always been happy. Not all PhDs have.

overnight at the Commodore Hotel, Grandpa Hudson's choice. From there I sent a letter that I would be arriving at Le Havre on the 24th of June on the Marine Marlin. This was the 13th June. On the 14th, I posted my last letter as I was boarding the ship. I said I would look for M. Dumas at dockside. If I did not find him, I would go to the apartment. If there was no one there, I would go to Mme Philbert's house. I had previously told her that I might have to stay there a few nights and she was very agreeable.

The 10-day trip on the boat was pretty tiresome, although there were many young people with whom to converse, some French who were going home. I don't remember much about the trip. Accommodations were scarcely better than on a troopship—perhaps two bunks instead of five. The food was not very good, but it was adequate. There was little to do except talk. The only conversation I remember was the discourse of a young Frenchman on how to prepare shellfish. "First," he said, "you must obtain them fresh from the sea, only an hour or two old. Do not wash them; save the seawater because it adds to the flavor. Then drop them into boiling water to which you have added however you wish for seasoning—onions, herbs, carrots, etc. the best part is then the broth to which you add white wine." He reemphasized that the seawater should not be removed. In many ways it sounds like the bouillabaisse I make, except I was never able to get shellfish as fresh as he recommended.

We docked at Le Havre and I walked off the boat wondering what to expect next; but there was no cause to worry because in the awaiting crowd, I spotted M. Dumas, all smiles. At that moment, all my concerns were put away. Here was the real thing.

I gathered up my belongings—a suitcase and a traveling bag—and M Dumas led me to the train platform. He paid for my fare, the first of so many payings that I cannot remember them all. This wedding was on him. I tried my French—better than before but still not very good. We kept up a fractured conversation all the way to Paris, through the Métro and up to the door of that dear little apartment. He had been telling me that Jeannine was eager to see me. So he stepped back on the landing and let me knock on the door.

It was flung open and there stood beautiful Jeannine—but not for long. In an instant she was in my arms, laughing and crying and hugging me so tightly. No one ever had been this glad to see me. We kissed and kissed. The violence of that first impact of our two bodies had knocked one of her earrings off and it was never found; perhaps it tumbled down the stairs.

Papa and Mamie[6] stood in awe of our wonderful meeting. In due time, our emotions settled down somewhat and we stepped back out of the door-

6. [Editor's Note] Jeannine referred to her parents as Papa and Maman. When

way into the apartment. In due time, also, I was able to pay attention to Mamie and give her a loving embrace.

I could not take my eyes off Jeannine (affectionately known also as Nin or Ninette). When I had left her two years before, she had been girlish and a little skinny. By now she was a lovely woman, well rounded and lovely. I knew what was in her head; I knew that she was as mature as a woman in her twenties. But she added to that a sense of vitality and eagerness that was truly her own.

We talked for a long time. There was so much to discuss. First, I had to learn about the wedding plans. Our letters, separated as they were by two weeks or more of travel time, had not permitted me to keep up with the arrangements that had been necessary in order to accommodate both the civilian and church ceremonies. Then I needed to talk personally with Jeannine. In some of my latest letters I had expressed my great eagerness for her in a physical way. This offended her, I think, and I was lucky that she did not change her attitude toward me. Instead, she had written that there was more to her than that and kept on loving me as before. I was suitably put down and things could now move along on an even keel. But eager I certainly was, being now 30 and never having been close to a woman.

Later, after conversation and affection abated somewhat, we were able to gather our things together and take the train to Epinay near the Fôret de Sénart where Papa had rented a house for the summer. This was to be our honeymoon abode, as well as our place to love Papa and Mamie. There was no place in the little apartment for me to sleep. This was June 25th and the wedding was June 29th. I had to stay somewhere. I remember sleeping in a small room of the house. Jeannine and her mother occupied a larger room; Papa stayed in Paris part of the time.

Jeannine explained the events of June 29 to me. She and I were to prepare ourselves in the morning. About 11 AM, we were to go to the Mayor's office and be married civilly. Then we were to go to the church around 1 PM and be married in the church ceremony. Then about 3 PM we were to go to the restaurant for the reception. And after that, Jeannine and I would go alone to the Epinay house. All this driving around was to be accomplished by a friend of Papa. He wanted to give a gift and, since he had a car, this was it—and a very nice gift, too. I had suggested a simple wedding but Mamie wanted Jeannine to be married in a church, and I certainly did not object. I was even willing to become a Catholic, but that was not necessary. The wedding became a marvelous occasion.

Craig and Jeannine had children, in young child-speech the names became Papa and Mamie. At this point in his telling of the story, Craig incorporated these names when referring to M. and Mme Dumas.

Two days before the wedding (June 27) we (Mamie, Jeannine and I) went to the church to have a talk with the priest. He wanted to make sure that Jeannine (who was a proper member of the church) would be in charge of the children's religious education and that I would not interfere with her relationship to the church or to her worship. I readily agreed to these stipulations and I think I signed a paper to that effect. It was an important step for Mamie who felt an attachment to the Church. For Jeannine and me, it was a mere formality because we had long since discussed our position with respect to religion: we were not religious. However, we also had decided not to influence the children's choices—but we would not give them childhood training. I was delighted to find that Jeannine was so mature and held strong views of her own.

The night of the 28th, we all stayed in Paris. Papa found a small nice hotel near the apartment, where I stayed. The activity at the apartment must have been intense. In the morning, Papa came to rouse me from what had been a sound sleep. There was no doubt now—nothing could go wrong; the wedding was on schedule; by the end of the day I would be married. An amusing thing happened, however. As usual, I slept naked so when I answered Papa's knock, I was only partially clothed. Later, I found that Jeannine had shyly asked "Papa, does he have hair on his chest?" when the answer was yes, she was satisfied. Papa had none. And to this day one of her small pleasures is running her fingers through the hair on my chest, now somewhat thinner.

I shaved and dressed in my dark suit. Papa came to get me, looked me over and said "That won't do." So we went to his barber and had a haircut (I looked funny in the wedding picture) and then a closer shave with a straight-edge razor, my one and only experience with that awful tool. My skin was rather tender and the second shave set it on fire. At first I was very conscious of that; but in the rush of events, I forgot it and, I suppose, my skin healed. At any rate, no one seemed to notice how red I was.

We went back to the apartment and waited in the foyer, at the foot of the stairs. On each step was a bouquet of flowers, the gift of the gruff old concierge—who was not gruff that day. Soon Mamie and Jeannine came down, Jeannine dressed in a white shimmery dress with a floating veil. Fortunately for us, the weather was favorable. The sun was out in a cloudless sky. Jeannine looked radiant and I had eyes only for her, but I am sure that Papa and Mamie's eyes were wet.

We got into the car, which was probably decorated with white flowers in the fashion of marriages, but I don't remember. In a few minutes we arrived at the Mairie (Mayor's Office) and were escorted into a kind of courtroom. Only two witnesses were required but there was a small crowd of people. Soon the Mayor came in, a short fat man with a large red scarf draped diagonally over his belly and a number of medals on his chest, his badges of authority. I remember him standing against the light of a tall window, with wooden railings marking off the desk area. He talked for what seemed like a long time but I was too flustered to understand much of it. Jeannine elbowed me and I said "Oui" which seemed to satisfy everyone. We had some signing to do; then it was back into the car for a stop at the photographers. The picture later turned out to be very fine of Jeannine. I seemed a little peaked with my hair cut in an unusual style. But everyone else was happy so I was not troubled.

The next stop was at the church where a large number of people were assembled. Some of them, I suppose, were simply off the street, curious about the proceedings. I understand that it was only a church, but it seemed like a cathedral to me. Because I was not a Catholic, our ceremony could not be held in front of the altar. Here Jeannine's and my memories differ. She remembers our being married privately in the small side room. I remember our being married outside the railing but in the main church, down in front of the altar but not close to it. The memory of my knees pressing on a step with the high windows behind the priest is still with me. In due time, with another prod from Jeannine, the ceremony was over. Then came the ring exchange (I had brought them with me and Papa had them engraved "Jeannine á Craig 1948" and "Craig á Jeannine 1948") and the book signing. Many years later, Jeannine's ring was stolen; since then, she has been wearing mine. Finally it was time to walk arm in arm as Mr. and Mrs. Hudson down that long nave and out into the sunlight. There in the large crowd, most of whom I did not know, were my two Paris friends: Mme Philbert and M. & Mme Beliz, the Russian émigrées, he an art dealer (we still have some of his gifts of etchings) and she an engineer. There was a large crowd, probably some gathered from the street, and Papa took pictures with a movie camera. The pictures were not very good, but they did show Jeannine radiant, like a white cloud in that lovely wedding gown.

The next stop was the Reine Christine, a small restaurant Papa had hired for the afternoon. The Reine Christine was located at the intersection of Rue Dauphine and Rue du Christine. This is in the Left Bank district of St. Germain des Prés near the intersection of Boulevard St. Germain and Boulevard St. Michel, two well-known avenues. There, we were served a wonderful dinner at about 2 PM. There were perhaps 12 of us lined up in seats on one side of a long table. Service was from the other side to minimize inconvenience. A number of courses were brought out. The ones I can remember were a large plate of saussison (hard, dry sausage) and sliced cucumbers. I loved it. There were sliced tomatoes and young fowl (perhaps squab) and roast leg of lamb with wonderful little potatoes. Then cheese (camembert) and probably a dessert. With it all was Papa's beloved Alsatian wine.

At the end of this wonderful dinner, during which Jeannine reminded me "don't eat too much; remember tonight," there were drinks of Calvados and cognac. And lots of stories—dirty stories mostly, which I couldn't understand, but which made Mamie and Jeannine blush.

As we went into the church, seeing that I was without gloves, Charles Sainsaulieu (a friend of the Dumas) lent me his nice white gloves. I never wore gloves except in the cold, so I didn't know what to do with them. Finally, I carried them in one hand, to look formal. But they were lost, probably at the restaurant. So after that, whenever any of us saw Charles, he always said (jokingly) "Tell Craig I want my gloves back." I know it was said in jest, but it bothered me every time I thought of Charles. So finally I bought a very handsome pair of gloves (not white, it's true) and we took them to France with us in 1987—almost 40 years after the white ones were lost. At a very formal dinner, in front of all his friends, I presented the box to him. He opened it and was so moved that he wept. So I was able to discharge my debt after all. I liked Charles the best of all the friends of the family.

The bar in the restaurant was served by the proprietress and she served all sorts of drinks, mostly cognac and calvados. I was tempted to drink with them but Jeannine whispered "remember tonight."

Later in the afternoon, guests began arriving. There was a table in one corner on which a small pile of wedding gifts began to accumulate. We had expected nothing, really, because we believed the wedding was rather private. But Mamie had sent out 70 invitations and even though most of them did not come to the reception, still there were many. The little restaurant, tables pushed to the side, was full.

After the meal was over, there was dancing on the small floor to the music of a record player. All the men wanted to dance with Jeannine, of course. And I felt compelled to dance with all the women. Meantime, there was plenty of cognac and calvados and the men tempted me to drink with them. But I understood their joke and limited myself. There was a particularly insidious trick called the "Norman Hole"—or something like that—in which the drinker opened up his throat and tossed down a small glass-worth of Calvados directly into his stomach. The purpose, of course, was to show off; but the consequence was to get drunk as quickly as possible. I declined to play the game. In fact, since I had enjoyed the wonderful wine with dinner, I allowed myself only one or two strong drinks. I remember the cases of wine, cognac and champagne sitting on the dance floor in one corner. This was obviously a great occasion for Papa and he treated his friends to a night seldom ever seen.

Around midnight—somewhat after, as I recall—the champagne was opened and they all toasted the bride and groom. Jeannine and I returned the toast with a glass each. Then Papa said it was time for us to go. He had hired a taxi with a driver he trusted (knew) to take us out to Epinay. We had the key of the Epinay house. As we left the restaurant, Mamie broke into tears and clung to Jeannine as long as she could. I knew for the first time how great a sacrifice she was making. I am sure Papa felt the same, but he was able to hold the tears back. There have been many times since then when I have been piqued by Mamie or Papa's actions; but I can never forget the sacrifice they made that day that I might be happily married.

Jeannine gathered up her beautiful wedding dress in her arms and we got into the back seat. By this time, Paris was dark and as we drove out of town, lights became few and it was black outside. I remember having the sensation that this cabdriver could take us anyplace and we wouldn't know. But in due time (about 10 miles driving) we stopped in front of the house under a street light. We thanked the cabbie who had been paid by Papa, climbed the few steps to the front door. With the key, we opened it and walked into the dark entryway. Jeannine's little dog, a toy white Pomeranian named Jou-Jou, was there to greet us, happily yipping and dancing about. The house smelled like flowers.

The house was dark and we wound our way carefully through the kitchen, up the stairs and at the top of the stairs, turned on the lights. The space at the top of the stairs was a library and it was full of white flowers—a marvelous sight! Ongoing through to the bedroom, we were struck by more flowers—perhaps two dozen large bouquets. I was very moved, and Jeannine was too. All she could utter were Ohs and Ahs. In the bedroom was the large bed made up with linen sheets embroidered and turned down the full 30 inches in the French fashion.

We clung together in a warm embrace for a long time. Then I began to remove Jeannine's wedding dress. But we were interrupted by the loud talking of 3 or 4 young men in front of the house under the streetlight. When they appeared to be approaching the house, I took the large revolver from the desk in the living room and we stood near the window overlooking the street at the ready. I felt the tensions rise as the young men, obviously drunk, moved about in the street. Finally they drifted off, and we could relax.

With some shyness, we undressed and climbed into bed with the light out. We clung together for long moments making no movement or sound. Finally we began our first lovemaking. Jeannine was as eager as I. It was the first time for both of us. Then, as we relaxed, she asked me to prepare her a basin of warm water in which to wash. She was fastidious about washing and has remained so to this day, nearly 50 years later. So I went down to the kitchen, built a fire in the little heating stove—with Jou-Jou dancing happily around my legs of course—heated the basin of water and brought it upstairs for her to wash. After that, we lay quietly together in bed, but sleep would not come. We made love twice more, each time with washing (the stove didn't even cool down). After that washing, we were able to cuddle in each other's arms and sleep. The following morning, we awoke to the smell of cooking. Mamie and Papa had come in and were preparing a 9 AM breakfast for us. They could not help but be pleased to see Jeannine come down so radiant with smiles.

We were scheduled to take the boat on August 4th, which left a little more than a month of free time. At first, this seemed like plenty of time, but very soon it was filled up. During those days, Mamie and Papa stayed with us at the house; but they were the epitome of discretion. Jeannine and I did very little to care for ourselves. Mamie cooked—wonderful meals—and did the laundry. We all helped with the dishes. Papa went to his shop each morning and returned each evening with food and delicacies. We ate very well. At times, at the house in the evening, we played cards. I taught them some games familiar to me. Mamie never got the hang of cards, but Papa was very good. A few times we went into Epinay to shop at the one store there, often for wine. Jeannine overheard gossip about the strange family— the tall American, the pretty young girl and the "countess." In general, we had no contact with the neighbors, however.

I have always heard (word of mouth) that the honeymoon was to be a time sacrosanct to the newlyweds alone, a time when they saw no one they knew. We found our honeymoon shared with Mamie and Papa to be glorious. We had privacy when we wanted it and we had help with household things when needed. The honeymoon could hardly have been nicer—I suppose this was in part due to the many thoughts we shared in our long letters—and we were able to enjoy many little things we had never talked about. One of these was the cold water shower in the garden, on the back of the house. The weather was very warm, upper 90s to over a hundred on one or two days. In that hot weather it felt so good to get into the shower. Perhaps it was possible to see us naked there from houses in the back. We gave it little thought. On a few occasions, I persuaded Nin to come into the cold shower with me—with much sputtering and squealing because she was unaccustomed to cold water. On Jeannine, the cold water was too much of a shock, so we did not repeat that. To this day Jeannine loves showers but the water must be just warm.

We were such eager lovers! For days and days, we made love once or twice a day. In due time, it became once a week for the rest of our lives, even accounting for menstruations, babies and separations, until in old age we had to slow down to once a month. It has been one of the bonds that made our marriage strong. Of course, there were many other factors, but one should not neglect the importance of physical closeness.

The town (village) of Epinay sur Orge is located south of Paris, near the Fôret de Sénart, in the Y formed by the joining of the Seine River and Yerre River (stream). To get there, one takes a train in the direction of Villeneuve St. George and getting off a little farther out at Montgeron. Down from the train, it is about two km walk through the town and out a short distance beyond was the house.

The house was two-story and built of a soft, light colored stone with rough surfaces and rough mortar joints. It faced the street and was surrounded by a high wall of the same stone, the top of which bristled with steel spikes and shards of glass. The roof was of the usual red tile. There was a garden in the rear of about 100'x100', with some fruit trees, berry vines, currants, stone paths, flower beds and an outbuilding (presumably for tools, etc, but we never looked into it).

The house was owned by a professional midwife who had let Papa rent it for a month or so. Part of each floor had been closed off to contain the owner's private effects. Downstairs was the kitchen, a bedroom and the dining area. The stairs somehow fitted into the middle of the house in such a way that under-the-stairs storage could be reached from the kitchen. Wood was stored there and was the source of fuel for the cooking stove. Upstairs was our bedroom and a rather good library. The owner's books were available in the library and I looked at some to see what midwifery was about. Furniture was left in place, at least in good part. There were a number of windows, but the house was still rather dark.

It was surely less than a kilometer to the forest, easy walking distance. It was an old forest, filled with oaks, maples and pines, a lovely place. On one of our two trips into the forest, Mamie and Papa came with us to make it a pleasant picnic. That was the occasion on which Mamie made a veal loaf spiced with nutmeg. It was delicious. She has made it several times recently but it never had the aromatic flavor of that first time, perhaps because ingredients in Albuquerque were different or perhaps because first memories are strongest. That picnic was a very pleasant time for all of us with balmy weather and soft leaf-strewn ground under huge trees (perhaps beeches). On the second trip into the forest, Nin and I went alone with a camera. I took a lovely picture of Nin sitting naked to the waist on a blanket in the soft light; we still have that picture, though by now it has faded considerably.

Jeannine's tiny pocket calendar of that summer notes the things we did. On July 1, Mamie packed a lunch and we all four walked into the Fôret de Sénart and picnicked under the big old trees. The ground was spongy with humus and we had a wonderful time.

On July 2, we went to see Pépé and Mémé,[7] Papa's parents. Pépé had been a farmer in Auvergne before WWI. He was gassed in that war and was pensioned. His small pension plus the money they brought with them allowed them to purchase a small house and yard at the edge of the Fôret de Sénart. Jeannine told me of many dear memories she had of living with them when she was five or six years old: riding her tricycle around the garden paths, playing dolls in a little entry-way, helping Pépé prepare snails and Mémé cook meals, etc. To her at that time, the house had seemed large and the garden huge. But I was hardly expecting the small scale of things I found. When I saw it, the house was scarcely 12'x18'; I could nearly span the dining room with outstretched arms. The yard was no more than 50'x50', with a high wall all around it as was common there; a few strong paces carried me across the garden. Pépé and Mémé were themselves scarcely five feet tall, so things for them were more to scale. They must have thought me a giant. But what they lacked in size they made up for in spirit. Even though I was taking their precious girl away from them, they were friendly and hospitable to me—but we could hardly converse. Jeannine, as always, was the interpreter.

Years ago, Papa had dug them a well and they had a large compost. Pépé did have a very nice little garden which must have pleased little girl Jeannine very much. To me, Pépé and Mémé—both shorter than Papa and Mamie—were sad people. Perhaps they didn't get out very much. Perhaps they were sorry to see Jeannine leave. However, they did live long enough to see Jeannine and baby Marc on the trip to France of 1951. I'm sure that pleased them.

On July 3, we took the train to Tourcoing, near Lille in northern France where much of Mamie's family lived. We also visited Roubaix. These three cities once constituted the center of the French textile industry and are still active today. Its origins reach back to the Middle Ages and perhaps depended on the culture of flax which was indigenous. In modern times, some of textile manufacture has moved to the Far East. But at this time (1948) I found the region to be prosperous and bustling. We stayed with the family, but there were so many people there that I have forgotten their names and faces. I recall only two names: siblings Samson and Delilah Lutz.

---

7. [Editor's Note] Victorine and François Dumas, parents of Jean Dumas; Pépé and Mémé are familiar names which Jeannine used meaning grandma and grandpa respectively.

In general, I was much taller than the French people I met; but in this group I remember one was taller than I and several were quite tall. One of them spoke English and we had conversations about WWI—he had been gassed too. They served us a banquet and I ate much more than my share of sliced tomatoes and saussicon. They were so good! There was a parade there in honor of the Americans on July 4, very much like our celebrations with marching bands, etc. and there was a dance. I was an awkward dancer; but Jeannine was good and much in demand.

We returned to Paris on July 5, back to Epinay. We had taken the fast train—in 1948 the bullet trains were a thing of the future—but this was fast and comfortable and quiet. We did take the bullet train (TGV=Train de Grand Vitesse) from Paris to Lyon in 1987. That was a thrill. The French rail system is a marvel. You can get anywhere—nearly—by train.

On July 7, we left Paris (Jeannine and I only) to go to see Mme Cochard in St. Mars La Jaille. Since the train only stopped at Nantes, we had to take a bus. All went well and we arrived at Mme Cochard's address. It was a small shop (laces, etc.) with her house in the back. We were received graciously and given the master bedroom on the second floor. Everything was white, clean and neat as a pin. We stayed there three nights and during that time, Mme Cochard had arranged for us to see some of the surrounding country. A friend of hers owned a car. He was a doctor, so he knew everyplace, and he spoke English. We did many things of which I relate three.

He drove us out to see an old-fashioned French farm. It was located on the edge of a small stream. Ducks and geese were everywhere, coming out of the water to leave the bank slick with mud and droppings. The house was large, a good part of it devoted to the kitchen and associated work rooms. Hams and sausages hung around the wall by cords suspended from the ceiling. There was a very earthy smell about the place, much like the buildings of the old Heinz farm at Peach Cove. There was a large table in the middle of the kitchen, well scrubbed and very old with big wide drawers. The drawers contained country bread loaves and chunks of ham—really dried ham, not like the tender meat that passed for ham in Paris. I understood that soup was a must at nearly every meal, as was wine, accompanied by bread and meat. I would have liked to have a meal there, but we weren't asked.

He drove us out to see a modern French country house. The house was beautiful in a fine brick veneer. There were no animals and the paths were well-tended. The garden in the back consisted of about ½ acre of vegetable beds (!) each surrounded by a low brick wall. The whole area was laid out in a pattern, the center of which contained a tree. Everything was properly weeded and the paths of sand nicely raked. It was a dream garden. All around the outer boundary were beds of flowers. The lady of the house invited us into a fine dining room, lighted by high windows. The furnishings were elegant. She served us some kind of dessert with wine.

On one of the evenings, the doctor took us out to hear the hunting horns. Men in the district, as a hobby, kept alive the old medieval tradition of blowing cornets (like a trumpet but without fingering) to communicate. We drove out to a small hill where there were only country noises and listened. The air was very still. It was dark. From one direction we could hear a horn. Soon it was answered from another and another and another—all around. The doctor said each horn had its own sound (pattern) so the men could be identified, which he did.

The doctor also told us a story about hunting ducks before the war. The Loire River enters the sea at Nantes. Huge flocks of ducks wintered in the estuary. Hunting parties went out in boats with shotguns. The killed ducks floated so they were picked up, brought home to be smoked or preserved for winter and spring. According to the doctor, a single hunt brought in hundreds of ducks to be shared among the families.

Mme Cochard's meals were delicious but one of them was outstanding. She had invited guests: her two sons, the woman who was the fiancé of the son killed in WWII, and some others. The food was delicious but what I remember was the dessert wine. The first bottle, encrusted with years of dust and dirt, was spoiled. The second proved to be one of my memorable taste treats—sweet as honey, one of the Loire Valley wines, well-aged.

We bade goodbye to Mme Cochard and all the nice people of St. Mars La Jaille. Most we never saw again, but one son, Andre, has kept in touch. In fact, his son, Louis-Marie, came to visit us in Albuquerque. Jeannine and our son Marc have visited them in Nantes; Jeannine and I met them on our 1987 trip and had another fine dinner.

There was a farm machinery dealership near St. Mars La Jaille. We visited it and I had a chance to see the French farm machinery. It was very much like that of the US; some of it was imported from the US. Two things struck me about the place. One, they had an old army jeep, lovingly cleaned up and painted. But they couldn't make it run. They hoped I could help them, but of course I could not. Two, they had a new 20-volume Larousse Encyclopedia—that I envied.

We returned to Epinay (by way of Nantes and Paris) just as we had come. Jeannine was not feeling very well, but she didn't complain. In Nantes, while waiting for the train, we found a confection store and I bought some candies and cookies and some chocolate balls for the ride home. Oh, those chocolate balls! They tasted so good but they were very rich and made me sick. I complained! We returned on July 10.

On July 11, we went to see my friend Mme Philbert on Rue d'Assas—the very street where Jeannine had been born 16 years before. We were given a fine lunch and talked for about two hours.

We had several days blissfully to ourselves, recovering from all the rich food and playing cards and reading. We, then, had visits to some of the Dumas' friends and on July 20 we visited M. and Mme Beliz for a lunch. They were the Russian émigrés, considerably older than I, and sad people. But they had a nice apartment from before the war and government policy did not allow the owners to raise the rent, which was ridiculously cheap. That was the last time I think I ever heard from the Beliz, who thought Jeannine was much too young for me. Little did they know.

On July 23, we went to the Georges' bakery and house for dinner. The Georges family had been friends of the Dumas family for years. I never met M. Georges but Mme Georges was a gay plump matron, somewhat older than Mamie, who had two children (Marcel and Jeanine).[8] I remember the party as rich with good food and happiness. In 1987 when we met with the Georges family, the bakery had turned into a bar on a very busy corner which the grandsons were operating.

On July 26, we had lunch with Mme Loreau. She lived at the Château in the past but we saw her in Paris. It seems to me that Simone Sainsaulieu was also there, along with Mamie and Papa. Mme Loreau was a once beautiful woman, but coarse—the stories she told! She was vivacious to the point of being boisterous. But she was good-hearted and had helped the Dumas out frequently. Because she was bossy, Jeannine as a girl had not liked her, but by this time their relationship was beginning to mellow[9]. The lunch, of course was delicious but the part I remember was the half of a cantaloupe filled with red wine. It was an attractive dish, but the flavor of cantaloupe with plain red wine was not appealing to me. After the first bite, I drank the wine and then ate the cantaloupe. Those little French cantaloupes are the best I have ever eaten. Seldom have I found one in the US.

That same afternoon, we went to the House of Baccarat. A friend in Portland had given me $25 to buy some nice crystal for his wife. So we

8. [Editor's Note] name corrections: M. Georges was Marcel; Mme. Georges' name was Marise; sons are Philipe and Thierry.

9. [Editor's Note] Mme Loreau was the overseer of the Château de Notre Dame de Gravenchon in Normandy. She ran and maintained the chateau and grounds around it for the owners. She had a son, Claude, and a daughter, Simone (married to Charles Sainsaulieu). M. Dumas made friends with the family during WWII and Jeannine spent summers with the family.

from unpublished manuscript *The Jeannine Françoise Dumas Hudson Story* by Jeannine Hudson-Green, 2010, p. 69–71.

went first to see what he could afford. Their sales room[10] was full of beautiful things, mostly too expensive. What really caught our eye, however, was the exhibit hall. All around the walls of this large room, were lighted crypts containing, behind glass doors, the duplicate sets of crystal designed for nobles, monarchs and rich persons over the years. Baccarat was the most famous maker of fancy crystal in the world. In the center of the room, on large tables, were all sorts of simple items, large and small, made in delicately-tinted crystal. It was an exhibit to take one's breath away. We stayed as long as we could, feasting the eyes.

On July 29, Jeannine and I went to a doctor's office to have her vaccinated against smallpox. Without that certificate, she could not enter the US as an immigrant. The vaccinations I had had consisted in scratching the skin of the upper arm with a vaccine needle. This doctor made an incision in her thigh with a scalpel and proceeded to press the vaccine paste into the wound! It was not deep and the bleeding soon stopped, tape covered it, we received the document and went on our way.

On August 2, we went back to Baccarat and I bought a tiny set of crystal glasses and matching decanter for my $25. It was a pathetic thing seen against the many pieces of real value; but that's what was available.

Now time was growing short. The boat sailed August 4. All of Jeannine's trousseau things along with two cases of Alsace wine were sent ahead to be put in the hold of the ship. They were not seen by us again until they were delivered to the 35th Street house.

On August 3, Papa had arranged to have a magnificent going-away dinner at a fine restaurant near the apartment. We had a private room for just the four of us. The dinner consisted of many of the things we liked, sliced tomatoes, cucumbers, saussison, etc. one of the dishes was a huge lobster, entire. The server cut open the tail and we all four ate from it. Then there were the claws. We were served vegetables in the French way (not just edible but delicious) and some meat. Then the server brought in a large cheese from which we cut slices. There was plenty of the excellent French bread and plenty of Papa's wines. Maybe we had dessert but by then I was stuffed and in a sort of haze. We spent the night in Paris in the small hotel near the Dumas apartment.

The preparations to leave France must have been hectic, but I was spared most of the details. I remember having to take care of some papers for ticket and passport affairs. On August 4, we all went to Le Havre and amid tears of departing, we boarded the *New Amsterdam*.

10. [Editor's Note] Jeannine noted in the margin of original manuscript "This was not a sales room open to the public. It was a warehouse and we were allowed into it only because Papa knew somebody there who was willing to let us in as a favor."

As the ship moved away from France, I remember looking back at the people on the dock and waving. Then suddenly we were alone and I felt the great responsibility of my situation for the first time. I had never had anyone permanently dependent on me before. I'm sure that Jeannine also felt a sense of panic, of being taken from familiar surroundings. Perhaps her inner thoughts were in turmoil, but she shed no more tears. We waved at Mamie and Papa on the dock as long as we could see them.

Many years later, Jeannine admitted that one of the strong motivations for marrying me was an urge—a strong urge—for adventure. Who would have guessed that demure, sweet Jeannine would harbor in her heart a thirst for adventure so strong that she would leave family and home at the tender age of 16! Never mind that history is full of such cases; it seemed so strange in the world I lived in. So perhaps her eagerness to leave France was in part due to the belief that this was the first step in a great adventure. Actually, her life with me has been full of adventure.

At first, even though second class, we were separated; later, the purser moved people around so that we had a room together. Shipboard life was at first exciting. We traveled second class and there were many people to become acquainted with. Some wanted to play bridge, which I enjoyed. I had learned many bridge tricks from games with Ellickson, Thompson and Stavseth at Reed; but Jeannine was really a novice.[11] There were games of all kinds to play, but the sheer pleasure of being on the moving boat, watching birds and waves, occupied much of our time; the rest was spent talking, reading and cuddling in our stateroom.

But after several days, life on shipboard became a little boring and we were pleased to see New York appear on the horizon. Somewhat to my surprise, Jeannine searched eagerly for the Statue of Liberty and I realized how much it meant for someone coming to America. It was announced on the New Amsterdam's public address system and we had to rush up on deck to see it.

Jeannine had begun a program of writing letters to Mamie, Papa and the friends and relatives in France—starting on the day we boarded the ship. These continued at the rate of several a week; she always managed some quiet time to be able to write, and it continues to this day although after Mamie and Papa came here, the need became much less. Those letters, all in French, would be an interesting view of what a young French girl saw in her great adventure.[12]

11. Later in Albuquerque we played bridge with neighbors in a sort of table rotating game. On one of these, Jeannine won first prize and she never wanted to play again!.

12. [Editor's Note] Jeannine's margin note "Mamie saved my letters and I have them." These are now archived.

Our last meal on board brought home to us a problem that was to beset us all the rest of our lives together: not enough money. We could not even give our waiter an adequate tip because I had to save taxi fare to the hotel.

There was great confusion when we docked. We could imagine the several procedures that needed to be done; but we had no idea how they were actually to be carried out. All went smoothly until we had to deal with the immigration officials. They held us up until all travelers had debarked. The ship was deserted. Finally our turn came. We presented all our papers, which were in order. Then the demand, "Where is her picture? We can't let you go without a photograph." We had not been aware that a photograph of immigrant Jeannine was necessary. By now, all of our luggage had been offloaded. "Don't you even carry a photo of your new wife in your wallet?" Of course I did and gave it up. That was a close call.

We went onto the dock itself and identified our several crates and trunks; we had to pay a little duty on the wine; but everything passed through customs and was routed COD to our 35th Street address in Portland. Finally we were able to get a taxi and go to the hotel, close to Rockefeller Center, where we had a reservation. There I had a very uneasy feeling of checking into a hotel for which I could not pay the charges. We were taken up to a most elegant suite; we should have declined it, but we were so tired and frazzled that I decided to change rooms the next night. And there, in those lovely surroundings, all Jeannine's pent-up emotions flooded up and she wept a fountain of tears. For the next night, we were changed to a single room and we stayed another night or two.

I called Grandpa Hudson and he sent me a check for several hundred dollars to cover expenses and plane fare. But the problem was to cash it. The hotel would not cash his certified check even with my identification! Finally I took it to the downtown office of the Maccabees and, since Grandpa was on the Board of Directors, they cashed it willingly. It was an experience to me, never before having been asked for credit references in a strange city. We were able to obtain reservations on a plane to depart New York City on August 13.

Meanwhile Jeannine's spirits rose and we left the hotel to get a glimpse of New York from street level. I had never had time to spend in New York City before, so we went out together to see the sights. Along the sidewalks were beautiful shops full of things that had not yet become common in Paris, and here and there were soft drink stands. Jeannine was greatly impressed by being able to have fresh oranges squeezed out into a glass while she watched; but she was very unimpressed by root beer, one of my favorite drinks, saying that it tasted like toothpaste (French of course!).[13] But the biggest surprise, one which she had looked forward to, was eating at an automat. She was fascinated by the idea of inserting a coin in the slot and out comes food—a door in a stall opens and you get whatever the door said—sandwich, pie, cereal, etc.

We found a tennis court in the shadow of skyscrapers! People were playing and we could tell that one of them was an instructor. We went to the Empire State Building and took the elevators to the top—one single elevator won't do it. Jeannine had never experienced such acceleration (perhaps ½ g) and nearly fainted. At that time, the Empire State Building was the tallest structure in the world and the view from there was spectacular.

We had dinner at the famous French restaurant in Rockefeller Center. We were dressed in the best clothes we had. There were 25 or so tables with four or five waiters dressed primly in black. We ordered and were served. But Jeannine's soup, a Madriléne soup, came cold and she declared it should be hot. We ordered the waiter to take it back. Now that caused a stir. All the waiters, one by one, were aware of it and nodded in our direction accusingly. Even the chef came out to glower at us. Much later we learned that the soup is optionally served either hot or cold and Nin was unfamiliar with the cold version. The rest of the dinner was quite fine and we enjoyed ourselves, even though the waiters were a bit huffy. Since that time, Nin has become not only well educated about foods generally, but very expert in the preparation of authentic French dishes.

The first part of the trip (NY to Chicago, I believe) was probably on a TWA Constellation. But from Chicago to Portland we traveled United Airlines. Everything about flying was new to Jeannine; and, truly, I had not flown very much myself. She was thrilled by the roar of the engines and the acceleration on takeoff; she was apprehensive about landing. She loved looking down on cities and farms, rivers and mountains, and clouds. In those planes, the windows were quite small and one could not get a very grand view; but the novelty of it flooded out any such limitations. She has always had a tendency toward motion sickness, and I recall keeping the whoopee bag at the ready; but I think she managed to avoid its use. Flying in those days was at about 20,000 feet, which gave a better view of the ground and of clouds, but at the expense of smooth ride. Part of the time we were roughly shaken by turbulence and that was hard for Jeannine.

13. Later, in Albuquerque, I taught her how to make root beer from the Hires extract, yeast and water and it became a family favorite.

9

Married Life, Graduate School, and Birth of a Son

When we landed in Portland, Mom and Dad met us and had their first look at the new daughter-in-law. They were probably a bit apprehensive at first; but she grew ever more beloved in their esteem. Certainly one of the reasons for this was Jeannine's eagerness to do everything in her new country and to be helpful to her new family. We went directly to Mom and Dad's house. Of course, Grandpa and Grandma Hudson met us there. Jeannine was pretty tired upon arrival, and slept half a day.

On August 19, Mother arranged a reception so we could meet all the family (possibly some friends as well, I don't remember). Jeannine was very quick to identify names with faces and was reasonably comfortable at the end of the afternoon. She did much better in Portland than I had in France.

Dad's vacation began August 21 (a Saturday) and he had planned an outing (camping) to Elk Lake in the Cascades. At that time (1948), it was a very rough place, a designated campground in a National Forest, but developed really for fishermen. The fishing was good there. The Hudson clan came along. We were: Harvey and Bertha, Craig and Jeannine, Dexter and Rosie, Marilynn and Neil, H S and Neva, and even Uncle Claus. This was his favorite place; he used to come years in the past with his friends from Benson Polytechnic School for fishing and camaraderie. We all slept on the ground in tents except HS and Neva, who rented a little cabin.

Shirley and Tab were absent because Tab could not get time off (he worked at *The Oregonian*[1]).

The lake was perhaps a mile across, cold, clear and pristine. All around it, the hills rose up, covered with a pine forest, to merge into the Three Sisters mountains. Under the sweet smelling trees, the ground was covered with a thick soft mat of needles. One afternoon, far away from the camp, in the warm still air, Jeannine and I made love on the soft mat. That was the true break from the life of Paris into the new world of the West. She has always loved the out-of-doors.

Meals were prepared on a stone fireplace in the middle of the camp. Jeannine did no cooking but always helped with the clean up. On one occasion, Jeannine, Marilynn and I took the trail to Green Lake. It followed a dashing stream and since it was a hot day, we often stopped to refresh ourselves. The others fished or played cards or simply rested.

On one day, Jeannine and I borrowed a boat and rowed around a point of land to a hidden inlet which was utterly quiet. The afternoon air was warm and still. No one was around. I had the idea that she would look like a water nymph, so she disrobed. The lake bottom was pure white sand only 2 or 3 feet down. But when she jumped into it, the fun disappeared; it was icy cold. There was a rush for the shore only to run into thousands of pollywogs in the shallows. We managed to get her dressed again and, after regaining our composure, returned to camp. The image of a beautiful water nymph was set aside. In later years, however, I painted a picture (from memory) of such a lovely scene.[2] With paint, the water is never cold and there are no pollywogs.

Claus was the big fishing expert and, although others caught fish, he was the one who dressed them and fried them. Fish (trout) everyday. I'm sure Jeannine had never eaten so many so quickly. I have always had trouble with the bones. Even though I like the fish, the bones put me off. In restaurants of today, trout are always deboned which makes them much more appetizing.

The end of the camp-out finally arrived and we returned to Portland on August 28. We lived with Mom and Dad but often saw HS and Neva—and probably stayed at their house. They got along very well with Jeannine. Mom and Dad were at first somewhat reserved, probably wondering what their son had got himself into, why a regular American girl wouldn't have been better.

---

1. [Editor's Note] major daily newspaper in Portland.
2. [Editor's Note] *Lady Bathing 1954,* see Appendix: Catalog of Paintings.

Lady Bathing, painted 1954

There were a number of visits by the Palmers and we visited my friends. I remember in particular a dinner at Herman and Marge Johansen's house in Milwaukie. At that time they had two boys. They lived there all during Herman's years at Reed. They were struggling to make ends meet and to keep Herman in school. They had about half an acre which was intensively farmed and they had a stand of corn, the first Jeannine had ever seen closely. Marge took off some ears and cooked them for dinner, which impressed Jeannine greatly; but she didn't much like it. Many years were to pass before she could enjoy corn and the other rough food of the west. There were two or three other couples there but I don't recall names. After a pleasant evening, during which Jeannine had said very little, and as we were going out to our cars, I overheard one of the women say to another, "That marriage can't last. She is too young." Later Marge said to me, "Pooh, pooh, pay no attention." And she was right. I asked Marge to teach Jeannine how to make bread, which she did. Marge's rule was "put as little into it as possible" and it has proved to be very good.

We also saw Marley and Ruth Brown, Eugene Snyder, Libby Carter[3] and probably others. On at least two occasions we went to the Reed campus,

3. [Editor's Note] Elizabeth (Libby) Nichols Carter.

but it was empty—except once we ran into Dr. Knowlton. He was very polite but I could see he too wondered about Jeannine's youth. All was not easy for Jeannine in those first days. But I had faith, which proved to be justified.

Part of our days was spent gathering together the things we would need to set up house in Eugene. We were given bed clothing by both Mom and Dad and by HS and Neva. Mom and Dad took us to the Meier & Frank silver department and had us pick out a lovely service for eight[4]. We still have that set, not a piece missing, and I still admire the pattern more than almost any other I have seen. Jeannine has always treated it as a family treasure. But we were short all the kitchen tools, dishes and bric-a-brac that make housekeeping possible. So there was a "shower," a real novelty for Jeannine. All the women in the family (both Hudson's and Palmer's) gave Jeannine the things they thought she would need: pans, utensils, glasses, etc. Uncle Maurice sent a set of dishes for four, complete. I think we have to this day the large platter that came with that set.

And, of course, in due time a truck delivered and left on the driveway the two cases of wine and the two large packing crates of things the Dumas had given Jeannine as a trousseau. Included were some very well-made clothes but a little out of Oregon styles, several sets of bed sheets, real linen, all embroidered with our initial, Jeannine's wedding dress, three cases of Alsace wine in good condition (!), and the wonderful set of china (Limoges but unsigned), a service for twelve for six courses. Not a piece was broken. We were all boggle-eyed at it. We have used these dishes literally hundreds of times and even today they are the central feature of Jeannine's wonderful dinners. There were no cups and saucers, as had been the fashion, so one of the challenges has been to buy cups and saucers that would fit. These dishes have become a sort of hallmark of our marriage. When she began, Jeannine knew little of cooking, having watched her mother but seldom doing much. She set about making herself knowledgeable in cuisine and Papa helped by sending the *Larousse Gastronomique*[5] (the book of books in French cooking).

The shower was on September 3 and on September 4 we packed up for a visit to Tierra del Mar.[6] Rosie's parents owned a piece of land very near the beach and it had a house on it large enough for six or eight, although the accommodations were rather tight. Dad, of course, wanted to go fishing and

4. Jeannine told me that Mother had sent to her, in Paris, some patterns of silver. So the choice had actually been made by the time I came to see them!.

5. [Editor's Note] First published in 1938, the *Larousse Gastronomique* is considered to be the foremost resource in culinary knowledge. Recent revisions allow it to keep up with the latest culinary advancements.
Random House, Inc, *Larousse Gastronomique* .

6. [Editor's Note] on the Oregon coast, south of Tillamook.

he, Rosie and Dexter took off. Jeannine, who has always loved the ocean, took pleasure in the fine, white sand beach. Beaches in France were often pebbly. At the house near ours, which was occupied all year long, a large log had been dropped—4 or 5 feet in diameter and 20 feet long—it served as the wood supply. The owner sawed off large slabs 16" thick. These were split into suitable pieces for use in the house. It was Jeannine's first experience with our large logs. Later, she would use this kind of wood herself.

We returned to Portland on September 6, rested and then went to Peach Cove. This was the first time Jeannine had a chance to see the place where so many of my childhood memories were formed—the river, the woods, the gardens, the old houses, the picnics, etc. That was all before the war when the properties were cared for. She saw it pretty much run down and probably wondered how it could have meant so much to me. But she was discreet. In Portland, there were still people to visit and things to prepare for our housekeeping to come.

In September 1948, I checked into the Oregon registrar, paid my tuition, was assigned an apartment at the Amazon, and presented myself to the physics department.

Finally the great day came: our move to the Amazon Apartments in Eugene. Grandpa and Grandma Hudson actually moved us down there –at least for the essentials. All went smoothly and in the late afternoon, HS and Neva left us to ourselves in our new home.

The first task was to move our things around into some semblance of order. There were two single beds in the master bedroom. We pushed them together and lay the mattresses crosswise, making a good double bed which served us the entire stay. Other things were left where we piled them.

Neither Jeannine nor I had had any experience keeping house. So for a few weeks we were constantly adjusting. Shopping for food was experience, too, since everything was new to Jeannine. There was a small grocery store in our building so we were always able to pick up extras; but their prices were high.

The first night we were in the apartment, it struck us both that we were on our own. Jeannine felt so far from the comfort of her family that she had a good cry in my arms. But she never did that again, ever; even from the first day, she looked around to see what needed to be done and did it. And she had an innate sense of order which allowed her to put first things first and never shirk. For my part, I was appalled to realize that I was now responsible for her welfare. I had never before had to look out for anyone but myself. Now I had to make her happy as well as to satisfy our needs. Fortunately she was more than willing to help.

New Wife, painted 1948

The Amazon apartments consisted of about 20 Army barracks that had been erected in an outlying part of Eugene in the swampy broad valley of Amazon Creek east of town. They were two-storied buildings stoutly constructed but without insulation. Each building was cut up into eight apartments, four on each level; each consisted of a living room-kitchen combination, separated by a divider, a bathroom and two bedrooms. There were ample windows for light. There was no bathtub, only a 24"x24" shower.[7] In its original form, the kitchen contained a small wood stove and there was a large wood heater to provide heat for the whole apartment.

The overall size of our apartment was about 25'x20'. In the approximate center was the chimney that served both our apartment and the one below. Originally there was a wood heater and a wood stove vented into it. At the top of the stairs, one entered into the living room with the kitchen

---

7. In fact, we never had an ample shower—nor was I ever in an ample private shower—until we built our house on Los Arboles in Albuquerque. It had always been pleasant to shower at Reed in the big 8-man shower where there was unlimited hot water; one could stay in until he shriveled!.

to the right. Across the living room were two bedrooms and a bathroom. The larger bedroom was ours; the other served as my study room and later also held son Marc's bed and armoire. There was one table and four chairs. Originally there was an ice chest; but ice was hard for us to get so it was not used. At the foot of the stairs there was a wood bin to store our fuel. For transportation, we walked and used the bus.

Besides the money we came with, in October, we received the assistantship check for $78. In November we added to that the GI Bill check for $79, a total of $157 and the rent was $31.50. In December, the income was $137, for an average of $124.

In 1949, our income averaged $221 which included money from the Forest Service for Indian Ridge fire lookout service. By spring of 1949, Jeannine had begun to keep good records of expenditures. The rent dropped down to $26 and the only other household expenditure was electricity at about $2.50 per month. We also had to buy fuel for the stove and space heater, but that was nominal.

Food for our first year in Eugene averaged about $75 per month. We did not eat well, of course, but that paid for an occasional bottle of wine and a bit of luxury. Jeannine set about making a good cook of herself and, when guests arrived, there were always French dishes.

I found I was to work for Dr. Norris, a man of pleasant personality but rather limited ability in physics. He taught freshman physics and a course in advanced mechanics. On one of our early encounters, he showed me my duties—to assemble a counter full of experiments already to work so that he could pass from one end to the other, lecturing as he went, and throwing switches as per my instructions. The students could watch but not touch. Teaching theory these days emphasizes hands-on lab experimentation over demonstration, but I still think demonstration is important. This arrangement continued for three years, as long as I was a graduate assistant.

Sometime in January 1949, Marc was conceived. We were both happy about it, but here was a situation completely beyond our experience. Because of Jeannine's tender age (still 16) I felt we had to have the early attention of a good doctor and we chose Dr. Kirk. I very well remember the day of our first visit: he showed surprise, but quickly settled down to being helpful. From that time on, we had to include Dr. Kirk's office visit of $15.

One day, probably in late 1948, while shopping for food in a large store, we encountered Elmer Gauche. He was working in the store as grocer's assistant. He had been employed there before the war when grocery clerking was a rather respectable job. By 1948, however, the supermarkets were coming in and clerking was no longer a reputable job so Elmer eventually quit to rejoin the army. We immediately renewed our friendship and he became quite fond of Jeannine (and later of Marc). There was a little store in one corner of our apartment building where one could buy occasional items; but main shopping had to be done at one of the stores in town, such as the one Elmer worked at.

We had trouble shopping because we had to carry bags of groceries about a quarter of a mile—until we eventually got bicycles, and finally a car. Jeannine felt very shy about shopping because she was young and because her accent and unfamiliarity with things in Eugene made her feel out of place. The first weeks were quite a learning experience for her. I could help, but I couldn't always be there with her. She was particularly ill-at-ease going to shop for needles, thread, novelties, etc. because she was waited on by little high school girls who made fun of her. She was their same age or younger (still 16); but she was already working at being a woman of the house while they were still tittering children.

We had a collection of friends at U of O, some of whom survived for many years. Herman and Marge, of course, were already dear friends. Marge and the children now lived in Albany, where Herman worked at the Bureau of Mines station whenever he had time. Herman had some kind of apartment (I never saw it) where he stayed during the week. He and I had one or two classes together but mostly his course work was limited to the Chemistry Department. During the first year, he used up his enormous energy after class by playing me out on the handball court. After that, we saw each other only occasionally.

We also met a man named White who was older than I and who studied philology and linguistics. We had some delightful sessions in the SU building over a cup of coffee discussing the origins of language. Until languages were written down (roughly in the Bronze Age), there was no tracer to connect one with another. At that time, in the 1950 period, archaeology had not traced people movements as well as they have now been traced. We now know that by Bronze Age times, there had been a thorough mixing of peoples; only the sedentary or agricultural peoples could evolve distinct languages, which they did. So the origins of the languages of the world owe much to agriculture, a matter I would have liked to discuss with White. But I have never heard from him again.

Another friend from those days was René Picard. He taught Jeannine how to cook petits pois princesse and suprême au chocolat, dishes she loves to make even today. René helped Jeannine mature: he gave her some values in French Culture, he encouraged her in French Literature.[8]

8. In later years we used to receive Christmas cards from him and his wife (whom he married about 1960). They worked as teachers in Lycees. Once they visited us at Los Arboles; once Jeannine visited them near Paris. Finally he died about 1980.

I met Leonard Jones early in our stay at the apartment. He had been at Benson High School and Reed College with me, but I didn't know him well. He was by now married to a pretty young woman, Louise. On a number of occasions we invited them over to play cards and have dessert. They were agreeable friends. Leonard eventually left U of O to take a job with Boeing Aircraft where he was quite successful. Each Christmas we receive a letter telling about their year, and once we visited them at their home near Seattle.

That first year, I took three significant courses: quantum mechanics, electromagnetism and chemical kinetics. Each of them introduced new material that I knew very little about. Each presented a strong basis for future expansion which continues to this day. Before, at Reed, science had been the study of the gross forces of nature; or at best, simulated atomic interactions. Professor Swinehart (chemical kinetics) talked about atoms having shape, about reactions taking time to fit things together, about statistics of reactions. A new world opened up.[9]

That first year in Eugene provided many new vistas for both Jeannine and me. We had no transportation but (except for the drudgery of bringing home bags of groceries) we managed to do much of what we wanted to do.

It rained often and hard and my walk to the university every day kept me in a constant state of sinusitis with the associated soiled handkerchiefs. These, along with the rest of the laundry, Jeannine cleaned without complaint.

The apartment was without insulation so it was cold in the winter and hot in the summer. Heating was provided by the large space heater and to a lesser degree by the cookstove. I bought both mill-ends and "pond-lilies" for fuel. The mill ends were easily started but gave off little heat. The pond lilies were the butts of big trees that had been cut off to square the logs for the veneer peeler. They were hard to split but full of heat. Jeannine had been used to wood-fueled stoves in France, but she had trouble with our fuel at first.

An amusing but nearly tragic event happened to the young, very naïve, couple who lived below and shared our chimney. The wife had let the space heater nearly go out one cold night. When the husband complained, she threw large chunks of wood onto the bed of coals. Of course, nothing happened. The husband became irritated and threw in a cup of kerosene. Nothing happened and then, in our apartment we heard a muffled explosion, our stove pipe shook and small spurts of soot came out into the room. I ran downstairs to find their door open and shrieks coming from their little girl.

9. I have added many books to my bookshelf (and discarded some, too) which have permitted my mind to encompass the whole field of physics even as it was exploding into astronomy, biology and technology. As I see the world today, having a PhD can easily mean the end of the line through specialization.

Inside, smoke filled the room down halfway, the space-heater was in pieces and there was soot everywhere. Neighbors came from all around to help and in a little while the fire engine came and the crew showed them how to clean up. It could have been a dangerous situation.

One wintery day in January 1949, there was a snowstorm that dropped about a foot of snow on Eugene. Of course, everyone who could get out did so and spirits were high on the street. To our surprise, about a dozen from the physics department pushed into our little apartment amid much laughter, stories and beer. For about an hour it was a joyous party; then they departed.

Herman Johansen and I took the chemical kinetics course together. The class opened up a new vista to me, that of trying to follow the progress of a chemical reaction by means of microwave absorption. In the physics department there was already a set-up for the study of the absorption, in the microwave region, of the flexure of the ammonia molecule. I thought I could extend this set-up to include a high temperature ($500°$ C) reaction chamber and study line broadening and eventually chemical reaction. It became the subject of my master's thesis and of the doctoral dissertation.

We had frequent visits with Elmer Gauche and his family. He was such a lonely tragic figure and we gave him spirit. One dreary Sunday he drove us up the McKenzie River to a picnic ground in the trees. There was a shelter so we could have Jeannine's nice dinner out of the rain, and I was finally able to get a fire going out of the wet wood there. In spite of the gray rainy day, we had a good time.

During the spring of 1949, time passed easily. Our records show a steady expenditure for Dr. Kirk. And, looking forward to diapers, we invested in a washing machine. Jeannine no longer had to wait to use one of the community machines. There were no dryers, of course, but plenty of clotheslines. We also had festoons of sheets and underwear drying inside the apartment on certain days because of the high humidity outside.

I had already applied for, and got, a Forest Service lookout post, with Jeannine. Then for the Easter break, we met the family for an outing at the beach. While wading in the bay, I cut my foot, probably on a clam shell. It became infected and I spent a week in the infirmary taking penicillin shots. I barely made a recovery in time to report to the McKenzie Bridge Forest Service Station, with Jeannine, for duty. The ranger was surprised that Jeannine was only 17 (employment requires 18 years of age) and five months pregnant as well.

But we were sent out to Indian Ridge Lookout, high above the McKenzie in some of the prime timber country of Oregon, with a month's supplies of food. The country was beautiful. When we arrived, the ground was still covered with snow (late May). We stored meat and bacon in snow banks; but it really wasn't very cold there and we had to eat the meat in less than a week. In three weeks, the snow was gone.

Finding water proved to be the hardest problem. There was a spring about 200 feet down the steep hillside; I had to carry water up in a backpack. Jeannine was very conscious of conserving water, which was her undoing. She drank too little and developed a bladder infection. A call to Dr. Kirk resulted in her having to be taken down from the mountain on horseback, accompanied by three rangers and myself. She went to the hospital in Eugene for a cure, and then to Portland to stay with Grandma Hudson for the rest of the summer. This was in July and it put an end to her glorious time as lookout. She had loved it so much.

I bought her a .22 rifle and she learned to shoot. In the early mornings, deer woke us up with their snorts and shuffles. The air was delightfully fresh and in the heat of the day, it was filled with the odors of fir trees, decaying sun-dried duff on the ground, ripening berries, and wild flowers. At night there was seldom a whiff of wind and the stars stood out brightly in the black sky. I had to cut wood for our stove and from some of these sticks I carved out some rough spoons. Jeannine kept one of them and uses it to this day for mixing bread dough. She says it is strong and fits the hand well; but I think it serves mostly to bring back those happy days when she was barely 17, exploring in the high Cascades of Oregon, pregnant with her first child, loving the adventure.

The second year at U of O was easier financially—we averaged about $200/month—but not as exciting. I took mostly math courses: modern physics, advanced calculus, advanced algebra. And of course, I spent quite a bit of time in the laboratory beginning my research project.

Marc was born in October and our lives were forever changed. There were doctor and hospital expenses. There were nursing and care problems. Finally Marc could be put on milk and I nailed a cheese box outside the bathroom window to keep the milk cool and fresh. Eventually it began to freeze and we bought a refrigerator. By now the apartment was becoming crowded. When he was old enough to sit by himself, Jeannine began to bathe him in the kitchen sink. Curiosity got the better of him once and he poked the two times of the kitchen fork into the electrical outlet next to the sink. There was a flash and a howl. The tips of the tines were melted. We still have that fork. Strangely, as the apartment house was repainted every two years, the cheese box was carefully painted also.

During this second year, our utility expenses held constant—$26 for rent, $3 for electricity—and food was only a little higher. We found a source of horse meat which pleased Jeannine greatly. And in March 1950, we replaced the wood cookstove with an electric stove. Summer could now be a cooler time in the apartment. Also in 1950 we bought two bicycles which made moving around a great deal easier. I built a small baby seat which I attached to the handle bars of my bike and we could take Marc with us.

This period cannot escape reference to Elmer Gauche. Elmer's mother lived near the Amazon and Elmer shared the house with her; he also had a brother and sister who came occasionally. Elmer's health was poor; he seemed to have inherited a bad stomach from his mother. But he loved photography, converted a bathroom in that house into a darkroom, and presented us with some very nice pictures from time to time. The best of them shows little Marc, age about 6 months, riding in a handle bar seat I had made for our bicycles. Now such seats are common place, but at that time, ours was the only one in town and caused quite a flurry of attention. We also had baskets to carry groceries so we took him shopping with us. Eventually we got a car, got rid of the bicycles, and began to take trips into the woods. On one of these, a Sunday picnic in an Oregon drizzle, Elmer came along. We had a hard time starting a fire; fortunately we were able to stop at a Forest Service shelter. It was one of the last pleasant times we had with Elmer.

Elmer was an unhappy and very lonely man. He rejoined the Signal Corps in 1950, at the time of the Korean conflict. He seemed to feel a little more useful, earned good pay, and was almost happy. On one of this visits home, he met a girl (who was much younger than he) who worked at the telephone switchboard. Against his family's advice, he married her and they went to his base in California. Some months later, she was back and he was in the psychiatric ward of a hospital in San Francisco. We never learned what happened. And a few weeks later, Elmer disappeared, never to be seen again. He had checked out fishing gear and left his street clothes in his locker. The Army declared him AWOL and cut off his wife's and family's allowances. In spite of numerous efforts to track down what happened (his family suspected suicide or accidental death), nothing clarified. I contacted senators in both Oregon (Sen. Morse) and New Mexico (Sen. Dennis Chavez) to no avail. Elmer's family allowances were not renewed; eventually we lost track of the Gauche family. Elmer's disappearance remains a mystery. Seven years after his disappearance the Army probably paid off on his life insurance policy.

During July and August of both 1950 and 1951, I found work as a plumber's assistant with the Peterson Plumbing Company. The pay was pretty good and I learned a great deal about everyday mechanics and electricity. Most of my experience was in the areas of heating and water lines of all sizes. But I learned something from Peterson, too. He was a Seventh Day Adventist and his life was very orderly and he enjoyed a fine reputation in town. Jeannine soon got used to me coming home tired and dirty and I think she enjoyed putting everything right.

The bicycles allowed us to tour the city with Marc, often with a picnic lunch. Our favorite place was the Pioneer Cemetery, but there were also many parks and gardens to visit, and even a zoo.

The car was always in need of repair, as old cars always are. But it made camping possible as well as visits to Portland. On one such visit, we stopped at Arthur's house in Albany with a boiling engine. It was Sunday afternoon and he couldn't help with repairs. He said, "The radiator is clogged. But you can probably get home by accelerating up hills and gliding down the other side with the engine off." And so we did. The radiator was later cleaned out.

The master's thesis was used to lay out the program for dissertation research. One of the members of my committee didn't like that, so all I got was a B grade. During the discussion of the thesis, Dr. Dart asked me a question about radio frequency modulation (not really related to the thesis topic). I described amplitude modulation. No, not that. So I described frequency modulation. No, not that either. I was stumped; they were the only modulation techniques I had ever heard of. To this day, I can't imagine what he was driving at. But it was Dr. Dart who offered us his house to stay in while he took Sabbatical.

The school year 1950–1951 was not very memorable. I took courses in applied advanced math and solid state physics. By this time, I was advanced to fellowship status with a little more money and more activities around the department. My laboratory research was going poorly because of my inexperience. But what really troubled me was my inability to calculate the flecture modes of molecules in the microwave region. Norris was no help; indeed there was no one at U of O who could help and few in the country at that time.

About this time, I met Makoto Takeo (Japanese) and Shang-Yi Ch'en (Chinese). They were at the university as student and professor, respectively. Ch'en was working on spectral line broadening, experimentally, and Takeo helped with theory. Neither could help with molecules. But they became good friends. One night, Mme Ch'en invited us along with some other students to a wonderful Chinese dinner she prepared; Makoto cooked a Japanese dinner for us at our house. They were very kind to us and we have maintained contact, mostly with Takeo.

In the spring of 1951, the opportunity arose to send Jeannine and Marc back to France.[10] After a crossing marred by seasickness (or course Marc was

10. [Editor's Note] Jeannine noted in the margin that a trip had been discussed but they did not have enough money for the trip. So Papa and Mamie bought the ship passage for Marc and Jeannine. Additional money came from cashing some bonds Craig

not sick!), Jeannine was welcomed into her family's arms again with ecstatic pleasure. And Pépé and Mémé (Papa's parents), who had never expected to see Jeannine again, not only had her but a grandson as well. I have always thought this must have been an emotional experience for them; but I never saw Pépé and Mémé again. This was a time of great mother-daughter empathy, more healthy I think than it ever was later. While Mamie lovingly tended Marc, Jeannine and Papa roamed Paris soaking up the sights, sounds and smells. I later learned that she truly loves this feeling of close association and she never feels worried or fearful there. I cannot easily express this feeling in words; but I marveled at it in 1987 when we were there together. It was a wonderful trip (almost three months) for them, well documented by photos in her album.

Back in Eugene, life for me was pretty empty. I filled the time while Jeannine and Marc were gone with study, an occasional outing (René, another French girl, and I went to the Oregon beach near Florence and froze), and some work. The period would be completely vacant except that I have pictures of the outing. I took a job with the Forest Service again, and discovered that my heart was too weak now for that sort of life. So I gave it up and went back to Peterson Plumbing.

One of the men in the physics department was Stan Lynch; his wife was Marilynn and they had two children. We were quite friendly. But Stan ran out of money and had to go to work. He eventually wound up as a sergeant in the Oregon City Police Department. We visited them on our trips to Oregon. Later, Stan became despondent and killed himself. We kept in touch with Marilynn and the children for a number of years.

In the time between Jeannine's trip to France and the winter of 1951, there was quite a bit of activity of a sort of intermediate level. The GI Bill money ran out in June 1951. Grandpa Hudson began sending $100 per month which was wonderful. But I felt very guilty about accepting it. The money was never paid back.[11] During the summer of 1951, Ray Ellickson got me a job driving his brother's agricultural lime truck. I had no experience with such a heavy truck (5 ton), but mostly all went well. I got stuck once because a farmer had not told me he had watered his field. Jeannine came out to see me once or twice. The country air was delightful in the early fall.

Jeannine did a little posing for one of the art classes. It brought in some money. But as 1951 wore on, it was clear that money was going to be a serious problem for the future. My master's thesis was written (it was not the exciting experience I had hoped it to be) and I was trying to complete the

---

had. It was a big effort to go but it was very necessary.

11. [Editor's Note] Jeannine noted in the margin that after Grandpa Hudson died, while Craig and Jeannine were living in New Mexico, Craig was working at Sandia Laboratory and tried to repay the money to Grandma Hudson. She would not allow it.

formulations of ideas about a doctoral dissertation. My research was not going very well so an outside fellowship was not in the cards. The university treated me as well as they could. But the future was beginning to look bleaker. The final straw came when I would have had to take my qualifying exam over. All of my feelings of inadequacy came to the fore and, coupled with the lack of funds, it began to look as though I had pushed this program of study as far as I could. I began to think about jobs, and to put together a mental image of what I had to offer an employer.

We bought a car in December which gave us mobility. Dr. Dart became friendly and let us stay in his house while he was on sabbatical—nice because Grandpa Hudson's $100 was not very much. We paid rent at the Amazon in December 1951 and in January 1952 we bought sawdust for the Dart's house. These two actions define this major change in our lives.

The winter of 1951–52 was a tense one; I was depressed over the slow progress of my thesis project. My advisor, Dr. Norris, was having health problems and I took over the teaching of his mechanics class. He was never much help to me but in that last year at U of O, he was unable to help much at all.[12] Jeannine had had 2 miscarriages and was feeling poorly, but she made life so happy for Marc and me: walks in the parks, little camping trips, special dinners, etc. She enjoyed little Marc so much. No young mother could have been more attentive and devoted. Jeannine seemed to realize that I was in turmoil: try to find funds and go ahead with the thesis research or look for a job. Great uncertainties faced either option.

A new Physics Building had been under construction for some time and it opened in late 1951. I was given my own office in deference to my title "Fellow." But I was a little sad to leave the old Deady Hall which had housed physics for so long. It was one of the first buildings to be constructed on the campus and Grandma Palmer had gone there as a young woman.

I had an electronics course to teach. That was a real pleasure because, instead of teaching the elements of radio, I developed a course around electron experiments. Of course, I also had to include the essentials of circuit theory, potential surfaces, etc. The culmination of it was the theory of the cathode ray oscilloscope.

I spent much time in Dr. Ch'en's lab and learned by watching how he performed "high" pressure experiments. By high pressure, he meant a few hundred atmospheres, nothing like the thousands of atmospheres I would deal with later. I also absorbed a great deal of optics from him. It was no longer the stagnant area of physics I had once thought. Over the years, I

12. His condition worsened and he died of cancer in 1953.

have taught myself a great deal of optics. Dr. Ch'en had been pleased to see my interest and helped me.

I enjoyed constant contacts with Herman and with Dr. Van Rysselberghe[13]. During the spring of 1952, I sat in on Dr. Van Rysselberghe's advanced thermodynamics class. I learned a great deal and occasionally we could be able to have nice little discussions about things that came up during the classes. He introduced me to the term "thermostatics" which he felt should have been the title for the usual equilibrium process. "Thermodynamics" would then refer to non-equilibrium processes which were becoming ever more, important in reaction rate theory. But his terminology, correct as it was, never took hold.

Then in December 1951, Mel Merritt came to Eugene, recruiting a staff for Sandia Corporation. It was a government contractor managed by the well-established Western Electric Company. I took his application and filled it out. One of the last acts I remember at our Amazon Apartment was having my picture taken against the front door by Jeannine to use as the necessary portrait.

My second language needed for the doctorate was Russian. My, how hard that was! Even though there are certain grammatical similarities with Latin and French, the strange alphabet and the new vocabulary made it difficult. I finally got to the point where I could sing a few Russian songs to Jeannine and read some scientific papers in Russian but the literary Russian was always out of reach.

Having the car made outings much more available and pleasant. We went to Portland several times and to the beach. The bicycles were sold. We could shop with ease. Our life style was inching upward. Income for 1951 averaged $286/month. Rent was still $26/month and food, clothing, books, etc. were a little higher than before. However, the coming financial crisis could be clearly seen.

There were not many companies offering jobs. GE and Bell Telephone both offered places in the East, but that was not very interesting. I had begun to put locale first and job second in my mind even though I very much needed the job. Albuquerque sounded romantic enough and it was not far from Los Alamos. So when the invitation for interview came, I jumped at the chance.

The letter of invitation required me to be in Albuquerque at a certain day in April 1952 and to buy my own fare. They would reimburse me later. I remember talking to Grandpa Hudson about it and he said that surely I could trust Western Electric. So I boarded a plane and went to Albuquerque.

---

13. [Editor's Note] Dr. Pierre Van Rysselberghe.

At the Albuquerque Airport, I took a taxi downtown to the old Franciscan Hotel, where I had a reservation. Later I found that it was made of adobe bricks, one of the tallest adobe structures in the world. At that time, however, it had a comfortable 1930s style interior with lots of dark wood paneling in the lobby. I had dinner at the City Café which was notable for a series of beautiful murals around the walls depicting Anasazi ruins. A fire ruined some of them years later, but some were saved.

Coming back into the lobby, I met Vern Garratt waiting for a friend! Vern had been one of my buddies in the army and I had tutored him in math when he started college. Vern now worked at Sandia Corporation as a technical writer. After I was hired by Sandia (where Vern was working as a tech writer), our families met from time to time. Eventually he and his wife had two children while we had four. It was never an intimate relation, but was always friendly. Somehow Vern had taught himself how to play the piano by ear (he was already doing this in the army) and now he got jobs playing at bars in town, providing background music mostly.

He and his wife were charming and easy to get along with, but they did not get along together (she was in and out of psychotherapy); and eventually they divorced. She went to California. Vern had always had trouble with allergies (he used to buy tissue by the wholesale carton) and after the divorce (feeling more free of responsibilities, I suppose) he moved to Houston to escape the Albuquerque allergens. There he took whatever job he could find: for a long time he was a coffee salesman on a restaurant route, more recently he worked for a laundry. He remarried in Houston to a pleasant woman whom we know only via Christmas cards.[14]

At the laboratory, Mel Merritt asked me to work in his division and we spent the day talking to other scientists and managers. The most frequently mentioned subject was that of security. The laboratory was on Sandia Base which was laid out in typical military fashion with guards and machine gun towers (armed, I was told) everywhere. They made such a point of this that I had worries about bringing Jeannine into such an atmosphere. And construction was going on all around at a feverish pace.

But overall was the wind and dust. This was April, the windy part of the year and the construction was loosing clouds of dust into the air. My eyes smarted, but I wasn't to know the extent of the damage until days later. The horizon was ringed by mountains in every direction, the closest of

14. Over the last 10 years or so, we have had occasional phone conversations with him. He is a very pleasant conversationalist; Jeannine is fond of him. And he visited us once. The last we heard from Vern was in Sept 1994, when he called again—for no apparent reason—and we had a happy time recalling old names. I sent him a letter outlining the essay on Temperature and discussing Free Will.

which were the Sandia Mountains (Sandia means watermelon) and Monzano Mountains (Monzano means apples). The names and definitions were provided by Mel, but I never found out from which language they were.

Mel and his wife treated me to dinner in Old Town, the first spicy food I had ever tasted. They also drove me around town to get a feel for living conditions, from the poor barrio to the rich valley, but especially on the East Mesa where houses were popping up everywhere. Finally, without ever asking about my own technical background, and not telling me what I would be working on, Mel sent me home. It was agreed that if they wanted to hire me, I would get a letter.

Back in Eugene, Jeannine had been dealing with being alone as best she could. Little Marc helped pass the time. In the years to come, she would have to suffer many more such times as I travelled.

My eyes felt gritty from the dust but it washed out in a few days. One spot however would not go away—in fact, it got worse. Finally I had Dick Carter (Libby's husband) recommend an "eye doctor." He found a cyst under the eyelid and easily lanced and drained it. It was my first experience with an ophthalmologist, and as a family we have never trusted our eyes to any other kind of eye doctor since.

Finally in June the letter from Sandia came: I was accepted. Starting salary was to be $550/month beginning August first.

Dexter and Craig in front of Notre Dame in Paris, 1945

Jeannine and Craig, wedding photo, 1948

Camping at Elk Lake in Oregon with Hudson family;
(L to R) Marilyn, Jeannine, Rosie, 1948

In Eugene, Oregon, (L to R) Craig, Marc, Jeannine, 1950

Amazon Apartments, circa 1952

10

Albuquerque, New Mexico and the Early Sandia Years

1952—1963

There was a great deal to do in the ensuing weeks. Jeannine was busy putting together all our possessions into shipping crates. We decided that we would take a last view of the Oregon we loved so much camping out with Marc. We left the Dart's house almost as clean as we had found it. We set off for Florence and from there up the full length of the coast, camping at various campgrounds. We spent the early summer in Portland at Mom and Dad's house and visiting with family. It was, however, the last time we were to see Grandpa Hudson; he died the following winter.

Our transportation to Albuquerque was to be by train, leaving in mid-July. The train left from Union Station in Portland. On hand were the parents and grandparents and even Marilynn. It was a tearful goodbye because we all felt the uncertainties of the time. We were full of the excitement of new adventure but very unsure of what we would find in Albuquerque.

We left Oregon on the train when the weather was hot—about 90°—and enjoyed 1st class in an air conditioned sleeper but it was small, rather stuffy. Little Marc was not to be put off by the comfort and whenever he could escape, he roamed the train looking for excitement, often in the smoking car. It was difficult to keep him down. Jeannine was pregnant (with Elianne) and uncomfortable in the stuffy compartment. The trip should have been continuous, but there had been a severe earthquake in Bakersfield area the day before and we were routed around it on a bus. My! That was a hot ride but it was interesting to see the damage—from a safe distance. So we looked forward with great expectations to the arrival in Albuquerque.

Those expectations were dashed when we stepped out into the furnace-like heat and blazing sun of Albuquerque. The sky was deep blue, the sun very hot—actually still in the 90s and Jeannine felt the impulse to hop a train back to Oregon. We found out that, even though the air temperature was about the same as in Oregon, it felt hotter in the sun because its rays were direct, unfiltered.

I had been keeping in touch with Bob Thompson—from my physics class at Reed—who was already working in the Field Test organizations at Sandia. That whole group was sent out to the first big US Atomic test in the Pacific (summer of 1952) and since his house would be empty, he invited us to live there in his absence. We were very grateful not to have to look for living quarters right off the train.

Fortunately one of Bob's friends was there with a car and we were taken to Bob's house. However, relief was not to be found in the house, at least as warm as outdoors. It was our introduction to a hot climate and Jeannine nearly wilted. Little Marc, of course, was not bothered at all and set about exploring the back yard.

In a little while, Jeannine had the house to her liking. Bob had left his old Chevy which we used for shopping. The afternoon heat brought an activities slowdown, but the nights were cool. The rainy season was just starting and from time to time we could watch a storm move over the land from the west; but mostly they passed to the north of us and we benefitted little from the cooling.

Jeannine survived the hot summer and seemed to be at ease in the house by October and I was doing well at Sandia. We knew that Bob would come back and that we would need a house of our own. A house came up for sale about a block away at 2938 San Rafael and we thought it would suit us. It had a large extra room in the back for Papa and Mamie when they planned to arrive in 1953—those plans were essentially fixed. So we set about trying to put together the down payment. Grandma Palmer lent us $1000 and Grandpa Hudson put in a little. We had been saving some of our own, so we thought we could do it. The transaction was being handled by Keenan and Welsh, a reputable real estate firm. But there were a number of details to be dealt with; Jeannine was busy with them while I was at Sandia. She also had little 3-year-old Marc and was pregnant six months with Elianne. But I never heard her complain.

Then in early October a small disaster struck. I was stricken with gall bladder trouble, during one night. Jeannine rose to the occasion wonderfully and found Dr. Roy Robertson, an internist, by looking in the phonebook—at midnight. Those were the days. He came out to the house (to Bob Thompson's house), examined me and had me off in no time to St. Joseph Hospital. Dr. Robertson made the diagnosis and Dr. Nissen did the surgery. I was at St. Joseph Hospital on Grand Avenue; the building is still there but is now used, I think, for nurses training.

My operation had been more extensive than usual because Dr. Nissan was trying to remove my appendix at the same time. But he couldn't find it, so all I got was a lot of air in my abdomen. I stayed about 10 days in the hospital. The nurses and aides made my time as pleasant as they could but the air and gas trapped inside the wound made life hell and I often retched and vomited. But after some days, the worst of it was over and I began to feel a little more normal. The incision was about a foot long and was slow to heal. It was still very tender and there was a drain of rubber tubing in it that Dr. Nissen came every day to examine and to sniff the dirty brown liquid oozing out. The nurses and aides were very helpful and made me as much at ease as possible; but Jeannine was very worried to see me so weak and pale.

During this time, Albuquerque had a snow fall of about six inches—very unusual for October. The days were warm so the snow melted into a crackly layer of ice at night. In spite of the slick driving, Jeannine came to see me every night. Jeannine had completed the arrangements to purchase the San Rafael house and one day she came with an attorney to have me sign some papers, at bedside. I don't know how she managed to pull all the loose ends together. The realtor had been a rather sensible man, as I recall, and he must have helped.

Once at home, I recovered from the operation quickly, although the scar remained sensitive for many months. At last the house was ours, but we had to wait several weeks for it to be vacated. Eventually we were able to move in, sometime in the middle of November. In the meantime Bob had returned from the Pacific and for a while we all occupied his house together. Of course, when we were in our own house, we no longer had the use of Bob's car. The last car gas we bought for his car was in early November. We now had to do shopping and other such trips by bus or walking. Bob was very kind and took me to Sandia each day.

We furnished our house with rudimentary furnishings. I had ordered a Simmons spring and mattress from Rubenstein's[1] in Eugene. They thought I was weird but I questioned that what I wanted could be found in Albuquerque. It could, of course, as I was soon to discover. The "bed" was laid out flat on the floor. I wanted to make our own bedstead, so later I ordered

---

1. [Editor's Note] Furniture Company, Eugene, Oregon.

materials from a lumberyard and began to build it. Jeannine was quite happy with the idea.[2] The dining table consisted of Papa's trunk covered by my old 3'x6' drafting table. But Jeannine made it into an elegant Christmas table with a fine cloth and place settings. She and Marc and I had a quiet but lovely Christmas dinner in our own house.

We enjoyed that first Thanksgiving at the house of Jay and Helen Todd,[3] with their two daughters, Edith and Melissa. I was so weak that I had trouble staying up for the dinner. But they were so hospitable and helpful. Jay had a car and he and Helen drove us back and forth to their house which was on San Mateo NE. Throughout all the years we have remained friends. Jay and I worked in the same department at Sandia.

I checked into Sandia on August 1, as scheduled, and found a very warm welcome. There was a certain time spent signing papers and I was made aware of the security requirements which were everywhere in evidence. Mel showed me my office and introduced me to the nearby staff members.

During the next few days, I was told about the problem I was supposed to work on. It was to theorize about the interaction of blast waves with structures. I was also invited to participate in the design of experiments using high explosives. There was a team of about 10 men working on these experiments in Coyote Canyon. Mel very proudly showed me that facility and most of my blast work derived from those experiments. I was not very pleased with the field work: it was hot out there (100°), the sun was so bright it hurt my eyes, the ground was covered with prickly grass and cactus, and the work was hard. After a long while, however, I learned to appreciate better what we were doing and to enjoy the good-natured crew at work there. I met Dick Jones there and he remains a friend to the present day.

Deke Palmer was in charge of the field operation. An engineer whose name I forget was in charge of electronics (instrumentation) and Warren Roberts was in charge of preparing the HE charge, which meant piling up the TNT blocks, setting the initiator in the pile and making sure there could be no misfire. Everyone worked on building the wall from 1'x1'x1' concrete cubes. The wall was six feet high, six feet wide and about 30 feet long. Instruments were located in one end only.

When the charge was detonated, a blast wave raced toward the target structure. It consisted of a very steep front followed by a slower decoy. The front was a shock and its time scale was in microseconds. The rest of the

2. We still use that bedstead.

3. [Editor's Note] Jay and Helen Todd, and their daughters Edith and Melissa, remained lifelong friends of Craig and Jeannine.

wave passed in 10s of milliseconds. The peak pressure was of considerable interest but instruments at that time could not respond in microseconds ($10-6$), therefore the peak of the wave was always cut off.

The instruments measured pressure typically in the range 0–100 psi. They were mounted flush with the surfaces of the wall. The wires leading to the recorder were buried to be out of harm's way. The explosion really shook the wall and usually displaced some of the blocks, but by that time the electrical signals had already been recorded. The recordings were full of noise and extraneous signals. When I got them, they had been cleaned up.

The pattern of pressure on the front of the wall was characterized by diffraction. The patterns on the other faces were characterized by vortices. Jeannine got used to me talking about diffraction and vortices.

The vortex problem proved to be intractable mathematically and I was only able to get graphical solutions. But the diffraction pattern could be described by Sommerfeld's approach (about 1900) and in the summer of 1953 I had the help of Hugh Dewitt (a physicist) and Frank Lane (a computer programmer) in rendering a theoretical formulation which quite closely fit the experimental results. Hugh was a mountain climber and with a friend tried to climb the Thumb in the Sandia Mountains. He seriously hurt himself but recovered (1954).

I had met some men at Sandia who were of interest to me: Mel Merritt, Jim Shreve, Dick Jones, Deke Palmer and Luke Vortman were all associated with Coyote Canyon and Tom Cook, Bill Perrett, Carter Broyles, Jay Todd (and others I can't think of now) were all from the weapon effects group. Both of these groups worked under Everett Cox, our department manager.

1952 drew to a close with new house, new friends, new climate, new job, and by now Jeannine was 8 months pregnant. We were full of plans for the coming year when Elianne would be with us and we anticipated the coming of Mamie and Papa. We were trying to prepare the extra room behind the garage for them.

In the spring of 1953, Mamie and Papa completed their emigration application and came to Albuquerque. Ever since Jeannine and I were married it was understood that they would join us. In a very real sense, I was marrying the family when I took the daughter. What came as a surprise was the timing. We had always said—and believed—that when we were established, we would send for Papa and Mamie. As it turned out, we did not become established very readily; and the situation in Paris seemed to be worsening for them. Considering what was happening on both sides, they probably came at about the best time. Papa was in slowly worsening health, growing too fat with inactivity and poor eating but he was able to recover himself; and he had enormous intellect and spirit and vigor. He was able to establish himself in the new country. He forever changed our lives by emphasizing the importance of skilled hands. It was a lesson for me to learn, and I am still profiting from it. The skills varied from working with wood to working with food. Our two boys grew up in the reflected light of Papa's skills.

However, in January of 1953, tiny Elianne was born. While Jeannine was in the hospital, receiving the best of care, Marc and I were at home alone. January was always a bad month at the San Rafael house because of the use of floor furnaces. It was bitter cold outside and these furnaces maintained an average 70° temperature inside (the house was not insulated) at the expense of creating hot and cold spots. In considerable part because of these temperature gradients, our colds became flu; Marc and I were violently ill, vomiting without reprieve. The house stank of it; our bed was dirty. So I called a nursing service. The very nice and competent lady who came cleaned things up quite well. We recovered, and in a few days Jeannine came home with little Elianne. I was so afraid that our flu virus would linger in the house and contaminate them; but they did not get sick.

Jeannine's problem with Elianne became that of trying to care for her delicate skin. To this day, 30 some years later, Elianne has a delicate skin that must be pampered. The struggles Jeannine had at that time reflected upon the fallibility of doctors. Our family problem, inherited from Mary Palmer, is a kind of psoriasis; the children and I all suffer to some extent; of course, Jeannine is free of it, and for that lucky condition, the degree of affliction in the children varies from Elianne (worst) to Cassandra (least). The doctors we had access to had little experience in this area; medicines proved to be of no benefit, even harmful. In desperation one doctor suggested bathing in cooked oatmeal for the tiny 10-weeks-old baby, probably an old Scotch myth; it didn't hurt but it didn't help and it was so very messy. In spite of her early difficulties, Elianne became a bright, charming young lady full of good ideas and love.

Elianne had difficulty falling asleep because her skin itched so. During the first year or two I always sang the two of them (Marc and Elianne) to sleep with the old negro and frontier songs that I had learned as a boy. Often, after repeated verses, when I thought they were asleep and started to leave the room, Elianne aroused herself and cried "more, Daddy," so Marc chimed in. There were times when I was so tired that the little tyke exasperated me by her inability to fall asleep—of which I am ashamed, now—but I guess I must have suppressed the feelings and let her persuade me to sing. Me sing! Only a loving child could beg me to sing, with my poor voice, the disappointment of my father's life, he who was such a fine singer. Even to this day, when he is 94, dad can sing on key and with clarity—until phlegm forces him to cough.

Mamie and Papa came in April. It was fortunate for us that they had not been allowed to leave France with very much because we had very little room in which they could store their things. The room behind the garage was not very comfortable, but we were already crowded into the other bedrooms. The garage was turned into a shop and there Papa made his first pieces of furniture—very nice semi-Louis XV buffets for some rather wealthy French families—who were very tight with their money! Nothing more was done for them. But first, Papa completed the bedstead I had begun—a very sturdy unhandsome frame for Jeannine and me to thrash around on. I had done much of the carpentry—of which Papa was not very admiring, and he finished it with a dark stain polished with his 'lac' (shellac) ponce finish. He tried to use this old French standby finish but it never did very well in Albuquerque—partly because it was so dry here and partly because people here demanded something more resistant to water and alcohol.

While we were at San Rafael, Papa got his business started. Fortunately he knew what he was doing—I surely didn't help much. Taking Jeannine around to translate for him was necessary at first. But he was determined to succeed and soon was on his own. In spite of quite a bit of trying, he was unable to make things that would sell. All he could do that was realistic was to make things on commission and to do repairs. But in these two areas, he became quite successful.

He needed transportation and eventually he purchased a car which he traded for another, and then for another, eventually winding up with a Ford station wagon that suited him well. He had "Jean Dumas—Ébéniste" written on the door panels and, with his beret, he soon became a familiar figure around town.

Papa built up a rather extensive repair and refinishing business, working on the antiques owned by many of the old local families, and some of the new ones. He expanded his business to Santa Fe and eventually his reputation grew far and wide. In one case, he refinished all the antiques a woman was planning to donate to a museum in the East. In other cases, he reshaped pieces of furniture—some, fine examples—which did not fit in their owner's modern settings. In this way, he obtained as castoffs the excess wood, often ebony, rosewood, etc., which we still have. Finally, his reputation grew enough so that people at some distance would write or call. In one case, a professor from Minnesota asked to price a large chair upholstered with a Navajo blanket; it proved to be too costly.

After a few months of Papa trying to work out of our garage, it was decided that he could not work in our garage; it was too small, too close to the house, too limited in power and light. He had varnished the bed I started there and had built perhaps one other piece of furniture there; but clearly it could not serve as a place of business, especially for one as ambitious as Papa.

We obtained a lead on an out-of-use carpet cleaning shop. When Papa first leased-to-buy the old building, it was a mess, with old carpet scraps and tools lying around, a big furnace hooked up for drying, and a poor little office in one front corner. But by dint of hard work, quite a bit of it Mamie's, the place became a house of business. Little by little, he accumulated power tools: a table saw, a lathe, a shaper, a planer, a drill press, and a band saw (which made possible some very convoluted and fancy work). He built himself a table—a wonderful heavy French-style worktable out of Douglas fir and beech wood. It will never wear out; Marc now has it and it will surely serve him as long as he can work. That table is the legacy of the ébénistrie background from which Papa came.

Our family increased again with the birth of another daughter, Cassandra, in 1955. Mamie and Papa were still living with us at this time and we began to be really pressed for space. Papa and I and Jeannine worked to dig a basement for our house. Papa and I did most of the digging and Jeannine helped to move the dirt out. Papa and I worked together with blocking and concreting the basement walls. I recall one event in the basement construction that was frightening. A big block slid down on collapsing sand and injured Jeannine's knee. This was about the time she was contemplating or had started ballet training and we thought she had suffered a setback that was irreparable. But medicine to the rescue! An injection of the new drug Cortisone cleared up the problem, although it has always remained tender.

Jeannine starting ballet at Krassnov's Studio in 1955 was a turning point in our lives. First, it gave Jeannine the chance she had always wanted to become expert in a field of knowledge and rather skilled in its practice. And second, it brought us into contact with Bob Bruning and Tom Hall, two of our most devoted friends, still very much a part of our lives.[4]

In the San Rafael house, things began to deteriorate. One of Mamie's lifelong traits of personality has been a deep feeling of rejection by everyone. And she tried to solve this feeling by cultivating the affection of the children, often to the destruction of Jeannine's effort at discipline. The problem grew so severe that eventually Jeannine had to ask them to look for other lodgings. I think Papa understood, but Mamie didn't and never forgave Jeannine—even though she clung to her with desperation.

4. Bob Bruning was teacher of the adult class at Krassnov's, consisting mostly of ladies trying to slim down with grace. Bob had once taught popular dancing at the Arthur Murray School. He studied at Krassnov's and quickly became their star. While at the Arthur Murray School, he met Edith Boettcher, who would also become one of our most devoted friends.

Mamie and Papa did have a social life of their own, in good part due to their efforts to achieve citizenship which involved going to a language school. I think it was here that they met a number of other French people, one of whom was Arlene Foster. Mrs. Foster, married to a doctor, asked Mamie and Papa to manage a duplex house while living in a small addition. This gave them a place to live but was very hard on Mamie—they did not have a car at the time—but Papa accepted it in good grace.

During the year or so that Papa and Mamie stayed at Mrs. Foster's place, Papa initiated a tradition that became a family mark of distinction. He and Mamie put on very special Sunday dinners for us. Often Papa did the cooking, serving all sorts of nice dishes that were unusual, often inexpensive, but very good. Mostly his dishes were meat, sausage, vegetables; but there were some desserts, too. A list of all the special dishes that our family now uses has been made, including these. Some of Papa's dishes have been taken over by Mamie (like couscous), who now is the ranking authority. A word here: Jeannine is much better at making all the dishes than Mamie, but she refrains when a loss of face would occur.

After they had been using the shop about a year, Papa found that the little house that adjoined the property at the back was for sale and he signed up for it! We thought he might never complete the mortgage contract; but he did (in about 10 years) and we had a celebration at the restaurant that had been the old Robin Hood, now Chez Hubert's. What a feast.

Papa left a legacy of good will, of craftsmanship, of interest in the arts, of expertise in food preparation. To his family, he was usually friendly, devoted and helpful—but he did have a darker side. While Papa lived, Mamie was usually in his shadow. He always gave the impression of treating her like a countess; but privately, she complained that he did not. We never could understand the rift. After Papa died, he became a hero in her eyes; nothing he had ever done was ignominious; she revered him. And she became the self-appointed arbiter of French culture. We knew she was sometimes wrong, but her French fervor was so strong that we hated to contradict her—and so it goes to the present day.

While still in our first year at Sandia Lab, Jay Todd and I and several other staff members took advantage of free trips to Los Alamos Scientific Laboratory (LASL) to listen to seminars and colloquia. It was a rather awkward arrangement and Jay and I thought that we at Sandia should have our own Colloquia series. Eventually in 1954, we proposed it to the vice president of research and he accepted, giving us a small budget (I recall that it was $1000 for all expenses including honoraria). At first, we shared the responsibilities but little by little Jay let me do more and more. I had some ideas about politics in science and we got Oscar Morganstern[5] to talk. Little by little, the stature of the Colloquium grew until finally we had Henry Kissinger[6]. By this time, Jay had moved to Los Alamos and was no longer interested at all. I found several times that we could attract scientists too specialized for Sandia's staff to relate to. This was embarrassing. Many times we got scientists from Los Alamos, Livermore and other labs and universities whose work was exceptionally interesting. Carson Mark spoke 3 or 4 times about test results, as did others.

The Kissinger affair was very interesting. The management would not let me introduce two speakers in all: Senator Anderson[7] and Henry Kissinger. But I didn't mind. We had a luncheon for Anderson and a special dinner for Kissinger at our house, where Jeannine and Papa put on a feast. There were a number of visitors: the Chabais, the Longhursts, the Aherns and a variety of people from Sandia.

At about this time, I was asked by Frank Hudson (no relation) to recruit. I joined the Bell Labs Team to recruit at Oregon schools. I got three excellent staff members from U of O. Later, I was sent to University of Illinois-Urbana where I got two more very good staff members; some of these made very good administrators as well as scientists. The recruiting adventure also allowed me to look for Colloquium people and since by now I had a $10,000/yr budget, it was possible to attract some rather good speakers on a fee basis. The best source of speakers, however, was local talent, scientists in the Atomic Energy Commission (AEC) and visiting scientists. All in all, the Colloquium series was—and still is—a great success at Sandia. But over time I was having problems: stomach cramps and stammering and other signs of acute nervousness. So in January 1961, I resigned as Chairman, aided by advice from Clarence Mehl that I should do more research. Perhaps it was a poor decision, but at the time, I felt I was on a downhill health path.

The year 1961 was important for us for two reasons: our son, Cyril, was born and we decided to build a house on the property in the north valley that we had purchased from Mr. Bolles. When we signed to buy the property (I think it was in 1957), we had some dreams about building on it; but we couldn't see our financial situation improving that much. My work with the Colloquium had made me pretty well known not only at Sandia but

5. [Editor's Note] Oskar Morganstern, an economist, http://www.econlib.org/library/Enc/bios/Morgenstern.html .

6. [Editor's Note] Henry Kissinger, a political scientist and diplomat, http://www.biography.com/people/henry-kissinger-9366016 .

7. [Editor's Note] Sen. Clinton Anderson, http://www.govtrack.us/congress/members/clinton_anderson/400841 .

at Los Alamos and elsewhere. As a result, my pay slowly increased and by 1961 Jeannine and I thought we might be able to swing it, especially if she could earn a little (by teaching French and ballet).

So in 1961 I began to sketch out the kind of house we thought we wanted. At the time, nuclear war seemed to be a possibility and I spent hours trying to conceive how a nice looking building could also serve as a bomb shelter. All across the country people were installing in their yards various types of shelters, some expensive. They must have proved to be wasteful investments. Looking back now on the situation, war seems unlikely for the time and nuclear war very unlikely. There was another reason, however, for all this effort. One of the surprises of the southwest is the existence of ice caves in places where it is very hot in the summer. Would it not be possible to use the same principles to construct comfortable houses? Yes, it would if. . . Needed would be walls about two feet thick of tufa with few windows and doors. I spent days thinking of how to achieve this kind of situation and ran into two major obstacles: cost and aesthetics. In the end, I had to give up any hope of using physical principles and go with cheap construction techniques, which have been developed over the years to solve the problems by active heating and cooling. Later when solar energy came in to offset the cost and pollution of hydro-carbon fuels, I had to be very skeptical because the heat (or cold) comes when one least wants it and storage for times like the annual solar cycle seem still to be impossible.

I finally completed the drawings to Jeannine's satisfaction (she learned how to read them!) and we set about finding a contractor. We had to give up any hope of a basement structure and finally got Mr. Goad to agree to build it—with certain modifications. Construction actually got started in June 1962. We sold the old house very quickly and rented a place in the valley in May. Cyril was barely one year old; the other kids had to go to school from a bit of a distance. Jeannine even canned peaches and tomatoes there at the rental house and Mom and Dad came down to have Thanksgiving there. Our house was built—with frayed nerves and cost over-runs—and we moved in, in December 1962, with so little furniture the place looked bare. We had a visit from Herman and Marge and bought a davenport that made into a bed for the occasion.

Papa had been extremely helpful. His shop by that time was well-equipped and he and I made many of the built-ins, of fine quality. Mamie did her share, too, by helping with the children and meals. When Mom and Dad came down to help (over Thanksgiving), Dad and Jeannine did a great deal of painting. However, as with all family projects, some things were put off to be done later; and when we moved away 26 years later, some were still not done. Judging one's abilities is so difficult.

The Twinkle Experiment changed my life. Until then, I had thought of myself as a scientist of a team, working primarily on the effects of nuclear explosion. After then, I became a person with a mission—even several missions. I will go over the important events.

In preparation for the 1962 high altitude test series (at Johiston I) , wherein a particular burst was to occur at 400 km altitude, many individual studies were initiated by both the AEC and the military support groups. People at Sandia got involved by trying to predict the size of the fireball at 400 km. The usual Sachs scaling laws were applied with unsatisfactory results. I attempted a quasi-nova type calculation on the basis of equations in Chandrasekhar's book *Stellar Structure*. But no one believed that either. Tom Cook was sympathetic and urged me to take it to LASL; but I was too unsure of myself. My result, however, gave a fireball that was very small and short lived, merely a twinkle. This, of course, raised the question of whether it could be seen against the star background. Cameras were carefully timed to catch the instant of explosion, but still there was an uncertainly of position.

At about this time, Gordy McClure had invited a visitor from University of Ohio astronomy department to speak at a Colloquium on the subject of computing the orbits of small planets (invisible except in good telescopes) around the sun. They were very strange orbits. I had dinner with this man and with Gordy, and during the conversation, the question of astronomical seeing arose. He had quite a bit of experience in this area and told me that under extreme conditions (usually near the horizon) it was possible for a star image to disappear for a fraction of a second. It was also possible for images to remain very steady for minutes—but under conditions of very poor general seeing. My quasi-nova calculation led to a visibility time of a microsecond, hence the concern. I believe, as I think back, that the question was also raised by a co-worker Bob Harris, possibly also Jim Hoffman. I began to study the theory of star twinkling and other scintillation effects and realized that here was a field just opening up which had been around for 200 years or more. The theory of turbulence had been advanced enough by the Russians (Kolmogorov) to permit simple models to be initiated.

The LASL calculations of fireball size led to longer durations and appreciable diameters so there was little worry that I could be right. On the other hand, if they were somewhat wrong in the direction of smallness, then new instruments should be installed. As time passed and the test date approached, the question resolved itself in favor of the LASL calculations (others also confirmed it), so a twinkle test was not really needed; but I was allowed to go ahead anyway to plan an experiment using the facility at Tonapah, Nevada.

A rocket was to be fired into the air in such a way that two or three tracking telescopes could be used to follow it down. On its nose was to be a bright lamp. It was to fall with little drift, very little sideways motion and a rapid but not free-fall motion. The rocket design required the use of a long U-238 nose (!) so it had to be recovered (and was). Its vertical position was measured by radar. Its altitude was 100,000 feet. With all these requirements (and others, such as accurate weather jet stream prediction), the Sandia facility was about the only place in the Western world where Project Twinkle could take place, except over coastal waters where observation would be poor. You see, it's best if the light trajectory approaches the observing cameras.

As I recall it, there were two tests, one in March 1963 and one in November 1963. I gave a not-very-good report to the department; the data had not been processed. We found that the principal contribution to scintillation occurred at about the tropopause, with relatively little below. A more detailed analysis showed that there was a frequency shift of the spectrum (the Kolmogorov number) from high to low in coming down.

These results were published in *Nature Magazine*[8] and picked up by *Time Magazine*.[9] On the basis of these results, I was asked to prepare a book. I accepted—but I never should have. The Book started out modestly enough; but I let it grow into a much too complete study. Without being very aware of what was happening, I tried to include all aspects of irregular wave propagation at a time when the effects of turbulence were being reported in a literature that was growing exponentially—and is scarcely slowing down now 20 years later. So the Book was too ambitious and I had to give it up without finishing it. This turned out to be much greater disappointment than I imagined at the time.

This ends Craig's own retelling of his life story.

~ ~ ~ ~

8. [Editor's Note] Hudson, Craig C., *Experimental Evidence of a Twinkling Layer in the Earth's Atmosphere.*

9. [Editor's Note] Time Magazine, *Astronomy: The Twinkle Belt .*

Craig had been writing his family's genealogy stories and his life story off and on for about ten years before his death, balancing his time between painting, traveling, writing essays, family commitments, and dealing with health issues. Craig's health finally deteriorated to such a degree that he was unable to write and sadly he did not continue the telling of his life story past his descriptions of the mid-1960s.

The journey of his life, though, took him down several different paths worthy of note. Although Craig marveled on Jeannine's regular volume of letters to her parents, he himself kept up a monthly correspondence with his parents until their deaths, as well as with other family and friends. Many of these letters have been returned to us. Craig also journaled several of the trips that he and Jeannine took and Jeannine maintained well-documented photograph albums (30 volumes). With the help of these riches and the memories of my siblings, friends and family, the following is my compilation of the remaining years of Craig's life.

Elianne Hudson

PART 2

11

Settling in New Mexico with Family and Work

As soon as Craig and Jeannine had purchased their first house in Albuquerque, they were immediately drawn to improving the garden. Surely much of this feeling was due to the shock of such a dramatic change in environment from Oregon to New Mexico.

> *"For the past two weeks we have been very concerned with the yard and prospective garden. Bob has taken us twice to a nursery and we bought a peach, apple and pear tree (Anjou pear, don't remember the others) at about $4 apiece and a good sized seedless grape vine ($2.50). We are very happy with the prospects, although at the present time they are just sticks in the ground. The grape and pear are large enough to bear this year.*
>
> *We are going back soon to get raspberries and boysenberries. I have written to two west coast nurseries for literature but things like that have to be planted here before March and I am afraid they'll never make it, even tho I think I would prefer Oregon plantings. The nurseryman says almost everything does well here, although some have to have special soil consideration and artificial shade. At least we are going to have wonderful tomatoes, lettuce, cucumbers and melons. I know those do well in the sun. . .*
>
> *The soil in this place is very nice indeed. I spaded up in half an hour a plot some 5x20 feet—it is darker than Bob's was, more*

189

humus, and still is sandy. When dry, however, it becomes quite
hard. At the present time there is plenty of moisture."[1]

Albuquerque, by 1950, had become a rapidly growing metropolis with
a population of about 98,000 people. Kirtland Air Force Base and Sandia
Laboratory were the two large employers. By the mid-1950s more than
4,000 people were employed by Sandia and the city's population had grown
to 175,000. Route 66 went through Albuquerque and delivered tourists to
the area. Commercial building kept pace with new housing and soon there
were shopping centers, a new city hall and bank buildings. By 1960, Albuquerque's population reached just over 200,000.[2]

At the beginnings of Sandia Laboratory, the Sandia site (Sandia Base)
was about 6 miles from Albuquerque. Many Sandia employees lived in
housing on Sandia Base and found it prohibitive to go into Albuquerque
for entertainment. The AEC and Sandia (which were co-located on Sandia
Base) decided they needed a community center and construction on Coro-
nado Club began in 1949. By the end of 1950, the Club had 1000 members.
In the 1950s, '60s, and '70s these private clubs were quite the rage. The Club,
providing Sandia and AEC a centralized forum for recreation, included a
four-lane bowling alley and game rooms in the basement, dining and bar
facilities on the main floor, and swimming pool and patio outside. It gave
Craig and Jeannine the opportunity to meet and socialize with many of
Craig's co-workers and their families as well as meeting new people. Jeannine's records show that she was cooking and entertaining at the house by
1957. Many of these people remained close friends with Craig and Jeannine
for years to come.

During their years in Oregon, camping was an activity enjoyed by both
Craig and Jeannine. It wasn't until 1955 that Craig and Jeannine and Marc
went camping in the Southwest. Their first trip was to camp at Canyon de
Chelly in Arizona. The two young girls remained with Mamie and Papa.
The trip had been arranged by friends from the Mountain Club[3]. At that
time the school district scheduled a two-day teacher's convention in October, making a four-day weekend for students and their families. This was an
opportune time to camp with autumn in the air, the cottonwoods turned
golden, and *usually* good weather. This trip to Canyon de Chelly in 1955 was
the first of what was to become a treasured annual family visit.

1. Letter from Craig to 'Mom and Dad,' 13 January 1953.

2. [Editor's Note] Albuquerque Historical Society, *Statehood Economy 1945-now*.

3. [Editor's Note] Albuquerque Mountain Club, established in 1952.

(1969) "We went to Canyon de Chelly again this year, in the teeth of a building storm, with Suzy to replace Marc. The weather turned out to be magnificent while we were there. Warm days and nights, no wind, the canyon floor was running with more water than we had ever seen (it's been a very wet year) and we had to wade across to White House . . . While we were there this year, we found a new trail down to the canyon floor. It is shorter and far less steep than the other one; I wish we had known about it when you were here because I am sure you would have enjoyed seeing the cliffs and bottom sands more closely. It follows a cleft in the rock that appears at first sight very rugged; but actually is made easy by stairs cut in the sandstone that weave in and out of crevices."[4]

In the early years, camping consisted of old Army down-filled sleeping bags on Army cots, all obtained by Craig from Army surplus. Shelter was provided by two large tarps overlapped and suspended by rope between trees. Camping became a yearly activity for the family until well into the 80s and in a letter to his parents in October 1982 he says they had *"come here 27 consecutive years less one (on that year we learned of a storm soon enough to change plans, and we went to White Sands)."[5]*

In addition to the annual trip to Canyon de Chelly in October, a springtime camping trip to Chaco Canyon was also for many years an annual event. In the years that no summer road trip to Oregon was planned, the family planned summer camping trips in New Mexico or Colorado.

Within two years of moving to New Mexico, Craig lost two family members who had had an impact on his life: HS Hudson in 1953 and Uncle Maurice in 1954.

"It was a very unpleasant surprise to hear of the death of Uncle Maurice. I have written letters of condolence to Ivy, Grandma and Bev and Bud and writing them brought back a flood of memories mostly of long ago when we were all children and Uncle Maurice was an uncle to me. I know you must be seeing these old times and hearing whispering voices of long ago, too, times when everything wasn't so serious. It is difficult to exhaust deep seated emotions like this. When you are calm and quiet on the outside no one suspects the grief that you feel in your heart. It would be this way with me if my brother or a sister died and I extend to you my heartfelt sympathies.

4. Letter from Craig to 'Mom and Dad,' 15 November 1969.

5. Letter from Craig to 'Dad,' 20 October 1982.

I think Uncle Maurice had lived out the most of a full satisfy-
ing life and must not have felt fear or repugnance of death. It is
more evident to me here, however, being out of constant personal
contact with them, that the spirit of men like granddad and Uncle
Maurice never dies. You tell me of the death but it is not of my
own experience. For me their actions and their personalities are as
alive as ever. I get a lump in my throat when I think that I would
not be able to see them were I to go there. But the real man is as
much alive to me now as ever because I have the memory of his life
locked up in my own mind. Grandad Palmer, too, is a man who
has gained in stature with his death. He never did a great thing in
his life, in a social or economic way. But in another way he was a
great man; he was always kind and good and honest and did not
hold unkind thoughts against anyone.

And let me add a little more, Dad. It always seems inappro-
priate, when we are together or merely exchanging letters, to say
these things; but I would like you to know that I think you are a
great and fine man, too. It is not everyone's way to do big things in
the public eye; it is at least as important to be a stalwart, respected
man of moderate tastes and mild manner, a support for your so-
ciety. This is the man I believe you have been and I hope I can do
as well."[6]

During those first few years of becoming acquainted with Albuquerque, they discovered the valley area where the Rio Grande River cuts a winding path, north to south, through the city. Here they eventually purchased
one acre of land in the North Valley not far from the Rio Grande River on
Los Arboles ('the trees' in Spanish) Street from Mr. L. C. Bolles. Mr. Bolles
was a horticulturist by profession and lover of trees. He had planted many
trees on his several acres of property. Craig and Jeannine's new property
included a black walnut tree, catalpa, honey locust, Osage orange, juniper,
several different variety of apple trees, and towering cypress.

The new house design included aspects of Spanish, American, and
French architecture. The living rooms were situated around a large gathering area in the middle. The center gathering area was designed it to be
a formal dining area with a cork floor for dance parties. The central area
maintained a feel of openness and light with tall windows reaching up to
cathedral ceilings. The large and well-appointed kitchen was designed to
the specifications of master-cook Jeannine. While one had easy access to the
formal dining room from the kitchen, Jeannine's French heritage required

6. Ibid., 7 October 1954.

that she be able to close off the kitchen's controlled chaos from the elegance of the dining area.

Craig continued to have occasional heart difficulties. In January 1962 Jeannine writes to Craig's parents *"Craig's heart has been misbehaving and worrying us. He has been home all this time with a very erratic heart beat which causes him to feel weak and dizzy."* Craig followed up with a letter relating it to his past history of heart difficulties.

> *"I hope you are not too alarmed about my heart difficulty. It is not an entirely new thing for me—the first time I recall clearly a heart flutter was on the bus one morning going to Washington high school—but certainly this last siege was far more severe than anything I had experienced before . . . the doctor restricted coffee especially, but also alcohol. He also prescribed a medicine which is effective in stopping the spurious beats. But the most important step of all was to recognize the difficulty for what it was and not worry about its being something else. I am convinced that the worry was the major part of my difficulty."[7]*

For years to come, Jeannine enjoyed planning and preparing elegant meals. Both Craig and Jeannine enjoyed the social interaction with stimulating friends and acquaintances. Craig's involvement with the Colloquium allowed them to meet many interesting people.

> *"The Hudson house is beginning to be a sort of cross-roads. I think I mentioned to you Prof. Chen's visit in Sept and the visit of the 4 Africans in Aug. To this we must now add the visit of Prof. René Picard, who we knew at Oregon, but who returned to France in 1952, married, and was on his way to Oregon again this fall. Then Dr. Dick Carter (Libby's husband) came down to a medical meeting at Santa Fe. . . There was also an official of the French AEC, whose name I've forgotten in Sept. And finally, there was Mr. Keita in Oct, assistant cabinet minister of defense for the little nation of Upper Volta. He was, of course, a Negro. We have become very respectful of the Africans—they are cultured, intelligent, and well trained in government . . ."[8]*

Jeannine kept meticulous record of her planned menus for dinner parties. She noted the names of guests invited as well as her planned menu.

The Los Arboles property was a constant work-in-progress as Craig and Jeannine enjoyed adding trees, flower beds, vegetable gardens, and pathways. Some trees were eventually taken out while new varieties were

7. Letter from Craig to 'Mother and Dad,' 20 January 1962.

8. Ibid, 12 October 1964.

added. And, always, the climate continued to be a tribulation to Craig's 'ultimate garden' dream.

> "I have my plans all drawn and approved and building permit issued to construct a new tool house to replace the one that burned last January. The insurance company made a very reasonable settlement that will allow us to rebuild it close to the house behind the carport . . . They also gave us an allowance for some cypress trees that were burned, and we have used the money to replant with arbor vitae . . .
>
> Our weather here has been exceptionally balmy the last few weekends, getting up to 60 and 65°. This was fortunate because I have a large amount of digging to do. First the irrigation ditches have to be dug; then the excavation for the new tool house; and finally this spring I have to dig our well down 4 feet because it is no longer pumping water. Marc has become very useful and has more or less cheerfully helped with much of the work. It is a pleasure to work with him.
>
> We have put in a number of trees and flowering shrubs. I am being quite careful now to choose the hardiest ones. We usually have nighttime temperatures of zero in the winter, and half the time the temperature drops to -10° or so. . . twice I have tried to grow raspberries here but the plants don't grow well. Could it be too cold? Also my boysenberries stay alive but don't bear. Do they need full sun?"[9]

The weather wasn't always accommodating but even when it was hot, they could find enjoyment in the coolness of the evenings. Jeannine described it with obvious fondness in a letter Craig's parents: "Our street is so quiet and full of honeysuckles in bloom that almost every night we go out just before bedtime, only the two of us, and we have a pleasant stroll in the dark.[10]

9. Ibid, 8 March 1965.

10. Letter from Jeannine to Craig's 'Mom and Dad,' 22 June 1965.

Camping in New Mexico, (L to R) Cassandra, Craig, Jeannine, M. Dumas, Mme Dumas (behind M. Dumas), Marc, Elianne (behind Marc), 1956

Camping in the Southwest, Craig, holding infant Cyril, 1961

Newly constructed house, 1962

Family portrait, (L to R, bottom) Cassandra, Cyril, Elianne, (L to R, top) Jeannine,
Craig, Marc, 1964

Jeannine and Craig at Albuquerque airport, 1963

12

A Flourishing Family and Working at Sandia to Retirement

1966—1972

In March 1966 Craig's brother, Dexter, was hospitalized after suffering a severe stroke. His left side was severely affected and he never fully recovered. After a year he was moved from the VA Hospital in Portland to a nursing home. The family felt that Dexter would receive better care at the hospital but as Dexter's son, David, recalls, the hospital was overburdened with injured soldiers from the Vietnam conflict. This calamity was a devastating blow to Dexter's wife and two children as well as the entire Hudson clan.

Dexter lingered for many years with some of the family watching and wondering if there would be any improvement. Rosie, Dexter's wife, had to continue to work and keep her family going. Craig and Jeannine were a good emotional support for her.

> "Dexter is the same as when you saw him last summer. About six weeks ago I had him to the V.A. Hospital for his check up and they [can] find no change . . . the folks still live in their dream world about Dex and his ability to recover . . . Craig, I believe you are the only one of the family that understands what happens when [there] has been brain damage as extensive as Dexter's was.[1]

---

1. Letter from Rosie Hudson to 'Craig and Jeannine,' 6 June 1968.

198

Craig understood his parents desire to see improvement and wrote many letters of encouragement. He also wrote of his sympathy for Rosie's plight.

> "We received a nice letter from Rosie recently . . . and we must sympathize with her plight deeply. She seems to be suffering very little from loss of physical things, but Dexter's disaster wrings her and the children out. Dex seems to be less aware of the tragedy than the family, for which we may be grateful.
>
> I hope he can be induced to better his condition slowly. Expecting a full recovery no longer seems possible . . . "[2]

November 1968 was an important year in politics and Craig and his parents added that conversation to their letters of family affairs.

> "Yes, we too were very pleased to see the change in political power. Here in NM it was really dramatic. Nixon won by a far larger margin than nationally. Republican gov. Cargo also won in spite of the opposition of the newspapers, many professional groups and the 2 to 1 advantage of Democratic registration. Also, our 2 Demo representatives were unseated. When you think that, in those three cases, the Demos were the better men, the voters are really trying to oppose the party policies of the past few years. That's what we did."[3]

Taxes were always a topic of conversation. Craig and Jeannine were young homeowners with four children. Craig's parents were living on a fixed income.

> "About now, Albuquerque is jumping on the band wagon of high taxes, too. You know we have a sales tax of 4% (1 for Alb, 3 for the state). 'We' have just voted a big increase in state income tax to cover the soaring cost of education in Alb. Schools. 'We' have also just increased property taxes by 30% at least. There seems to be no end in sight for tax increases, and no one is willing to cut off anything the money buys."[4]

By the late '60s, the situation at Sandia Laboratory was beginning to change with the shifting of politics and military funding.

2. Letter from Craig to 'Mom and Dad,' 10 July 1968.
3. Ibid, 11 Nov 1968.
4. Ibid, 8 Feb 1969.

(March 1969) "My office is in one of its periodic upsets now, a reorganization that makes everyone feel nervous. Not about job security, but worry about finishing favorite projects."[5]

(November 1969) "My year-long efforts to get a program started at Sandia finally seem to be working out. On the basis of my Ajax study, which showed the feasibility of making remote observations of surface conditions on the Moon, Mars and Venus with Sandia developed technology, we are finally making contact with NASA. This would be a much less expensive way to get some of the information NASA is after, and would be an exciting thing for us to work on."

(April 1970) "My working situation is changed again. I have known for some time that this was coming. The old freelance group I was with has broken up, and now I must spend more of my time on specific technical programs. The free-lance work was very exciting—it lasted for 5 year—but now it's over and I must get back to more mundane problems. During that time, however, I initiated some studies which are continuing and which are very interesting: underwater light transmission, planetary exploration by probes, radio transmission in a nuclear fireball, and the transient response of the human eye to flashes of light, to name the most appealing to me."[6]

Craig's work often required that he travel. The prospect of a trip in the summer of 1969 to Washington D.C. was too much for Jeannine to pass up. So the two of them traveled together and in D. C. enjoyed visiting museums as they had in Paris. They managed to include a visit to old friends: Herman and Marge Johansen.

"Last week I had to make a trip to Wash D C and Jeannine wanted to go with me, to replace the vacation we had planned together but missed. Since Pittsburg is on the way, we stopped by there to see Herman and Marge . . . It was one of the pleasant visits in memory. Then we went on to DC and while I attended my meeting, J took tours, visited museums, had a wonderful time. She'd never been there before. She is one of the few people who can say she walked thru the Smithsonian barefoot because her feet hurt! We did get together for a few things: two nice dinners, the Nat'l Gallery of Art, the Lincoln Memorial . . . "[7]

5. Letter from Craig to 'Mom and Dad and Boyers,' 1 March 1969.
6. Letter from Craig to 'Mom and Dad,' 15 November 1969, 5 April 1970.
7. Ibid, 27 July 1969.

In August 1969, Marc married and, shortly after, joined the Army. He wanted to take advantage of the training the Army offered and he chose meteorology. He enlisted for three years to avoid the draft. After completing the training (April 1970), he would be assigned to a post.

> *"[Marc] believes he is to be assigned to central Alaska. He is quite thrilled and so are we all. He will have a chance to retrace some of his dad's footsteps, will be pretty much out of danger, and will learn a great deal from that experience."*[8]

Confirmation came in April 1970 for Marc to be stationed for two years in Alaska near Fairbanks. *"Suzie plans to join him in Alaska some time in June. Things may be a bit rough for her there but she is determined and courageous . . ."*[9] commented Jeannine about Marc's wife in a joint letter with Craig.

During the holiday season of 1971, the family suffered another death in the family. On December 31, 1971, Papa died in his sleep from heart failure. He had suffered a heart attack earlier in the year. Mamie was devastated; Jeannine made all the arrangements for the funeral.

> *"Jeannine had planned it to have an elegance that is relatively uncommon and the testimony of the presence of so many friends and associates (ours as well as the Dumas') made it a heart-warming affair, even in the midst of grief . . .*
>
> *Mme Dumas chose to receive flowers (instead of the cold gifts to a fund that are becoming common these days) and the chapel was filled to overflowing, with flowers even down the aisles . . .*
>
> *The estate (what a grand word for these small holdings!) will have to be settled pretty soon. Mr. Dumas' good name and the work he left behind him are the greatest part of it. Some people have already come to the shop asking to buy anything there, even little trial carvings, anything having his name associated with it."*[10]

The year (1972) was difficult for Craig and Jeannine. In addition to the sudden and devastating death of Papa, there were changes coming to Sandia. The climate for jobs in science in the '70s was quite different than during the '60s. There was more reorganization at Sandia; Craig and his friends were concerned. There were fewer jobs and many young scientists applying for every job.

---

8. Ibid, 5 April 1970.

9. Letter from Craig and Jeannine to 'Mom and Dad,' 12 April 1970.

10. Letter from Craig to 'Mom and Dad,' 8 January 1972.

"Last Friday, I was notified that my 21-year-old relationship with Sandia will come to an end as of 29 June 1973. As you can see, that day marks my 55th birthday, and according to the new rules, I can (and must) retire. The conditions of retirement are fairly liberal. I will receive ¾ year salary separation bonus plus 1/3 my present monthly salary each month as long as I live and in any case until all the retirement money is used up. I shall also have some other benefits not yet specified. Others were not so lucky . . .

Well, it's a shock to be terminated, but really I can not shed too many tears. In recent years the excitement of working at Sandia had pretty much disappeared, partly due to the change of management and partly due to curtailment of AEC funds for Sandia. The Bell management just about killed the laboratory by refusing to allow various groups to bring in new sources of funds when weapons money declined. We were not sorry to see the weapons money go—that indicates easing of tensions—but we sure hated to see the lab crumble. Even now it may crumble, tho the new pres. hopes to build it back. It is still rumor, but stories have it that a large part of the old Sandia management are walking out—people I know. LASL is still healthy. Their management actively invited other work as weapons declined.

My retirement money will assure that we do not want; but in order to maintain the house, I shall have to get another position . . .[11]

Also during that year, decisions had to be made about the property and building that made up Papa's shop. It was decided to keep the property. The front half of the building would be converted into two apartments, while maintaining the rear half as a woodworking shop for Craig and Marc (and potentially Cyril).

Housed within the shop were all of Papa's supply of special woods and all of his tools. In addition, over the years Papa had collected, sometimes in trade, pieces of fine wood for later use, such as carved wood panels, table legs, even a solid wood cabinet. For a number of years, Marc, Craig, and Cyril did make use of the shop. In later years much of the wood and tools from Papa's shop was relocated to the small shop space at the Los Arboles property giving Craig easier access for his projects. As Cyril grew older, much of the wood and tools were also incorporated into his own woodworking endeavors.

Mamie's social security was not sufficient to keep up with the costs and taxes on the property with the house as well as the property with the

11. Ibid, 25 February 1972.

shop. An attempt to rent or lease the shop was unsuccessful. Finally it was decided to convert the front portion of the building into two apartments. Much had to be done to the structure of the building, however. In addition to new walls and fixtures, the floor had to be cut out so that sewer and water systems could be installed where needed and insulation was added. Craig, Marc and a friend planned to do the remodeling themselves to save cost.

> "... Of course, money will have to be borrowed, but even paying back plus operating costs still leaves a good margin for her [Mamie]. She is quite anxious, naturally, but understands the problem and sees that this is the best course of action ...
>
> We are expecting to start work on the apartments in mid-March. Since we cannot put much time in, even with the help of a friend, they will not be finished until mid-summer. I will have free time after the end of June so that anything left over will be completed in July."[12]

Mamie was very anxious about the progress of the work, the noise, the changes to the property, etc. In June, Elianne went to France as an exchange student from June 1972 to June 1973. A continuous correspondence between Elianne and Mamie served as some distraction during the construction of the apartments. The process was longer than they expected but the apartments were finished and rented, and did supply Mamie with an income until she sold the property in 1990 to move in with Craig and Jeannine.

12. Ibid, 25 February 1972.

13

Switching Places from Workplace to Home

In June of 1973 Craig's retirement became official. As with all the transitions in his life he looked forward to what was to come. A man with his background and years of experience could be of value as a consultant. With a serious reduction in monthly income, Craig and Jeannine were also concerned about maintaining their home for the coming years. By the end of that retirement year he had obtained more than one consulting contract. The largest was with GE TEMPO.

> *(Nov 1973) "I have signed one consulting contract, probably the largest one, and expect to begin work in a few weeks. I know the second one is coming along and I should sign it this month."*
>
> *(June 1974) "My work at GE seems to be settling out at about 5 days ($500) per month, which is just great. It leaves me time to do other necessary things, and the work is interesting . . .*
>
> *Before our money ran out, we decided it would be best to get some extra . . . So we took out a second mortgage. . .we are very happy now that our ownership of it is not endangered because we love it here. We'd like to be free to travel to Oregon, though."*
>
> *(July 1974) "My work with G E TEMPO has been very satisfactory so far. I have had two months' work of about 4 days each . . . The happy part of the story is that I seem to be moving toward*

some rather permanent work programs for them in which I can continue to participate, so that the work will extend into the future as far as I wish. It is work that I like, and the rate of pay is more than I asked for in the contract. I think I could probably push the amount of activity up to 10 days a month if I needed to. The other contract, with CSC, has not yet produced a penny and I am thinking of terminating it."[1]

By 1974 Mamie's apartments were rentable and there was less concern about her income. The year began with the birth of Craig and Jeannine's first grandchild, Alethea, born to Marc and Suzie in January. In addition, attention turned to plans for a spring wedding at the Los Arboles house for Elianne.

By the summer, Jeannine had realized that her position as ballet teacher would not expand into more than it was—a much-enjoyed but nominal-paying position. She began to look for employment positions. She eventually went to an employment agency for help finding a position. The result was an offer by the agency for a position of jobs counselor with the company; Jeannine accepted the position. Although only the youngest child, Cyril 13 years old, remained at home fulltime, Jeannine's work schedule brought new aspects to the already new situation of Craig's retirement.

(June 1974) "Today is a momentous one for us. Jeannine begins to work at her new job. It means a complete reordering of our lives—I have to take over some of the household chores, she has to settle into a fixed routine.

No specific plans were made before her ballet performance. She had been looking around, but didn't take anything very seriously. Then she went to all the personnel placement agencies. Some immediately undertook to place her, and some considered her for a position in their own offices as counselor. She finally chose the latter and begins training in Snelling & Snelling, one of the largest national organizations. She will be assured of making about $4000 per year, and her boss tells her she may exceed $10,000 . . .

We were a little worried, however. My work was slow starting and J. wasn't confident she could sell herself. Counseling doesn't require an education, just a level head and a pleasant personality; so she felt this would be the best thing to try. And her confidence grew as she searched."

(July 1974) "Jeannine is just now finishing her study-work period with the employment agency and is to take her state exam Friday. She has been making a little money (about $300/month)

1. Ibid, 3 November 1973, 5 June 1974, 1 July 1974.

and soon hopes to double that. But most important of all, she feels that she is becoming important. The ballet was beginning to look more and more like a dead end. Her recent success, certainly the best thing she had ever done, was not likely to be repeated very soon, and didn't pay anything—which we have to think about now. Teaching simply does not have the potential we need."[2]

Jeannine reported to Harvey and Bertha in July of that year that Craig "*is very helpful with cooking and cleaning up after dinner and breakfast. Since he is home most of the time he is also 'mother' to Cyril.*" As Cyril was still in school, the scheduling worked out well for Craig to take on a teaching job at Menaul High School, a private school in Albuquerque. He taught math and physics during the 1974–75 school year. By the following year the money concerns were beginning to ease.

> "*I just returned from a consulting trip to Mississippi (Corps of Engineers Lab). It's beautiful there. I have a task to try to develop a municipal transit system for Albuquerque. It will be a challenge. I'm also opening up a business in technical writing. Jeannine is very busy, and quite successful, in her placement profession. Times are slowly improving.*"[3]

Craig and Jeannine's house and garden continued to give them much pleasure. Every spring Craig would ready the vegetable garden, the ditch irrigation system, and enjoy planning the year's crops. These usually included tomatoes, zucchini, and green beans with the occasional venture into corn, grapes, asparagus, raspberries, and blackberries. The several types of apple trees, the plum trees and a quince bush regularly produced fruit. The growing season was long but uncertain from year to year because of the possibility of late or early hard frosts as well as extended very dry and hot conditions.

> *(Nov 1973) "Our garden has been fabulous this year. Jeannine froze about 15 pounds of beans, and I just picked the last of them Nov 1! Our apple crop has been excellent. J. made jelly from our blue damson plums and it tastes like boysenberry."*
>
> *(July 1974) "The weather here has been record-breaking hot. Never in all the years that records have been kept has the temperature been so high (105) nor lasted so high so long (17 consecutive days over 98 and still going). Naturally, it has been hard on everyone. . .but it has been good for the garden. Yesterday I picked a ripe tomato from my own plant before July for the first time ever.*

2. Ibid, 5 June 1974, 1 July 1974.
3. Ibid, 30 October 1975.

*Last year had been a complete bust for tomatoes, but this year is
going to be fine. However, I fear there will be no fruit; late freeze."
(Oct 1975) "The delphiniums were one small plot of my garden
this year. Overall, it was much more successful than it had been
last year. We still have ½ bushel of tomatoes ripening to eat. It has
now frosted and everything has stopped growing."*[4]

Many celebrations took place in the house or on the property: holiday
parties, dinner parties, Easter picnics and egg hunts, Halloween parties,
Fourth of July picnics and celebrations. In the early years the back section
of the property, which had not been cleared for the house, was full of trees
and underbrush—much to the delight of the children—with only one or
two undefined pathways. In springtime, under the blossoming apple trees
in front of the house was the spot for picnics. Later a large picnic table was
built behind the house in the shade of the trees for picnics, formal and informal. Craig and Jeannine continued to enjoy entertaining and Jeannine
could make even a simple picnic a delightful repast.

Over the years, their group of close friends grew to include 4–6 regu-
lars. Even a birthday, spring picnic or holiday get-together of "family and
friends" could involve a dozen or more people. The large gathering room in
the center of the house served as both formal dining room and entertaining
space. Furniture was limited and could be moved to nearer to the walls to
allow for dancing or when the number of guests was small, furniture was
moved closer together to allow a cozier setting. Christmas celebrations always made use of the large gathering room with its tall ceiling to house a tall
tree. Over the years, the house was the venue for anniversaries and several
family wedding celebrations. Jeannine and Mamie, with help from Craig,
always planned and cooked for these occasions.

In January 1976 Craig had back surgery from which he recovered
quickly and fully. Craig never revisited his childhood experience with Christian Science religion; he was always dedicated to science and retained his
curiosity about how the world worked—even during a painful back ailment.

(Jan 1976) *"At about Christmas time, I began to have a rather
sore back and pain began to travel down my right leg. The inten-
sity increased during the holidays and eventually I began to need
medication to control the pain and to be able to sleep at all. The
pains passed into the muscles of my right leg and foot, and my
toes and foot grew numb. If I tried to walk very far, more than a
few hundred feet, my right leg began to weaken and failed to keep
pace.*

4. Ibid, 3 November 1973, 1 July 1974, 30 October 1975.

So I went to see our doctor, who is the one who gave the rather strong pills to control the pain, and he referred me to a bone surgeon. His initial diagnosis was that I had a ruptured disc (the buffer between vertebras), so I went into the hospital a week ago yesterday (Jan 7). For that first week, I lay 'in traction,' with weights pulling to stretch my back bone and to encourage the disc to pull back to normal. I also had a 'heat treatment,' a hot pack on my back for 20 minutes a day.

But after the week, very little improvement could be noticed. I felt good in traction and under the heat pad, but within a few hours (over night), the problem was back again and I had to take the pain killers.

Consequently, yesterday I underwent some diagnostic tests to clarify the situation. The first one consisted of pushing little electrodes into the right leg muscles to see the position and character of nerve impulses. Sure enough, the impulses of the painful muscles showed abnormalities which could be traced to a point on my right hip. The second one, a mylogram, consisted of an ingenious (and rather painful) experiment on the fluid of my spine. It is normally transparent to X-rays, so a hollow needle was inserted between vertebrae into the spinal canal and a fluid was slowly injected which was opaque to X-rays. The X-rays then showed in outline the nature of the problem. I was able to see the picture myself on the fluoroscope . . . As they tilted me, the dyed fluid sloshed around. The doctor even touched the nerve (with the needle) next to the bulbous disc and I felt a sharp twinge pass down into my numb toes . . .

His solution is to remove the offending bulb surgically (a lamenectomy) after which he believes things will return to normal."

(May 1976) *"My back is quite strong now and I have been working in the garden regularly. I don't try to lift heavy things (I keep it below 30 lbs) but this still leaves me with essentially no disability."*[5]

Although it seems there was discussion about Craig and Jeannine moving the family back to Oregon, they decided against it. They continued to make trips to Oregon every couple of years and enjoyed both worlds. They usually drove, but as air travel became more convenient and less expensive, and as they had to juggle two work schedules, they occasionally flew.

(April 1976) *" . . . we will not permanently leave Albuquerque. There have been times in the last 2 years when I thought of selling out here, but it would be a hardship to do so. My health insurance plan, which has been good for all of us, is invalid outside the*

5. Ibid, 15 January 1976, 1 May 1976.

Albuquerque area. Jeannine fears for her and Cyril's health in a damp climate (perhaps unjustifiably). I could not do consulting up there (it's a funny business—depends on friendships). And we love our self-designed house more and more. And there is Mrs. Dumas . . . So I see us as visitors to Oregon rather than as residents."

(Aug 1976) "We arrived home on schedule after a very pleasant trip. First thrill was flying just to the south of and a few thousand feet above the peak of Mt. Hood. Every detail was sharp and clear since the air was transparent. I had never had such a close look at Mt. Hood before! And we could see mountains from Mt. Adams to Broken Top beyond the Three Sisters. A magnificent panorama . . .

Arriving at Denver, there were rain storms all over the mountains, which looked beautiful in the setting sunlight . . .

The flight from Denver to Albuquerque was made in 1 hour, just after sunset. Storm clouds piled high on every side, but we rose above them and sailed peacefully along just over their tops. What a marvelous view to see the boiling cloud tops apparently frozen in place, with quiet 'meadows' here and deep, dark 'canyons' there. The predominant colors were rose and violet . . .

It is hard indeed to leave all that lush greenery and the wonderful tastes of sea food. But our dry atmosphere does have some compensations and I have become quite fond of chili!"[6]

After two years working at Snelling & Snelling, the changing civil rights laws and the politics of the day were having an impact. Jeannine was uncertain that her position as employment counselor would continue to be advantageous.

"Jeannine is very upset just now. Her job seems to be running on hard times and she is in the process of looking for another. Not only are applicants very few for the jobs available (but there are many many unqualified applicants), but the recent civil rights legislation is making things difficult. She may not say if the applicant is white or colored, of course; she may not give his religion. But she also may not say if he(!) is male or female, nor give his age nor his birthdate nor his state of health nor his education. So the purpose of her being there is being eroded. Naturally the entire office is pretty upset. One office in the East is being sued by the Labor Department for giving information about an applicant, and she visualizes the action moving across the country. She is worried about even giving the name of the applicant because Lucero or Chan or Goldstein, etc, have racial associations. She is not allowed to make notes even to herself about these matters because

6. Ibid, 1 April 1976, 31 Aug 1976.

inspectors have access to the records and personal notes and such information could lead to a labor suit.

I doubt very much if the people who drafted the age and sex discrimination law imagined that it would be used in this way. Jeannine (and her co-workers) are unusually exposed because they are so tightly regulated. But employers in general are treating the law quite differently. They want to hire a male, 20–30 yrs old, high school education, etc, for a particular job. And they find excuses to reject every one else who applied. For the employer, it is selection, for every one else it is discrimination, against the law.

Where this will end is anyone's guess. Some liberties are going to be trampled in the name of protecting other liberties. The Supreme Court is going to have to make some pretty tough decisions in the coming years. Civil libertarians have had their day, and I foresee a swing away, toward social and employer liberties, in the future, but the legal process is so slow.

So right now, J is in the delicate position of trying to find a new job without yet giving up the old one. It is certainly making her upset, and I can sympathize. I hold her hand and try to make things pleasant at home; but in the end, she is the one who has to fight the battle . . .

I remember reading in my history books about the collapse of the Middle Ages in Europe because the regulations about who could work on what and where became too restrictive. I wonder if we are not approaching that situation in this country.[7]

Jeannine soon found another avenue for her talents. By September she was training with New York Life Insurance Company, a company she would remain with until retirement. Craig's consulting work which had had up-swings and down-swings was now keeping him challenged.

(July 1976) "Jeannine is almost certain now to leave Snelling and go to NY Life. She has an offer from NYL and has passed their qualifying exam with high ratings. She expects to get the formalities worked out next week. The training class would start in September. Naturally she has worries about her ability to sell life insurance; but if she can the rewards will be double or triple what she is making at Snelling, and there is a very fine retirement program associated with NYL. The one type of job for which she has had a standing order— and the one she can never fill—is insurance agent. Albuquerque seems to be a pretty active center for insurance just now.

I have quite a bit more work now. The TEMPO contract is developing along new lines. I have two instrument design plans

7. Ibid, 17 May 1976.

going, both of very advanced type; one measures very subtle and rapid air density changes and the other measures the components of the strain (movement) tensor in the ground. TEMPO's new objective is to develop an instrumentation capability, which I think is just great. The other project is to design a public transit system that is more efficient than those in existence. It's a real challenge!

Anyway, I believe our futures will be brighter than our recent pasts. Jeannine is looking forward to the new work that will get her out of the office and into contact with people . . .

Jeannine can almost always have her way with some one if she has a chance to talk long enough. She never gets sidetracked from the main point. And she is very competent with numbers. I think she has a good future as a salesperson."

(August 1976) *"Jeannine reported for work Monday and is now deeply engrossed in her training program. She was very frightened of it at first, but has now settled down since she found that afterall it wasn't so hard.*

I received a call . . . to show up Fri morning for some consulting. It seems to be very interesting, having to do with instrumentation in strong shock waves, and may turn out to be quite an upcoming project."[8]

From the first stirrings of Craig's interest in world history and culture during high school literature and history classes, through his time spent in Europe during the war, his connection to the Dumas family, and on into his later years, Craig's enthusiasm for culture never waned. The children were brought up in the company of books on art, history, antiquities, and literature. Every so often Jeannine would instigate a poetry reading with everyone reading or reciting one of their favorites, be it even a nursery rhyme. When they were old enough, they accompanied Craig and Jeannine to museums, the Civic Symphony[9], theater, and the Santa Fe Opera.

During the mid-1970s, Craig began volunteering his time to The Museum of Albuquerque and the Albuquerque Archaeology Society. At the Albuquerque Archaeology Society he was Vice President in 1974 and 1975 and then President in 1976. As he had with the Sandia Colloquium, Craig brought in scientists to speak at the Society's meetings.

"In the mid-1970's Craig Hudson enlarged the scope of the Society's lecture programs presented at regular meetings of the membership.

8. Ibid, 8 July 1976, 31 August 1976.

9. [Editor's Note] Albuquerque Civic Symphony established in the 1932 (later known as Albuquerque Symphony Orchestra and eventually New Mexico Symphony Orchestra).

> *Up to that time, programs largely concentrated on traditional ar-chaeological or anthropological subjects.*
>
> *As Vice President and program chairman from 1974 to 1976, Craig invited a number of scientists to speak at Society meetings on topics that might have archaeological implications related to their scientific specialties at such places as the Los Alamos and Sandia National Laboratories. Society members were informed about X-ray fluorescence, analytical organic chemistry of archaeological materials, the impact on human behavior brought about by clima-tological changes, dating methods, computer uses in archaeology, pollen dating, and metal working in historical antiquity.*[10]

In 1976, as Chairman of the Special Events Committee for the Mu-seum of Albuquerque, Craig conceived and designed an energy symposium scheduled for early the next year.

> (July 1976) *"I am now chairman of the Museum of Albuquerque Special Events Committee. One of the tasks I have is to direct a symposium on Energy. It is presently planned for late next year. I'm sure it will be a very interesting symposium."*
>
> (Nov 1976) *"I am project manager for an energy symposium (3 days all day) to be held in Feb, supported by a NM Humani-ties Council grant (I'll get $1800); and technical directory of the concurrent energy artifacts exhibit to be held for 1 ½ months at the Museum of Alb. That may bring $1600. If we can publish the results (another $2000), I'll be editor. It should attract nationwide attention."*
>
> (March 1977) *"Well, Feb 5, 12, 19 have come and gone, and the Energy symposium was a big success . . .*
>
> *The Energy Exhibition will close tomorrow. It has been open since Jan 30 and has been the most attended exhibit the museum ever had. School classes have poured through, scheduled about as thick as they could come. I planned the exhibit and selected the materials, but the staff put the exhibit up."*[11]

All the while work with GE TEMPO continued with *"projects in making butane out of natural gas by use of radioactive wastes from nuclear reactors; of measuring super high pressures near (at the edge of) a block of exploding TNT;*

10. Olsen, N. H., & Bice, R. A., *The Albuquerque Archaeological Society: The First Twenty-five Years*, 1966–1991, p 15.

11. Letter from Craig to 'Mom and Dad,' 8 July 1976, 13 November 1976, 12 March 1977.

of predicting the collapse of earth near explosions."[12] New projects presented themselves with Craig's friendship with Iben Browning.[13]

> *"I am still working for GE TEMPO on the Hi Pressure gage; but also I have recently submitted a study for a gage to measure dust in the air. I think it is a better design than is presently available. They seem to need something like that. But a new project has just come up. In 15 days, I am to present a theory which will allow the prediction of yield of corn (or wheat) 10 years into the future! Sounds crazy? Maybe not. I'm working with my friend Iben Browning who has been gathering data of this kind for years. Now he wants to assemble it into a formula (rather complicated) which will do the impossible—predict the rainfall. I am sure we can write the formula and maybe we will have enough data to make it work."*[14]

Craig wasn't the only one volunteering his time. The Hudson photo album's first recording of a connection with the Alliance Française[15] is in 1975. Over the years Jeannine (also Craig and Mamie to a degree) attended meetings and functions. Jeannine eventually became involved with the leadership of the Alliance Française. Several times she and Craig hosted the July 14th celebrations in the gardens of the Los Arboles property.

1978 was a busy year for Craig and Jeannine. The summer had many get-togethers with family and visiting friends. In September Jeannine and Mamie took a trip to France and Yugoslavia (to visit Mara, the foreign exchange student who stayed with the Hudsons during the 1971–72 school year). Money was tight; staying with friends in France saved them the cost of living expenses. Craig left the house-sitting to the now grown children and, with monetary help from Bertha and Harvey, visited family in Oregon.

> *"I can hardly find the words to thank you for the pleasant stay in Portland. It was a wonderful two weeks for me and seeing old friends and family was the kind of inspirational experience I need. It was wonderful.*
>
> *I left Marilynn with information about how to get help for Mom if she needs it. It's a heavy burden for Marilynn to carry and I will always be available if needed. Also Rosie said she would*

12. Ibid, 20 May 1977.

13. [Editor's Note] Dr. Iben Browning (1918–1991) was a biophysicist who studied climate cycles.

14. Letter from Craig to 'Mom and Dad,' 30 January 1978.

15. [Editor's Note] The Albuquerque chapter of the Alliance Fran.aise, which is dedicated to fostering the French language and culture, was founded in 1962 by Claude-Marie Senninger and her husband Truett Book.

like to help and I think she may be able to come over more readily than Marilynn.

Seeing Dexter again was both pleasant and pathetic. The logic part of his mind seems to be relatively unaffected and it was like old times to discuss things with him. But he did not recognize me at first, so a portion of his memory is gone. After a while, however he seemed quite at ease with me and I was very touched when I tucked him in bed and he said 'good night Brud'; it was so familiar.

What a momentous 2 weeks! I am sorry I can't do it more often. Thank you for all your help."[16]

Also that year the Department of Labor began an age discrimination suit against Sandia Laboratory. Craig and some of his co-workers who were pushed to take early retirement were encouraged by their lawyers to cooperate.

(April 1978) *"The Department of Labor is suing Sandia for age discrimination in a major case to test the new law. I'm to be a guinea pig, a situation I don't relish. But Tom Ahern, my lawyer, says I should cooperate."*

(Aug 1978) *"The Labor Department is suing Sandia Labs for the early retirement (age discrimination) of me as well as others. The case comes to court in January. I have very mixed feelings about it. On the one hand, I would like to benefit from a judgement that would replace my lost income. But on the other hand, I fear that the confrontation would put me in a difficult situation with respect to my friends still at Sandia who would have to be witnesses. The Labor Dept lawyers say I have a responsibility to see that the law is tested to the best of our ability; but I say that it will be a rather trying experience not obviously worth the possible gain. However, I probably will not have a real choice in the matter, since it is a class action suit."*[17]

By the end of 1979, Craig suffered two major losses. His brother, Dexter, died in May and his mother, Bertha, died in November. Bertha had mentioned health problems in a letter dated Jan 16, 1979, *"Dad is taking care of me like a baby and I let him. I am free of the arthritis pain in my wrists and knees, but my hip still won't hold me safely, so I use a cane. My biggest problem is that I am so short of breath. Dad has me 'deep breathing,' and I have been plagued with itching of all things! Must be what Mom called 'shingles.'"*[18] Craig's sister, Marilynn, reported in an April letter of taking Bertha to a

---

16. Letter from Craig to 'Mom and Dad,' 17 October 1978.

17. Ibid, 7 April 1978, 18 August 1978.

18. Letter from Bertha Hudson to Craig, 16 January 1979.

doctor and ". . . *he put her on heart medicine, diuretic medicine, potassium medicine. She was having congestive heart. She is much improved . . . is up off the davenport and doing some of her chores.*"[19]

Craig returned to Oregon for Dexter's funeral service and again in November for his mother's. "*The moments of solitude at Dexter's graveside will remain indelibly impressed in my memory. My heart ached for him when I saw him so crippled, and his death in this sense is a welcome relief. But seeing his name on the little grave tag affected me profoundly. It is a vision I will never be able to forget.*"[20]

On the canyon floor, Canyon de Chelly, Craig on the left, 1970

19. Letter from Marilynn Buley to 'Shirl and Craig and families,' 6 March 1979.
20. Letter from Craig to 'Mom & Dad,' 30 May 1979.

Craig in front of his chalkboard at Sandia Lab, 1972

Craig and Jeannine, 1979

14

Rediscovering Painting

1980—1985

In March 1980 the volcano Mt Saint Helens in Washington State erupted, and again in May, blowing off the side of the mountain. As a boy growing up in the Portland area Craig was used to seeing the beautiful snow covered peak of Saint Helens on the skyline and camping at Spirit Lake. The eruption drew much attention of scientists and the media. Craig was very interested in the event and would in 1982 paint several paintings related to it. Craig and Jeannine with son Marc had planned a road trip to Oregon for the end of May. The drive took them past the Grand Canyon and Glen Canyon and the Redwoods in California. The photo album documents them near Woodland Washington but it was a cloudy day with not much to see, save for the dust and ash on the road. The return trip took them by Yellowstone Park, Jackson Lake and the Tetons, and Black Canyon of the Gunnison. Several of these places would be reflected in Craig's paintings.

St Helens Erupts, painted 1982

By the summer of 1981, Craig and Jeannine's children were grown. Cyril, the youngest was 20 years old. All the children were occupied with school, work, relationships and each one, from time to time, found support and encouragement with the parents. Craig wrote a beautiful, heartfelt letter to his father contemplating fathers and sons.

> *"In part this letter is a tribute to you on Father's Day . . . It is impossible to recall the many times—let me assure you the number is large—when I have been able to repeat to my children some lesson or some attitude or some experience that I have learned from you. That is the way of the father-son relationship. The subtlety of it is often lost except in retrospect, when you were grateful it was there. Some people have never had that relationship and I think the world is the worse for the lack. I try to keep Marc and Cyril coming to me with their problems. . .and I think we have a pretty warm relationship, just as you and I have. That's the way I like it. There is no problem too difficult to talk out, though some of them are unpleasant or awkward. I have been very impatient with the boys to settle down and become dedicated to a goal. They have been equally impatient with what they envisioned as their options in view and have been trying to broaden their experiences and their options. I remember how I was, how impatient you must have been to see me settle down, and how considerate you were.*

*When I look back on what Jeannine and I did, I really wouldn't
want to change much of it. Making more money might have been
a possibility by changing jobs, but even that doesn't seem so important now, and in part the realization of that was due to you and
Mother who taught me to moderate ambition with contentment.
So, thank you Dad, for all your help and advice and, especially, the
quiet example you set. I'm trying to pass it on."[1]*

Even after Craig retired and money became tighter, they always tried
to save a bit aside for concert tickets. Family and friends knew how much
pleasure Craig and Jeannine derived from music and often aided them in
their endeavors with birthday or Christmas gifts.

*(June 1981) "Mme Dumas gave us tickets for the June Festival
this year, the Guarneri String Quartet[2]: six concerts. The last is
tonight. They have been wonderful; it was a gift for our birthdays
and we will enjoy the memories for a long time. "*

*(July 1981) "We are not planning to attend the Santa Fe Opera
this year—too expensive."*

*(Aug 1981) "Our friends have been very nice to us this sum-
mer. Suzie Pool gave us two tickets (front, center at $35 each)
to the Santa Fe Opera and we saw Hindemith's "News of the
World"[3]. . .Suzie also gave us tickets twice to the Santa Fe Music
Festival . . . "[4]*

Craig always had projects around the property that involved his time
and he continued to research several topics that interested him, but by 1981
his consulting work was at a standstill. *"There are many things that need my
attention around the house, but we also need money and it is not certain in
this economic climate that J. will continue to be successful—though her work
still looks promising . . . I'm trying to simplify my life but still to leave open the
possibility of making money. So I may go back to consulting soon."[5]* And into
this period of uncertainty, Craig returned to his painting.

*". . . I have finally returned to painting pictures! It seems so simple
in my mind to do things but when I pick up the brush, it suddenly
becomes difficult. It is clear that I shall have to do a great deal of*

1. Letter from Craig to 'Dad,' 10 June 1981.

2. [Editor's Note] Guarneri String Quartet, renowned string quartet founded in
1964.

3. [Editor's Note] Craig is probably referring to the opera *News of the Day* by Paul
Hindemith.

4. Letter from Craig to 'Dad,' 10 June 1981, 20 July 1981, 24 Aug 1981.

5. Ibid, 4 Nov 1981.

painting before I can recover my former proficiency—and I would
like to surpass it by a wide margin.
    Dear Jeannine is the one who is making this all possible. She
works hard at her life insurance selling and she is getting to be
pretty good at it."[6]

Also, Jeannine was now quite involved with the Alliance Française.
She formed a restoration committee and was a moving force behind the
restoration of New Mexico's Boxcar[7] from the Merci Train,[8] the entire
process encompassing more than ten years.

> *"Jeannine Hudson, a Parisian married to an Albuquerque resi-*
> *dent, formed a restoration committee comprised of the Alliance*
> *Française, members of the Forty and Eight, the Historical Society*
> *and the Railroad Club of New Mexico. With the support of New*
> *Mexico's Governor Garrey Carruthers, the committee recently*
> *launched a fund-raising campaign for the boxcar."*[9]

By January 1982, Craig had plans for a one-man show for November
of that year. Although consulting was still an option, Craig fully intended to
sell his paintings to supplement their income.

> *(Jan 1982) "I have painted 2 Canyon de Chelly pictures for my*
> *new show. I'm getting better all the time. At this point, I have*
> *about [$]15,000 worth of paintings for sale. I hope some of them*
> *will sell soon. I can gross about [$]12,000 without losing Social*
> *Security. This year will be the year [for] me to try to figure out how*
> *to market my paintings."*
>   *(May 1982) "My plans to have my painting exhibition in No-*
> *vember still hold. I must do quite a bit of painting between now*
> *and then, since I plan to finish seven new works in the next few*
> *months and get ready a number of old ones. The idea is to have*
> *an invitation only show here at the house to serve as a 'debut.' My*

6. Ibid, 3 Dec 1981.

7. [Editor's Note] In 1981 public attention was brought to the condition of the
boxcar (forgotten, weathered and used as storage space) in an article in the *Albuquerque
Journal Magazine Impact* (V5 No4, 10 Nov 1981). .

8. [Editor's Note] Merci Train also known as the French Gratitude Train, was a
train of 49 French railroad boxcars that had been filled with tens of thousands of personal gifts of gratitude. The Train was sent to the American people, one boxcar to each
of the 48 States and 1 shared between Washington D. C. and the territory of Hawaii.
The gratitude of the French people was for the hundreds of boxcars of relief goods that
Americans had sent to the French people in 1948.
Bennett Sr, Earl, *Merci Train*.

9. Conley, Manuel A., *What Ever Happened to Those Forty And Eights?*.

new paintings are all going to be on scientific subjects (more or less) and since almost no one is doing painting of this kind, I hope to become professional. If I can make an extra $5000 a year, I will greatly relieve the pressure on Jeannine and I will be able to do something I have always wanted to do. Consulting does not seem to be very good just now (no work for a year), but it could pick up. However, I'd like painting better."

(July 1982) "My plan is to send out 300 invitations, mostly to individuals but in some cases to groups. The invitations will be printed and will not be very costly. I have made a list of people to whom I would like to send invitations and the list is much longer than 300. . . in any event, only 300 will be sent—to scientists, doctors, lawyers, friends, neighbors, artists, political figures—a rather select group."[10]

During the '50s and '60s Craig painted about a dozen paintings. Some were landscapes and some portraits. In 1982 Craig had shifted his attention and efforts from the practice of physics to painting. Between 1982 and 1983 he completed 55 paintings! Craig's first one-man exhibit, *Natural Forces*, was held in November 1982 at the house—his home gallery. Craig painted 26 paintings in 1982 for this one-man show.

The year 1982 held other notable events as well. Daughter Cassandra was married; son Marc married again. Jeannine was president of the Alliance Française of Albuquerque and maintained a normal work schedule. Being president of the Alliance Française included being involved with several functions. All those obligations took a toll.

(April 1982) "Jeannine was in charge of the ceremony honoring our friend Claude S. by the French govt. The French consul came from LA and with the Mayor did the honors at the Museum. It went very well. This week, two more distinguished Frenchmen are here—an organist who I heard last night play a program of modern pipe organ music (wow!), and a historian we hear tomorrow lecture on the history of science. We have dinner with both men."

(May 1982) "Jeannine was so keyed up for the wedding, running here and there to attend to so many details and at the same time serving as president of the Alliance Française (there were three major functions involving notables from France in the 10 days preceding the wedding!) and on top of that trying to maintain a normal work schedule at NY Life, that it is no surprise to learn that she had a breakdown. She has had a couple of these before when things became too tense so now I am beginning to know how

10. Letter from Craig to 'Dad,' 27 Jan 1982, 20 May 1982, July 1982.

to deal with it. She becomes physically lethargic and needs to rest constantly; but her mind cannot stop and goes round and round over the same problems. It takes much patience and sympathy to console her and eventually to help her back to a normal way of life. This time it has lasted about 10 days but now she can face up to the office again."[11]

The painting portion of Craig's one-man show was complete by the end of summer. Then every painting, when dry, had to be framed and a plan made for hanging 25 paintings. This was a large endeavor, but Craig was excited to be painting again.

(Aug 1982) "I am nearly finished with my paintings, tho many of them need final touches . . . I have drawn a layout of the living room wall space and identified the place of every picture (22 of them) and only one has not yet been started. On the wall over the French doors, where there is plenty of space, I have the St. Helens trilogy: a picture of the St. Helens area before the explosion (actually a satellite radar relief map which does not show vegetation); then the explosion picture; and finally a picture from the ruined Spirit Lake looking back into the new crater. In the place where the old French tapestry hangs, there will be four 24"x30" pictures of astronomical subjects—the largest area and the most spectacular views; everyone who sees them is awed. But I like them all. One of the most interesting parts of my exhibit, in my view, is the fact that each picture has a story which will be associated with the picture. Some of the stories are little scientific lectures, telling why the picture is important. Some of the stories are just about the history of the picture. For instance, I use the portrait of Grandpa Hudson to tell about my training with Sidney Bell."

(Sept 13, 1982) "My show is still on schedule. It will certainly not be a grand affair, and Tom Hall is a little aghast at the simple frames I am making. But for such a high risk venture (and with our finances the way they are), this is all I think is justified. So it will have to do."

(Sept 22, 1982) "There will, finally, be 25 'scientific' paintings in the main exhibit called "Natural Forces." That pretty well fills the walls of the living room. There will be about 20 paintings in the retrospective exhibit in the playroom, which also fills the walls. Some are quite large (35"x45") and a few are rather small (12"x15"); most are intermediate (20"x30"). The frames have been a great deal of work to make and still are not very nice—simple but rugged."

11. Letter from Craig to 'Dad,' 21 April 1982, 20 May 1982.

(Oct 1982) *"So far as I know, none of my out-of-town friends is coming to see the show . . . Actually, it is gratifying that so many people have acknowledged the invitation: a long letter from Edgely Todd (Colorado), another from Hugh de Witt (California), a telephone call from Sabiha (John) Worrell (Texas). It has been fun, too, receiving calls from friends in town. One of special interest was from Wilson Hurley, my hero of sorts, who took up painting after a career as an attorney. He is now, after 10 years, a very successful artist and is building a $600,000 home/studio. . .If I can be only partially as successful as Hurley, I will be quite satisfied. We paint the same style but different subject matter. And I have not been so happy and pleased with myself for a long time. Being an artist-scientist really agrees with me."*[12]

The "Natural Forces" one-man show opened on Sunday November 7, 1982.

"The show opening on Sunday was not as well attended as I had hoped, but even so it was a grand occasion. About 50 people attended (I had hoped for 100) and some I had especially wanted to see did not come. Perhaps they will show up Saturday for the 2nd reception.

The weather was delightful so we set up a table in the patio for serving wine and cheese and had coffee and cake in the kitchen. As a social event, it was warm and friendly. And the little booklets I had put together to help interpret the pictures were in great demand. Some of the visitors took the booklets in hand as they walked around and carefully read each essay as they looked at the pictures. There were only 3 booklets and I could have used 5. A few people inquired about price and showed some interest in buying, but so far there has been no commitment."[13]

Within two months, Craig was painting again and planning the next one-man show for early summer.

(Jan 1983) *"I have started painting again, preparing (I hope) for a show in May. This one will be a little different in the sense that a number of the pictures are going to be familiar, of canyons we enjoy in the southwest. I'm going to continue to paint pictures of microscopic science (only 4 this time) and I hope to include one astronomical view. So the title will be 'Natural Forces II,' but this will be a much smaller show than the last. Planning and painting these pictures is the most pleasurable activity I have had in many*

12. Ibid, 17 Aug 1982, 13 Sept 1982, 22 Sept 1982, 20 Oct 1982.
13. Ibid, 9 Nov 1982.

years. It is unfortunate that some of my old friends think I have gone soft in the head—without having seen the pictures. So it is with considerable anticipation that I look forward to the article that Linda Mitchell wrote about me. It is scheduled to appear in the Journal 'Impact' (the magazine section) in the next few weeks. It will show some of the pictures (in black & white) and will describe my motivation in choosing those subjects."

(Feb 1983) "I have already finished 2 Canyon de Chelly paintings and nearly finished one of Black Canyon—which may be the biggest and best thing I ever painted. It will be very dramatic. Still to come are 2 large pictures (91) Chaco Canyon and (2) Saturn's rings; and a number of small pictures."[14]

The article about Craig was printed in the *IMPACT / Albuquerque Journal Magazine* in February 1983. Jeannine sent the article to Elianne, mentioning that while it had a few little mistakes, it was generally good and represented Craig well . . . *"One thing really annoys him (in a funny sort of way). Several times in the article he is referred to as having worn a lab coat! The poor ignorant journalist couldn't know how demeaning it would be for a theoretical physicist to be confused with a lab tech. She has only seen scientists in movies . . ."[15]*

It was an extensive article. The journalist did capture Craig's thoughts and motivation concerning his paintings. *"I can no longer look at anything and simply observe it as to its exterior appearance. I no longer have an ordinary view of the world,' said Hudson. 'I keep seeing in it underlying forces and underlying factors. You can't escape it.'[16]* The article also allowed the reader an insight in to how Craig would give new life to scientific images. He would choose a small black and white photograph that interested him from scientific journals and research the phenomenon. Then he would transform the image by enlarging it and adding color and an arrangement that he felt would best tell the scientific story.

With science moving to the background and painting moving to the foreground, Craig made plans to pass along his collection of scientific books, journals, and magazines that he had saved over the years. *"I have found a university in the Congo that needs scientific books and magazines, and I am donating mine. But money has to be found for shipment. So that is in progress—not accomplished, but I think it soon will be."[17]* All the while,

14. Ibid, 14 Jan 1983, 9 Feb 1983.
15. Letter from Jeannine to 'Elianne,' 8 Feb 1983.
16. Mitchell, L. A., *A Scientific Eye for Art*.
17. Letter from Craig to 'Dad,' 28 March 1983.

day-to-day living and interests continued with the garden, the family, and camping.

> "I have painted 9 pictures for my next exhibit; three of them are quite large—1500 sq in or more. And they are surely (all of them) the best paintings so far. I have planned 7 more pictures, one of the 1500 sq in size, which I am sure I can finish by May. I price my pictures at about $1 per sq in although that is only an average. Jeannine serves as agent; but so far there have been no further sales even tho she is rather busy at it . . .
>
> We are planning to have an outing in the middle of May, a family camp-out at Chaco Canyon. You may remember it as the valley in which about 7 ancient Anasazi pueblos have been found and excavated. It is now a dry desolate place but the archaeological evidence indicates that it was once much more livable and supported squash, deer meat, etc. It is a fascinating place to spend a few days walking through the excavations. We began taking the children there 20 years ago . . .
>
> April will be a time to try to catch up on our bills, to try to pay the income tax, to finish my paintings and get ready for the show (and to make a lot of frames!). Also a time to start a garden and for Jeannine to get back on her feet [from a bout of the flu]. That is a lot to expect of April."[18]

Springtime also brought other concerns for Craig; he had developed pollen-related allergies and was afflicted with itchy, watery eyes, sinus and throat symptoms. He was not able to take antihistamine and decongestant medications because they interfered with his blood pressure and his heart, so when possible, he tried to travel to Oregon to visit family and friends for a couple of weeks to get some relief. Jeannine mentions Craig's difficulties in a letter to Elianne.

> "I am going to try to get Daddy on a plane to San Diego sometime around March 17th. He could spend a few days there and then fly to Portland with Grandpa who plans to be in San Diego much sooner . . . Even though this week was encouraging I have no money to show for it. I may have some in April or May if I am lucky and all goes well. Still, I think Daddy should go even though some bills will have to go unpaid . . .
>
> The California storm finally reached us last night but it had mostly dissipated on the way and all we received was a sprinkle of rain and wind. When the clouds go away and the sun shines again it will be spring for us. Daddy will be anxious to work in

18. Ibid, 28 March 1983.

the garden: just the thing he can't do. Best for him to be gone. Even
painting is difficult if your eyes itch and water."[19]

Craig made the trip and had an enjoyable visit with his father. He was
also able to collect more information concerning the genealogy of the Hudson and Palmer families.

(May 1983) "My notes and all the papers and names I collected
up there are untouched in my briefcase. As soon as I can, I'll get
to them and have much more to say to you about the success of
the trip. As for my allergies, as soon as I got back into the desert
atmosphere, my nose began acting up again. The visit to Oregon is
very helpful—but it isn't long enough."

(June 1983) "The pictures—all 19 of them—are finally done,
the frames made and hanging on the wall. I have to put the final
coat of paint on each frame and the final varnish on each picture;
but if worse came to worse, the exhibit could go as is. And it is
really a nice one. All the pictures have eye appeal. Last time, some
of them were scientifically significant but not necessarily appealing
to the eye. And I think this may have hurt the exhibit. This time,
I have not written essays because the material doesn't really need
explanation: it's obvious . . .

In addition to the 19 new paintings, which are hung in the
living room, Jeannine has included her favorite 9 pictures from the
last show, hung in the playroom . . .

I have collected together the major pages of the genealogy of
our family—that is, we four children, our children, and our ances-
tors back as far as good information was known to me—and I
have had copies made for each of us and for you. Things have
been too busy to send them, but I'll get them in the mail soon. This
genealogy can serve as a central starting point for spreading out
in the directions of marriage, families or for extending backward
in time. I'm interested in the historical aspects, but as you know
it's pretty difficult to obtain good information earlier than 1800.
Perhaps I'll be successful later."[20]

Craig's second one-man show, "*Geology of the Southwest,*" opened July
10th. Jeannine's letter to Elianne reported a beautiful show.

"It is too early to assess whether it was successful or not. It was
certainly a beautiful show. . . 29 people came last Sunday; 26 came
yesterday. Then on July 14th, Thursday, when the Alliance had its

19. Letter from Jeannine to 'Elianne,' 4 March 1983.

20. Letters from Craig to 'Dad,' 16 May 1983, 26 June 1983.

annual celebration in our backyard I made an announcement that
people were welcome to enter the house and enjoy the paintings:
21 or more did so. Last November, at the first show, we had had
82 people in 2 days. Obviously we had fewer this time. But on the
positive side: one painting has been sold already from this show."[21]

Never one to have only one project in the works at a time, Craig completed that year built-in wooden bookshelves and display case in the playroom. He also planned for some public exposure for his paintings.

(Sept 1983) ". . . *I have built Mother her long-desired corner cup-*
board in the playroom, complete with 5 doors, a 'vitrine' in which
to exhibit her little treasures, a place for the TV. Attached to it is
a huge bookcase that covers the entire east wall. Around the fire-
place is a fine display of wood paneling (not yet finished) . . . The
new studio, in your and [Cassandra's] old room, is now beginning
to take shape as my journals & papers are boxed up and books
moved out to the new bookcase . . ."
(Oct 1983) *"I have (at great effort) moved my science papers*
out of the yellow bedroom and made it permanently into a studio
. . . I have a painting of flowers (morning glories) on the easel
now, not yet finished. My first attempt at flowers in recent years.
Mother is quite pleased, I am also going to exhibit 5 paintings
publicly in Nov . . . Show will be downtown in Pub Serv Bldg, in a
rather nice lobby area. We will be eager to see how it goes. I need
the public exposure—but not in a bad show."[22]

The exhibit at the Public Service Building of New Mexico in Albuquerque
was in pleasant surroundings for an exhibit. Jeannine was disappointed as
"there was no publicity and it was in a room hard to find, without even a
poster to show the way," although according to Craig *"it did not go badly and*
I can now claim a public exhibit."[23]

The end of 1983 found Craig working on future shows: *"I am well*
into the pictures for my Feb show—not half finished yet, but nearly. You'd like
them. The big show will be Nov 84, pictures of fluid motion. I'm putting lots of
effort into that."[24] And that year Craig and Jeannine made a decision of a
gift to each of their four children which they would repeat numerous times
over the following years: *"As our gift for Christmas 1983, we have decided to*
give each of our children one of Daddy's paintings . . . Any painting is available,

21. Letter from Jeannine to Elianne, 17 July 1983.
22. Letter from Craig to 'Elianne,' 8 Sept 1983, 17 Oct 1983.
23. Joint letter from Jeannine & Craig to 'Elianne,' 18 Nov 1983.
24. Letter from Craig to 'Elianne,' 2 Dec 1983.

no matter how big, how small, how old or how new. We hope that this very personal gift will convey our feelings of great pride and love toward you."[25]

In early 1984 Jeannine reported that Craig received an *"invitation to submit 7 photographs (black & white) of painting to be considered for the Salon de Nations exhibit in Paris in June . . . if he accepts the cost is $1,000 + shipping to Long Island and back. I am urging him to try for it . . ."*[26] He did try and was accepted. He sent five paintings. The exhibit opened on the 4th of June.

> *"As I write this, the exhibit in Paris has been open for about 6 hours. Jeannine and I are very excited. We hope it will be an entrée into the European market. More realistically, we hope it will not cost us too much!"*[27]
>
> *"My Paris exhibit has finally wound down and I am expecting to receive the pictures back any day. Nothing seems to have come of the effort except an entry on my resume. Sad. But I am painting on the next show; one picture is finished, a second started—of 25."*[28]

One of the projects that Craig took on in the mid-80s was building furniture using the tools and the fine wood from Papa's shop. Craig and Papa had previously collaborated on the design of furniture and Craig had learned a few things. Craig didn't have the sophisticated training that Papa had achieved, but his artistic abilities served him well. Their collaboration probably began as a result of the language barrier that Papa encountered when he first came to America and attempted to set up a business. Customers would first communicate their furniture ideas to Craig and/or Jeannine and, while Jeannine translated to her father, Craig sketched and relayed the customer's ideas.

Included with the wood in Papa's shop were several carved wood panels that Papa had collected over the years. Craig had the idea to use the carved paneling as doors for cabinets and buffets. Craig eventually built, either from original wood or from pre-existing panels of wood, one cabinet and two buffets. Marc and Cyril helped with lathe work for the legs and door knobs. The cabinet was equipped with shelves for wine bottles and hanging stemware rack and has carved wood panels for the doors. One of the buffets was an old piece made of cherry that Craig rescued from years of dirt and

---

25. Letter from Craig & Jeannine to 'Elianne,' Dec 1983.
26. Letter from Jeannine to 'Elianne,' 11 Feb 1984.
27. Letter from Craig to 'Dad,' 4 June 1984.
28. Letter from Craig to 'Elianne,' 13 Aug 1984.

disuse; the other Craig made from oak from the shop and carved panels. Family members still enjoy and make use of these fine pieces of furniture.

Craig had only one exhibit at the house in 1984. The "Flora and Fauna" exhibit included 9 paintings of North American wild flowers and 14 paintings of the prehistoric cave art of the Périgord region of southwest France. It opened May 13, 1984.

Aurocks Gambol (Lascaux), painted 1984

> *"We are finally all ready for the show—except for the food & drink and clean-up in the yard, last minute things. The flower pictures are brilliant—but small. When I began them, it was with the idea of developing a line of bright little gems—and for a beginning they are OK. They have metal frames and I would like to move into inlaid wood frames, rather like the style of medieval icons . . . So on Sunday, we will learn if this style of 'art' is worth anything."[29]*
>
> *"Our 'Flora & Fauna' exhibit went nicely in the sense that it was fairly well attended (75 so far) and that there were several inquiries; but so far, no one has bought a painting except David [Hudson]."[30]*

The 'Flora and Fauna' exhibit was the beginning of a busy summer. Several friends made overnight visits and Craig worked on home improvement projects and *"on top of that, we have had 2 small burglaries. Up to now, we have felt it unnecessary to lock everything up. But after the second one, I put strong locks on our outbuildings. The things we lost were not large and certainly could not have been stolen for profit. But they had to be replaced . . ."[31]*

In early July, Craig and Jeannine made a road trip to Oregon taking Mamie along with them. The trip took them almost a month and included

---

29. Ibid, 9 May 1984.
30. Letter from Craig to 'Dad,' 22 May 1984.
31. Ibid, 4 June 1984.

visits with family in Portland, Marley Brown and his wife, Herman and
Marge Johansen, and a few nights at a rented beach house near Waldport.
The trip had several objectives in addition to visiting family and friends: give
Jeannine a much-needed rest, allow Jeannine to visit a client in Idaho, locate
the boxcars in Utah and Idaho, enjoy the beautiful countryside. Craig later
wrote a commentary of this trip. The drive to Oregon took them through
Utah, Idaho, and up the east side of Oregon and along the Columbia Gorge
into Portland.

> *"July 10—Driving north to Moab took us along a beautiful skyline
> off to the east in Colorado, the La Sal mountains with peaks as
> high as 12,000 feet, still snow covered. We had to pass Arches with-
> out stopping, but the road up through that gorge was beautiful . . .*
>
> *July 11—The drive from Salt Lake City to Boise is not very
> interesting. We spent two nights in Boise; the extra day was to al-
> low Jeannine to look up a client living near there on a cherry farm.
> We found his place in the later afternoon. They talked for awhile;
> then he invited us to pick a sack of cherries to eat while driving.
> The mosquitoes were thick so Mamie stayed in the car while J. and
> I picked—and ate! They were delicious and our sackful lasted two
> days . . .*
>
> *French Boxcars—One of the objectives of this trip was to let
> Jeannine see what other states had done with their French box-
> cars. There was one in Salt Lake City, another in Boise and a third
> in Astoria. I had already taken pictures of the one in Astoria. The
> boxcar in Salt Lake City was standing in the open in a pleasant
> park setting. It was nicely painted, but had no decorative plaques
> on it. At least, it was in good condition. The boxcar in Boise was
> inside the old prison which was being remodeled into an exhibit
> hall for big, rough items. It, too, had no decorative plaques but it
> was nicely painted. However, it was located in a rather dark hall
> so that details were difficult to make out . . . Of all three boxcars,
> the one in Astoria was by far the best displayed. It was placed
> under a roof, protected by a chain link fence, and painted and
> decorated in a manner that resembled its original form. It was
> located in a grassy park under large trees."[32]*

The return trip took them south through Grants Pass and into California to visit the redwoods. Then they went east across Nevada, cutting the
southeast corner of Utah around St. George and down into Arizona to their
favorite Canyon de Chelly and then home to Albuquerque.

---

32. Unpublished commentary *Trip to Oregon 1984* by Craig Hudson, 14 June 1995.

"*July 31—. . . Just over the border into California, we came to the Jedediah Smith Grove, a marvelous stand of the largest redwoods, a state park. It was so quiet and peaceful there. We took a number of pictures, showing how huge the trunks were . . . of course, the tops were out of sight. Then we drove down to the Lady Bird Johnson Grove. Here the trees were not as big, but it was a little more open and we could see the trunks tall and straight, their crowns hidden in the ocean mists . . . I later painted one of these scenes, showing Jeannine standing on a 'Forest Trail' (the name) which has been a favorite . . .*

Aug 2—. . . In the afternoon, we drove on, through some beautiful country, to St. George in Utah. But on the way we drove through the old mining towns of Pioche and Panaca. Between the two is Cathedral Gorge, a Nevada State Park. There was a little water there (in the midst of dry alkaline desert), a nice picnic area under trees, and all around us were the spectacular spires that gave the park its name . . .

Aug 3—This day's drive took us through some of the most amazing country of the entire trip. From St. George, we drove east through the southern part of Zion Nat'l Park through beautiful mountains to Kanab, then to Fredonia . . . we hurried on along route 160 through Kayenta (lunch in a blistering heat), then to Chinle and Canyon de Chelly . . .

Aug 4—We spent the morning out at Spider Rock overlook. We have seen it many times and it loses none of its appeal. We stopped at the new overlook at Wild Cherry Ruin which shows a spectacular piece of canyon. On a later visit I took an afternoon photo which I then painted into '5 O'clock Shadows,' one of the good ones . . .

What a trip! We arrived in Albuquerque, dropped Mamie off at her house, and fell into the arms of our welcoming committee at Los Arboles."[33]

Craig's records show an exhibit of four paintings at the Statesmen Club in Albuquerque in August. A "One-man Exhibit" at the First Interstate Bank, City Center, in Albuquerque included 12 paintings.

Craig and Jeannine had been considering moving to smaller property and dwelling to ease their responsibilities. Advanced age, infirmities, allergies all conspired to force Craig and Jeannine to think of moving to a smaller space. The property upkeep was getting to be difficult and required so much time they didn't have time for other pursuits.

---

33. Unpublished commentary *Trip to Oregon 1984* by Craig Hudson, 14 June 1995.

(Nov 1984) "Jeannine has talked to Mamie about our hopes to move into an apartment in order to be a little more free to do the things we like. Mamie was quite upset at first, since she can hardly appreciate the things we like to do . . . But little by little, she is beginning to feel more comfortable with the idea . . . Next we need to tell the children, and I suppose they, too, will require some time to get used to the idea."

(Feb 1985) "Our plans concerning the house are slowly formulating and so far things seem to be fine. As you know, the main objective is to try to arrange things so that Jeannine and I will be able to do things we want to do instead of taking care of this property. So we have selected a real estate agent and as soon after Elianne's wedding as possible, the house will be put on the market. We expect, because of the value of the property, that it will take most of the rest of the year to sell it."[34]

The house was put on the market in May 1985 and Craig and Jeannine worked their busy lives around people touring the house, a few each month. Craig began painting again for an exhibit at the house, hoping for a summer date—but that became unrealistic. Many things had to be done to keep the house and yard ready for visitors. The Home Gallery exhibit finally occurred on December 6, 1985.

Karman Street, painted 1985

---

34 Letter from Craig to 'Dad,' 16 Nov 1984, 15 Feb 1985.

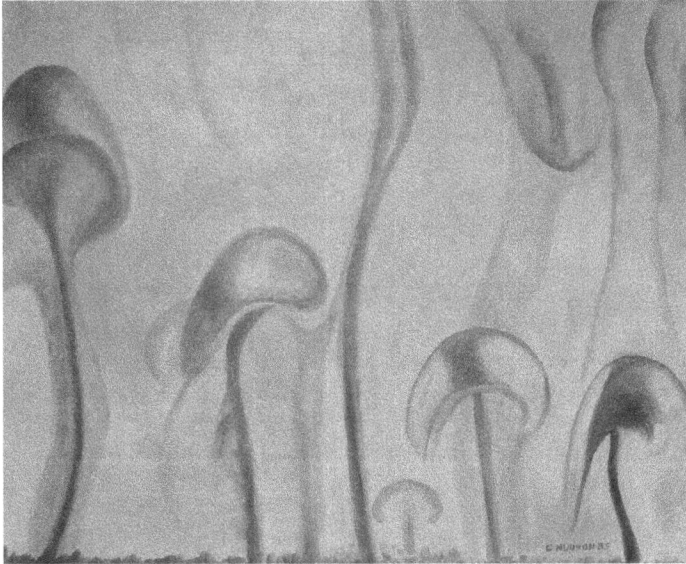

Thermals, painted 1985

(June 1985) "I have also been working to finish my suite of pictures for the next exhibit. We don't know when it will be for certain, because I am only half thru painting. We will have 6–8 weeks time after the decision to sell is made, so I hope to be able to squeeze it in."

(July 1985) "Some interested people have come to see the house, but there is nothing definite yet."

(Nov 1985) "I am now in the final stages of the exhibit "Beauty of Fluid Motions." Invitations have been sent . . . I am just now finishing the final 3 paintings . . . Frames have been ordered and will be here this week. The exhibit plan is all ready but there will be a lot of work to carry it out.

We may have a buyer for the house. A family has been here twice to look at it and shows a great deal of interest in both the property and the neighborhood. Not sure yet, however. We were this close once before."

(Dec 1985) "I finally pulled everything together, with Jeannine's help, for the opening of the exhibit today . . . For this show, I had 24 paintings . . . and 3 of them were 36"x48," exceeding the number of large paintings of any other show. I think my paintings are better now than ever before. I am more able to make things appear as I want them to be seen, and I'm trying more difficult subjects, too.

> *There seems to be some progress on selling the house. We have had an offer; we made a counter offer; they made a counter-counter offer; we made a counter-counter-counter offer . . . As soon as the offer is accepted, we will have to look for an apartment seriously; we have already checked out several and know approximately the range of prices and services. It's going to be strange living in an apartment . . . We are pleased, though, at the prospects of having more freedom to travel."*
>
> *(Dec 1985) "In some ways, this exhibit has been the most successful one so far, although none of the pieces sold. But I think the paintings are the best I have done so far. It is a big relief to have it over so we can get into our Christmas season activities."*[35]

Christmas was a bitter-sweet time and the year ended with a potential sales contract on the house. . .but still nothing definite.

> *(Dec card 1985) "I think we may now have a valid sales contract for the house; it is being examined by our attorney now. However, it is contingent on the sale of the buyers' house, so we will surely be here through the winter."*[36]
>
> *(Dec 1985) "The prospect of leaving this house in which so many memories were born has been sobering on us all. The children don't talk openly of it, but we can see the nostalgia appear in so many unguarded moments. Jeannine has often had sad sessions with herself, with me, with the children, and with good friends when fun times were recalled. I guess I am the least affected of the family because the house, while full of good memories, has also been the source of many frustrations, dogged work and exasperating disappointments. The sweet part of Christmas was the wonderful gathering of the children and friends, and the invitations to their houses, too. It was a warm and gratifying spirit that enveloped us all this Christmas.*
>
> *Cyril's huge Christmas tree (he cut it for us in the Jemez mountains near Cuba) was the largest we had ever had . . . it fills the [living] room so that Jeannine had to trim a little . . . it was one last, grand splurge of Christmas in the old house."*[37]

This sales contract for the house fell through as did several others, leaving Craig and Jeannine on a rollercoaster of emotions for several years. They took the house off the market for a time and then later listed it again.

35. Ibid, 19 June 1985, 8 July 1985, 25 Nov 1985, 6 Dec 1985, 9 Dec 1985,.
36. Christmas card from Craig and Jeannine to 'Dad,' Dec 1985.
37. Letter from Craig to 'Dad,' 30 Dec 1985.

The house finally sold in July 1988. The intervening years were, as usual, active and filled with painting, work, and family matters.

For most entries to exhibit his paintings, Craig was required to send photographs of the entries. Craig and Marc worked together to keep up with the photography. If accepted the framed paintings had to be taken to the exhibit space for hanging. Out-of-town exhibits also involved the problem of transportation of the paintings. If they weren't taken by car, they had to be crated and shipped, which was costly.

> "Marc is helping me to take color slides of some of my painting to send as entries to the "Images of the Universe" exhibit in Iowa next spring. If they are accepted, we will have to consider how to get them there; taking them by car is a possibility, which would interfere with our trip up the [Pacific] coast. But it is a rather long shot anyway. As you know I submitted a proposal to the Oregon Arts Commission for the OSU Computer Building. There were some 75 entries and only about 10 winners; I was not a winner. In order to win at this game, you have to have experience, which is slow in coming. But we have sold another picture (that makes 6 so far), so there is a little bit of success to talk about. And there has been another invitation from Europe (this time a gallery in Paris) wanting to show my pictures. I'd like to send them some (and to Geneva, too) but at this time I can't afford the expense."[38]

38. Ibid, 30 Dec 1985.

15

The Canyon de Chelly Suite of Paintings and Finding a New House

1986—1988

By spring 1986 Craig and Jeannine were visiting with Mamie almost every day while Mamie continued to live in her own house. Jeannine maintained her schedule at New York Life and persevered with her efforts to restore the Boxcar. Craig had begun a series of paintings of Canyon de Chelly, their favorite camping spot.

(April 1986) *". . . We have a regular routine now: we bring Mamie over for dinner every evening about 6:30 and she stays to watch a program or two (if there is any) and we take her home at about 10:00. Of course, some evenings we are invited out. For her part, Mamie repays us by doing the laundry.*

Jeannine's efforts to restore the French 'Merci' 40 & 8 boxcar have taken a new turn. The old car was such a wreck (nothing like the fine Oregon car) and the undercarriage was missing. So she began inquiring in France if replacement parts could be found. Finally after months of waiting the French Railway answered that they had found such a car and would sell it at 'cost.' The cost proved to be about $2000 plus transportation. So now the problem is to raise the money. Many people were interested when it didn't cost anything. Now that money is involved, some have backed off. However, there is a core, still, of interested people led by the NM Historical Society. So she presses ahead trying to find

236

the funding—and trying to find a place to locate it where it will be cared for. The 'it' now is a little uncertain. The old car is owned by the state; the new car would be owned by whoever pays for it. At the present time money is being raised on a rather broad front, so she has some uncertainties ahead. One of the members of her committee is an attorney as well as an official of the NM Historical Soc so I'm sure something will be worked out.

I have started to paint my 5th series, this time on Canyon de Chelly. I'm finishing the second and ready to start the third. I am trying to represent the many beautiful shapes and colors that we have seen out there. Sometimes we could capture the effect in a photo, but more often we just catch the essence of the scene on film and I have to supplement the rest from memories. I love painting the glorious colors, but there is almost nothing scientific in this series (to be 20 or 25 pictures).

(May 1986) "I have now finished 5 paintings of the new Canyon de Chelly suite of 1986 ... I expect to have the suite finished by the end of summer. Then, if all goes well, Jeannine and I will pack them into a van and take them on tour—Oregon first, of course."

(June 1986) ". . . All of them [Canyon de Chelly paintings] will deal with various aspects of that beautiful place, from views of the Canyon itself to views of the ruins. I located some very old photos in black and white (from 1920s) which show a very different view of White House (ruins) than we now see and I expect to present them in full colors, along with more contemporary views. I might even add a reconstruction of White House in its prime—a little artistic archaeology. At any rate, I expect to have these paintings ready by fall and perhaps I will be able to bring them to Portland to exhibit. I have already written to the Alumni Office at Reed asking if I might be able to show the suite there. And I have written to the Mt Angel Abbey on another matter (tracing Grandpa Palmer's birthplace) and if they are friendly I will ask to show the suite there, too. This got started when Marge Johansen showed some of her tapestries there and sent me a name to write to."[1]

The exhibits at Reed College and at Mt Angel Abbey were scheduled for spring and summer of 1987. The remainder of 1986 included a trip to the Northwest with Mamie to visit family, friends, and the Oregon beach. Just before Christmas, Jeannine had surgery on both feet to correct troublesome bunions and convalesced over the holiday while the family pitched in with household duties.

1. Ibid, 3 April 1986, 4 May 1986, 9 June 1986.

Cool Shade (Canyon de Chelly), painted 1986

Spider Rock (Canyon de Chelly), painted 1987

Craig's fifth one-man show "Canyon de Chelly, an Intimate View" opened at the 'home gallery' on February 1, 1987. As Craig writes to his father in February, the year was shaping up to be a busy, exciting year.

> "*The exhibit has gone very well . . . Unfortunately I had the flu the entire time and was not able to visit with the people as much as I would have liked. However Marc, [Cassandra], and Cyril helped out and Jeannine was a fine hostess (with Mamie's help). No paintings have sold yet, but there have been nibbles.*
>
> *I had a letter from Mt Angel (which I answered with a phone call) and everything seems to be in very good order so far as we can tell. There is supposed to be an announcement of the exhibit in "Oregon" magazine. And they have other means of advertising, I am told. I also learned that we are not permitted to have receptions with food within the Library; so that problem need not be faced. Of course, Jeannine and I will plan to be there on the opening few days to greet people . . .*
>
> *I also had a call from Reed College. They seem to want to exhibit some of the painting in the summer alumni show on campus. I said it would be fine. The timing is a little wrong, but somehow it will work out.*
>
> *Tom Ahern is dead, as you know. But his wife, Virginia, knows a painter in the Grants Pass area and they have set up a possible exhibit there later in 1987 or 1988, at the Fine Arts Museum of Grants Pass. I'm delighted; it is wonderful country to visit and both Jeannine and I hope it works out . . .*
>
> *If there is another exhibit of the Canyon de Chelly suite in Oregon, I may have to return to pick it up. Of course, I should not say 'I'; without Jeannine I couldn't do these things at all.*
>
> *We are also sending brochures to galleries in Europe and perhaps we will find other possibilities for shows later. Meanwhile, I have planned my next series of paintings (this time of people) and I'll get started immediately.*"[2]

The brochures that Craig mentions never came to be, although a photographer friend did photograph Craig, in situ, in September 1987 for the purpose of the brochures. Jeannine notes in the photo album of the time that ". . . *it became clear that this fold-out [pamphlet] would be extremely expensive if one wanted a good color reproduction.*"[3] So they gave up on that idea.

2. Ibid, 21 February 1987.
3. Notes by Jeannine from Hudson Family Photo Album #14 1987.

Craig kept a diary of the Mt Angel Exhibit trip which began on March 26, 1987. The trip included an ambitious schedule: make new contacts, set up the paintings and be at the opening of the Mt Angel Exhibit, visit friends in the Portland area, visit with daughter Elianne and husband in the Seattle area, and visit the Oregon boxcar of the Merci Train in Astoria. They would be gone just over five weeks. Mamie was to fly to Seattle, on her own, to meet them for the visit with Elianne. Craig and Jeannine headed out with the paintings packed in the car along with their luggage.

> "3/26/87—We made ready for our trip—our great adventure— and left Albuquerque on the morning of March 26. We stopped by to see Mamie and left about 10:00AM, destination Flagstaff. Leaving was quite a thrill, not a little apprehensive, because we were driving out with a relatively untested car (the Dodge Caravan) into uncertain weather, with a big load of my best paintings packed in cardboard boxes of untried design, with the idea of testing out our hopes of a new lifestyle—painting pictures and exhibiting them in places across the west.
>
> After we passed Gallup, we began to feel lighthearted and finally cut ourselves loose from the worries about leaving. These worries stemmed partly from my leaving a painting unfinished, from leaving the house in the hands of Andy (not knowing what problems he may have), from leaving Zizi's business in some one else's care, but mainly from leaving Mamie alone in her house, wringing her hands in self-pity. It was to be the longest time she had been left alone; and the longest trip Zizi and I had ever taken together in all our years of marriage, alone.
>
> Crossing into Arizona prompted Zizi to spring a surprise on me: stop at the 'Petrified Forest.' The car was running well, we were comfortable, time permitted, so we pulled off into the Nat'l Mon entrance. The northern part of the park, called the Painted Desert, was much like the area near Canyon de Chelly and of modest interest. But later we arrived at the southern part and the thrill of the great araucaria logs frozen into varicolored stone was powerful. We took a few photos to trigger memories; but the great fun will be retelling the experience. Some of the stone logs were the size of redwoods . . .
>
> 3/27/87—. . . We drove on through Kingman and Needles without incident and came eventually to Mojave to spend the night. We had passed thru the so-called Mojave Desert which seemed no more a desert than the area around Albuquerque; but we had seen many Joshua trees, a treat for Zizi . . .

3/28/87—Driving out of Mojave took us up thru a steep canyon at Tehachapi, the walls of which were lined with hundreds of wind mills of various designs to generate electric power. I had heard about this site (perhaps the biggest anywhere) whose purpose was an engineering experiment to test the economic feasibility of wind power generation. There seemed to be no obvious problem, but we heard that it was not working very successfully and been largely shut down.

The next leg of travel took us thru Bakersfield and up along the western side (following 15) of California's great central valley. There we saw agriculture functioning on a giant scale. Water was pumped up (south) from the Sacramento River and allowed to flow down (North) irrigating along the way. Fields were very large, hundreds—even thousands—of acres, all neatly planted & cared for. A popular crop was wine grapes, thousands of acres of them; also there were walnuts and almonds, and some vegetable crops. Crops that can be harvested by machine are certainly preferred over hand pick. California production of wine, especially common wine, promises to be huge in the near future. We later learned that this great irrigation project is beginning to slow down because of salinization. The effluent cannot drain efficiently and irrigation picks up too much salt and selenium. A more direct drain to San Francisco Bay is needed and probably will be soon—at great cost, of course, but this grand irrigation project is certain to bring agricultural billions to the area eventually . . .

3/29/87—This day led us through some lovely country thru the Siskiyous [Siskiyou Mountains] of N. California and S. Oregon . . . We hurried on to Margery Overacher's house in the deep hills S of Grants Pass. What a pleasant arrival that was! Margery proved to be about 65 years old but very alert and lively. Her friends were about the same age. We all 6 sat down to a dinner she had waiting. Talk was about art: they had enjoyed seeing those of my pictures in the thinner two boxes; they wanted me to comment on their works and especially on their plans to show in the Kimo Gallery. What could we say? They do lots of swishy painting which seems to be akin to therapy work. But they seem to be serious and will paint and repaint an area to achieve the 'best' color match (by some inner standard I don't understand). They still take lessons (!) and apparently their teacher instructs them on such topics as color matching, free flowing lines, balanced 'masses,' etc.

3/30/87—. . . We next stopped at the art museum in Grants Pass, to see what it was like . . . and a show by Curtis Otto was being hung. Otto is a skilled enough painter who seems to work in the Andy Warhol tradition: everything must make a 'statement' about our culture. He came out to the car to see some of my paintings and—so far as was apparent—he seemed to be much impressed. Since he influences the museum's program I suspect we can have a show in 1988. Some talk was to the effect of coordinating a science show with the Abbey in 1988 July . . .

3/31/87—. . . We drove up thru Reedsport (which I later learned had been named after Mat Reed, Mary's father;[4] on up the coast past familiar sights; and into Portland by way of McMinnville . . .

4/1/87—. . . the day was spent catching up with Dad . . .

4/2/87—. . . we drove down [from Portland] to Mt Angel and arrived just in time to meet Darlene Strand leaving. She graciously allowed us to go in and begin setting up the exhibit. After looking over the [wall] panels . . . we agreed upon a scheme (Zizi's) that gave space for 14 paintings in mid-floor and 5 more along walls, with a 6th space for the autobiography . . . We found that organizing by numbers, as at the home gallery, was not feasible, so we ignored numbers and put similar together. The whole operation took about 4 ½ hours, even counting adjustment of the overhead lights. There were no surprises . . .

4/3/87—. . . we went over to [Cousin Ruth's] apt (a very nice place) . . . We spoke much about Claus' family which had always been a mystery since he was orphaned and raised by others as their own; she seemed to want to make much of the Messings, perhaps (like Dad) to balance out the overwhelming Palmer influence. Her apartment was just what we had looked for in Albuquerque but could not find: a nice building, security, nice view, about 1400 ft², all for 600/mo. Albuquerque has no such place except for twice the price . . .

4/4/87—The show opened at the Abbey at 1 pm. Before that we checked in at the guest house, into a very nice small room. things were very slow at first but about 2:00 pm Fran, Ralph, Nancy, Kelly & Elianne drove up and things brightened . . . We stayed till 5 pm, then went to our room . . . Father Bernard had been very much in evidence and very friendly; he urged us to see the library and meditation room. The meditation room contained Marge's tapestry . . . The tapestry is about 3'x8,' mostly blues and light creams. I watched her compose it and knew it was to go to the Abbey (when I was there in 1986) and she admitted to being constrained by a committee. It is not her best work and even with a written description, one cannot get a clear idea of what it is for, what it is to show. But, like a mother, she loves every offspring . . .

4. [Editor's Note] Craig is probably referring to Mary Reed Palmer.

4/5/87—. . . The show opened to a happy throng of relatives and friends responding to my invitation . . . Eventually most cleared out, Darlene Strand came and we 5 had a little party in the staff-faculty room for an hour . . . After a pleasant visit at the coffee table, we all went separate ways, we into Portland . . ."[5]

Craig and Jeannine spent several days in Portland visiting old friends and family before driving west to McMinnville to visit and stay overnight with Herman and Marge. In the mid-70s Herman (having retired) and Marge had moved back from the East coast and purchased several acres of land just outside of McMinnville.

"4/8/87—. . . Both seemed to be in good spirits and we chatted about health, art, politics, until bedtime. We had had a nice dinner of Marge's special fare. But they are turning a little bit to health foods now, not so much to my taste . . .

4/9/87—We had hoped Marge would come with us to Astoria, but she declined. Instead, she took Jeannine out to a wild part of the property where trilliums could be found and we got a fine picture of a large trillium already past its prime and turning purple. Then [Herman and I and Jeannine] set out for Astoria, taking the sunset Highway thru the Tillamook Burn[6]. *No longer is the landscape seared and black. New trees have sprung up and in a few places, where reforestation was undertaken promptly, the forest is quite impressive. Back some miles from the road, of course, where reforestation was more difficult, the land (where not too steep) is covered with brush; conifers will come later. One of the stories Herman told during this drive was one I had not heard before. He and a man "Fred" were very close during the dark days of fighting on the Italian front. It was a dangerous and slow task to drive the Germans out of their prepared positions in the mountains north of Florence. One day, he related (giving a great deal of interesting detail which I cannot recall), he and Fred were at their ease during a lull in the fighting, standing near a dirt road enjoying the sun. Suddenly the silence was broken a short distance away by a loud 'whuff' and, closer, another louder 'whuff', signifying a line of incoming shells intended to bracket the road. Fred jumped into his foxhole, nearby, while Herman dashed a few yards toward his. The third 'whuff' hit Fred's foxhole and killed him. The fourth round stirred the air at Herman's ear and buried*

5. Unpublished *Diary of Mt Angel Exhibit 1987* by Craig Hudson, Spring 1987.

6. [Editor's Note] Tillamook Burn was a devastating series of three forest fires in the Oregon Coastal Range mountains west of Portland between 1933 and 1951. Decker, Doug, *Tillamook Burn* .

itself in the ground just ahead of him, a dud. He leaped over it and into his hole and the rest of the shells fell harmlessly. He felt after that that he had a new lease on life. Much later, as he was looking through the McMinnville phone book he happened upon an entry for Fred—. On impulse, he called and spoke to Mrs. Fred— in a rest home. Upon visiting her, he found her rather bitter about life, about how barren it was for a war widow who no one cared for. She had suffered a severe paralyzing stroke and, while her mind was clear enough, she was unable to enjoy life. He continued to visit her occasionally until she finally died.

. . . During the rest of the day, we went first to the Marine Museum in Astoria—a wonderful place, full of marine lore and artifacts, mostly having to do with shipping in and around the mouth of the Columbia River. I learned that the Columbia is the only major river in the world too young to have a delta, which is supposed to lead to its peculiar shifting sand bars, causing numerous shipwrecks, a graveyard for ships . . .

After the museum, we crossed the Columbia Bridge (a thrill in itself since [it] spans the channel at 300 ft height) to the Washington side. There we walked out to the North Head light house which was operating (beams oriented slightly separated) . . . Finally, after a charming time with Herman (who recounted that as a boy he used to cross the ferry with his bike and ride out these 20 or so miles just to while away a Sunday) . . . we went with Herman to gas up, sent him off to a long ride home in the dark, and went back [to the Inn] for a pleasant night. It had been a great time with the Johansens.

4/10/87—. . . After some talk about the exhibit at the Abbey and other such things, we drove off in the rain . . . we drove to the Flavell house [Astoria] and took some photos of the French boxcar, trying to show the undercarriage. It was pretty dark to photograph and I doubted much would be seen. We used the flash and hoped for the best. Then we headed out of town for the Longview Bridge. Across the Columbia and into Kelso [Washington], we stopped for a cup of coffee and a marvelous homemade cinnamon roll . . ."[7]

They continued to drive north to the Seattle area to meet with Mamie, who had flown in, and together they visited with Elianne and Kelly. The visit included a trip to the Olympic Peninsula and the Olympic Rainforest, which made quite an impression on Craig.

"4/10/87—. . . Late in the afternoon, we arrived at Elianne's to find that Mamie had come in by plane that morning instead of the evening before. She had left late from Albuquerque, missed

7. Unpublished *Diary of Mt Angel Exhibit 1987* by Craig Hudson, Spring 1987.

*the connection in Denver and had been put up at a fine hotel by
the airline. She was a little shaken by the experience, but none the
worse for wear . . . [After a family dinner] plans were laid for the
next day to leave for Port Townsend and later Quinault . . .*

*4/11/87—We followed each other (Elianne and me in one car
following Mamie, Zizi and Kelly in the other), down to the ferry
landing . . . Finally we drove onto the ferry, a very large ship, and
got underway. It was also a fast boat and crossing the sound took
hardly half an hour. Mamie was at first frightened but we climbed
to the promenade deck where seats and tables were provided in a
warm enclosed area and she soon loosened up and became quite
gay—especially when provided with a cup of coffee. Out on the
water, it being Saturday, hundreds of sail boats took advantage
of the stiff breeze as their occupants playfully tested their skills
against the risks of keeling over, racing this way and that across
the water as far as the eye could see. Once on the shore, Kelly led
the way to Port Townsend . . .*

*4/12/87—We departed midmorning for the drive to Lake
Quinault . . . The first night was one of trying to stabilize our
health problems. Mamie had been very ill on the road and Zizi
and I both had colds . . .*

*4/13/87—After breakfast, leaving Mamie in her room to
rest, we four [Craig, Jeannine, Elianne, Kelly] took a trail from
the parking lot [of Quinault Lodge] up into the woods and had
a marvelous walk through the rain forest. The sun came out on
occasion and it never really rained. So we had a fine walk of about
3 miles through wonderful woods. The path was often graveled to
keep our feet dry; but sometimes we walked over moss and even
corduroy bridges lain over swamps. The return path took us down
steeply thru giant Douglas firs, under a bridge and finally along
the edge of the lake and finally up to the gazebo which was visible across the lawn from the dining room. On this trip, we took a
number of pictures which could describe the Olympic rain forest
very well. We picked up Mamie, took her down the road to the
edge of the Douglas fir grove, and had a pleasant lunch . . ."*[8]

Craig's painting *Olympic Rainforest*[9] was a reproduction of a scene
that he photographed on this trip. The group stayed several nights at Lake
Quinault and several more days in the Seattle area. On the 20th, Mamie flew
back to Albuquerque, without delays or surprises. Craig and Jeannine and
Elianne continued on to the Portland area for more family and friends, and

8. Ibid.
9. [Editor's Note] see Appendix: Catalog of Craig's Paintings.

to check out the exhibit hall at Reed College. Craig's diary includes notes on composting in the Northwest (surely with dreams of his Albuquerque garden in mind!) and his observations on some of the new developments in downtown Portland.

"4/21/87—. . . I took a drive out to the Mt Tabor Fuel yard with Ralph. There I saw my dream working: a 6' diameter x 18' steel mesh drum made to separate mixed bark chips (read compost) into 3 bins of 3 sizes while a moving belt fed material into it. A wonder, that I had wanted so much to have at Los Arboles, for compost. The yard was full of all kinds of chip material for the garden. While driving around the Northwest, we have seen very large operations of sawdust—sand—peat moss composting using frontend loaders, bulldozers, scrapers, etc. soil preparation is big business and it really shows in luxurious growth & flowering . . .

4/22/87—We took E. to the appointment at Reed . . . and showed her the exhibit hall. Things seemed to go very well and she grasped what she needed to do instantly. All is set for August, I hope . . . After this, we went to the Rhododendron Garden and spent the rest of the afternoon walking those well-kept paths among giant azaleas and rhododendrons mostly in glorious bloom of rainbow colors. Such a marvelous display; such a marvelous park . . .

4/24/87—. . . we packed a lunch and Dad, Marilynn, Zizi, and I went to Peach Cove. It was a very fine day. The place is pretty run down. Blackberries and grass over run the gardens and flower beds that used to be. I have memories of what was then nice, but it is hard to communicate them. I took Zizi around to see as much as we could. Dad is no longer able to do any work up there; even the tools are broken. Pretty much the same is true of the Palmer place, too, and even Ted Todd manages to keep only some of the wilderness down. Expensive memories. On the way back, we stopped at the old Riverview Cemetery for Civil War Veterans (I took pictures and hope to have a better description from them). Marilynn finally spotted the old Grandpa Best tombstone and we noted some ways to mark it . . .

4/26/87—This morning opened a completely unplanned day, one of very few on this trip. Finally we decided to go downtown, which Zizi had wanted to see, and to have dinner at the Newport Bay on the river, which Marilynn had recommended. We drove down via the Banfield freeway (I-84) in only 10 minutes (!), circled thru the new Chinatown arch (quite fine, with great dogs on either side with a pagoda traversing 3rd street), drove along Waterfront Avenue at the southern end of the 'esplanade.' There is a beautiful concrete walkway 20–30 feet wide all along the frontage along *which people promenaded. Mostly they were rather trampy looking, but certainly there were many neat handsome people with children and old folks. Back of the sidewalk were shops of all kinds with several restaurants and one hotel, the Alexis. All was very new. It will take some firm discipline to keep street people and rowdies from dominating this area (already there are some), but perhaps gentility can win out. There is a long sward of green lawn in one place running down to a beach. It was a rocky beach but the invitation to swim was present; perhaps spreading sand will help since there is no tide to wash it away. Couples lounged in happy ease all across the lawn; children ran and played. We went into the Alexis and found a fine place to display paintings (the ones in place were mediocre). We went into a bookstore and found it well stocked. This marvel of waterfront improvement, which included a small sheltered 'port' for boats to tie up, extended perhaps ½ mile on the west side roughly from Ross Island Bridge to Burnside Bridge. It was an admirable development. Of course the unseasonably good weather, bringing out several thousand people, helped a great deal. An area of condominiums stands between this harbor frontage and Portland streets . . . we drove up town to see (a)the auditorium waterfall park; (b) Pioneer Square and Portlandia close up, (c) other public & private statues. The waterfall is glorious and obviously entertains many people (mostly urchins, I suspect, but others too). Pioneer Square seems to be overrated. It is built on the old Portland Hotel land near Meier & Frank and consists entirely of red brick, attractive enough. Unhappily, it attracts a small crowd of pushing and shoving young cocks whose shouts intrude and threaten the peace. There was also a cluster of rag-tag musicians with an aged electric guitar; the music was inconsequential; what was amazing was that they could play at all and that they swing with the gyrations of rock artists—and there was no one to watch! I know from news reports that Pioneer Square is very popular, a focal point for Portland youth activities, so it has this kind of success. The Portlandia figure is awesome, standing high above the street and beckoning to people on the sidewalk below, a truly powerful figure for Portland. Unhappily, it is poorly lighted, but a relatively small change should solve that, putting the figure out over and dominating the intersection. The carved and cast figures of people and animals in downtown Portland is very impressive. Their arts commission has rejected attempts at 'modern' sculpture; with few exceptions, there is no junk there . . ."*[10]

Craig and Jeannine returned to Mt Angel Abbey on April 27th, the day after the close of the exhibit, to dismantle the exhibit. The paintings were

10. Ibid .

returned to their boxes and the boxes were stored at Craig's friend's house (Marley Brown) until August. At that time Elianne would orchestrate the setup of the exhibit at Reed College. After an exciting beginning, they made the return trip to New Mexico in four days.

> "4/29/87—We drove from Pendleton to La Grande against a very stiff head wind. At one place, on a level road, with the gas pedal floored we lost speed from 55 down to 45 (!). On impulse, we took the road from Baker up (down!) the Snake River to Hell's canyon Dam. Most of the road was very good and quite scenic; but when we finally got to the last 20 miles, it was literally cut out of a vertical wall of rock, mostly without railing, and often rising to 500 feet above the deep lake. It was very scary for me to drive, scarier when Zizi drove. I kept my nerve, but it disturbs me how little calm I have in such a situation. When I recall youthful days . . . "[11]

Before finishing the trip home, they set out to find Shoshone Falls where "there was no water flowing (irrigation used it all) but I took reference pictures."[12] Craig remembered his Grandfather's stories of Shoshone Falls and had a plan for a painting which he completed in 1990.

Shoshone Falls, painted 1990

11. Ibid .
12. Ibid .

Within a month Mamie, Craig, and Jeannine were in Europe. They visited with old and new friends and members of Jeannine's family as well as historical places, museums, and the Opera. Mamie stayed with friends while Craig and Jeannine fit in a trip to Dijon, France, where Jeannine checked on the boxcar that had been purchased for New Mexico, a trip to Périgord for Craig to see prehistoric cave paintings (copies of which he had painted from photos), and a trip to Austria. Craig described their trip to his cousin Louise and her husband Dick, with whom he had recently renewed a friendship.

> *"The trip to France and Austria depended on our being able to stay with friends; we could not have afforded 6 weeks in hotels. The purpose of the trip originally was to visit these friends; but once there, we made use of the opportunity to hear music, to see exhibits of art; but most importantly, to see what only Europe can offer—the artifacts and structures of early Man. In that we luxuriated. We were reading Jean Auel's 'Valley of the Horses'[13] as we went along which added a charming background to our excursions thru Neanderthal and Cro-Magnon cultures. One special trip into the Périgord, to Les Elyzies, gave us the opportunity to try their marvelous food while seeing the famous caves of the region."[14]*

Before leaving Paris they took photos at old memorable places.

> *". . . Back in Paris, we went to the place where Jeannine and I first met. We took each other's picture in front of Notre Dame in memory of my meeting with Dexter on this spot in 1945 . . . We went up to the door of the old Dumas' apartment for Jeannine to shed a tear over memories of those old times . . . "[15]*

Returning from nearly six weeks in Europe, their life in Albuquerque returned them to their respective jobs. Craig was occupied with finishing a painting for entry in the Fine Arts Show of the NM State Fair, mailing a painting as an entry to the First National Parks Painting Competition, and continuing work on the portraits.

> *"I have been working on a new series of paintings, this time doing people. It is quite a change from my previous work, one which I needed to make for disciplinary reasons as well as for the pleasure of painting people I love. So far, I have nearly finished my third*

---

13. [Editor's Note] *Valley of the Horses.* Jean M. Auel. Random House Publishing Group 1984.

14. Letter from Craig and Jeannine to 'Louise and Dick Godfrey,' 14 September 1987.

15. Letter from Craig and Jeannine to 'Dad,' 25 June 1987.

out of a suite of 15—and the work is going slowly. In part, I have been distracted; but mostly the work is more tedious and harder.

A new kind of exhibit is opening here in about a month, of which I will be a part. Artists from across the country who combine science with their artistic skills will join to show off their work. So far as we know, it is the first exhibit of this kind attempted and quite a bit of publicity is being planned nation-wide. But you know how things like this go: it could flop. One thing I am sure of: busloads of school children will come and since Jeannine and I have agreed to be docents, we will have our hands full."[16]

The house was put on the market again, bringing up those bitter-sweet feelings again and the press to consider future living conditions. In Oregon, Cyril, Elianne, and her husband Kelly set up the paintings at the Reed College Alumni Summer Art Exhibit which ran August 3rd—24th.

The year came to a close with the birth of a granddaughter (Aubrey), a firm invitation from the Fine Arts Museum of Grants Pass to exhibit the Canyon de Chelly paintings in April 1988, and an exhibit of some of Craig's science paintings at the *Art and Science Exhibition 1987* at the Fine Arts Gallery at the New Mexico State Fair Grounds in Albuquerque during the month of October.

"The exhibit closed on a pleasant note. The lady from New York who came out here representing the AAAS, a world renowned science society based in Wash DC, stayed at our house 4 days and was very pleasant and interested in everything. It was her first visit to the southwest . . . "[17]

Craig recognized that 1988 would also be a busy year. He had planned much in way of painting and exhibits.

"My year in painting is shaping up to be a busy one. In some cases, I have to apply to a jury to be able to enter; in other cases, I have scheduled exhibits:

Date	Place	Jury	Exhibit
Feb	Alb	Arts & Crafts	—
Mar	Alb	—	Home Show (8)
Apr	Grants Pass	—	Canyon de Chelly [19]
Jun	Alb	—	Arts & Crafts [12]

16. Letter from Craig and Jeannine to 'Louise and Dick Godfrey,' 14 September 1987.

17. Letter from Craig and Jeannine to 'Dad,' 2 November 1987.

Jul	Wyo	Natl Parks (1)	—
Jul	Mt Angel	—	Natural Forces [18]
Aug	Alb	State Fair (1)	—
Aug	Silver City	Local Show (1)	—
Oct	Alb	—	Art & Science (6)

The numbers (3) etc mean new paintings; the numbers [18] etc mean existing paintings. So I have a lot of work to do, since we will be traveling for 2 months (Apr & Jul). It's a big year and it may get more complicated with time. Of course, Jeannine will be working as hard as possible to make some money while I am painting."[18]

Craig was wise to predict entanglements for the coming year. Youngest son, Cyril, married in February at the Los Arboles house; granddaughter (Olivia) was born in May; Craig was hospitalized for hiccups and heart problems in June; the boxcar from France was delivered on June 28th; the house sold in mid-July and Craig and Jeannine moved into an apartment one week before leaving for their second northwest trip.

(Jan 1988) "Day by day we are moving into the new year and it is already becoming busy with a number of interlocked engagements. Tomorrow Jeannine goes to Santa Fe to talk to Governor Caruthers about a bill that is being introduced into the Legislature for her boxcar . . . Cyril's wedding is only a month away now. I am trying to complete 3 new paintings to enter the jurying for the Arts and Crafts Fair in late June. . .my own home show is scheduled to open Mar 20 and those paintings are not ready yet either (may have to postpone it). And then we must leave in early April to get to the Grants Pass opening. Nothing has come up yet; but I am expecting to enter two exhibits in Aug, sent an entry to the Natl Parks Competition in Mid-July and have 4 new science paintings ready for the Art & Science Exhibition in October—if it comes off. Beyond these things, I can't think straight. Of course, Jeannine is pursuing her work at NYL to keep some money coming in; and the French Boxcar is causing a lot of activity, many phone calls, committee meetings, etc.

The only thing that could complicate matters more than they are is for the house to sell. No one has been to see it lately; but there could be a 'sleeper' out there, I suppose."

(Feb 1988) "Jeannine's Boxcar activity is coming to a head. Her visit to the Governor 2 weeks ago brought promise of some money

18. Ibid, 2 January 1988.

for transportation; and a State Representative has found at least temporary lodging for the car at the State Fair. So she is almost ready to tell the French Gov't to send it!

I am preparing the paintings for the July exhibit at Mt Angel; we will bring them up in April."

(Mar 1988) "Cyril and Sundee's wedding came off beautifully. Jeannine had planned everything in detail and there were no mix-ups . . . it was a fine party . . .

I am trying to finish 2 paintings for the Nat'l Park exhibition and one for the State Fair before we leave. And there is still work to be done getting ready for the July exhibit at Mt Angel."[19]

Craig journalized the two Northwest road trips. The drive would take at least three days, if they didn't make detours. Craig and Jeannine enjoyed the ride and each other's company. They took turns driving and sometimes packed picnic lunches for themselves. The April-May trip took them to Grants Pass and Mt Angel for the exhibits, the Portland area for family and friends, a stay at the Oregon beach, and the Seattle area for the birth of Elianne and Kelly's daughter, which being overdue, made their schedule tight for the return trip.

"Mon Apr 4—. . . Finally we got off and, with a feeling of excitement and freedom that only comes with an adventure, we sailed up over the shoulder of the Jemez Mts to Cuba [New Mexico]. We had done this so many times before; but this time was a little special. The ground was still damp with moisture from the recent snow and the colors were beautiful; Jeannine remarked about the "Hunter's Point" painting and how it reminded her of the great red rock cliff near Jemez Canyon. I remark on this because I like to do such paintings and it is pleasant to know they are appreciated. In fact, it was the only one of the three accepted for the June Art Fair . . . In this sense, Jeannine has an unerring sense of the appealing; I must learn to control my stubborn desire to satisfy innate demands that seem to grow out of my science background and which have low artistic appeal—to others. These raw geologic scenes seem trite—even tho fun to paint; but they are liked! . . .

We found the Caravan to be comfortable, conversation pleasant, and the road slid beneath us like a smooth ribbon. We stopped for lunch at Dove Creek, at a small war memorial park in town. For a small town, there was lots of activity as farmers began to get ready for spring planting and school kids jogged around the roads.

19. Ibid, 2 January 1988, 20 January 1988, 15 February 1988.

In a way, I regret not being able to jog anymore; but what I can now do in its stead is really much more fun . . .

Tues Apr 5 — . . . I must remark on the road up away from Moab, across the Colorado and past those wonderful red cliffs. We had driven up there with Marc, Elianne and [Cassandra] in 1956, along a very steep narrow road, in our old Pontiac with the worn out tires, I with my heart in my throat, out over the desert where the sand blew across the road so that at places it was obliterated. Some starving cattle wandered around looking for something to eat but there was almost nothing growing. Strangely, as we looked now out of our nice car gliding along a new superhighway with green grass and shrubs on all sides and a sign here and there of human habitation, Jeannine's recollections of that first trip were much less somber than mine. She had seemed to have complete confidence that all would work out—as it did, of course; but for me, not the least of my worries was that we saw not a single car for 50 or 60 miles on that long ago trip. I guess I worry too much . . .

Wed Apr 6—As we left Twin Falls [Idaho], the conversation touched on Shoshone Falls, which we learned was again dry. Apparently my only hope is to reconstruct the entire falls from those pictures I took last year of the dry rock bed. The water will be permanently used for irrigation unless something happens. Our car rolled happily across the long Idaho prairie on the concrete highway . . .

It had been our original intent to spend another night on the road; but Zizi felt so comfortable driving—and relieved me so often—that finally, after having a late lunch at Farewell Bend of the Snake River, we decided to drive on into Portland.

The miles rolled by and we stopped at our first sight of the Columbia for a coffee break; then on down the Gorge into the sunset with such beautiful scenes that I photographed a few from the car . . .[20]

Craig and Jeannine had only a night or two in Portland to connect with family and pick up Craig's paintings that had been stored at Rosie's house. They drove to Grants Pass set up the paintings and were present for the opening. They left the show in place and drove back to Portland. On the way they made a side trip to Mt Angel to check on the gallery space there. By Tuesday they were driving north toward Seattle where they would spend time with daughter Elianne and her husband, who were expecting their first child within the month. *"It was a lovely reunion and fun to see Elianne all*

20. Unpublished journal *Spring Oregon Trip 1988* by Craig Hudson.

puffed up with a baby. She was tired, it's true, but she was so happy."[21] One evening Craig had his first interview with a reporter.

> *"Wed Apr 13— . . .[in the evening] I received a call from a [report-*
> *er] of the Grants Pass 'Daily Courier' and I gave him an interview*
> *by phone. He wanted to know about my time at Reed and U of*
> *O, my work as a scientist (Sandia & consulting), my art training,*
> *and how I prepared myself to paint the Canyon de Chelly suite*
> *(by working from photos). He also asked about my 'emotional'*
> *interest in the subject matter. I told him Monet was my favorite*
> *artist and that I liked to build up a painting by layers until, as a*
> *final step, I sprinkled the little accent brush strokes which give the*
> *picture character. I spoke for several minutes about the effects of*
> *atmospheric turbulence on seeing. He seemed not to understand*
> *very well but went on ahead anyway. We also discussed the sci-*
> *ence paintings to be shown at Mt Angel—he already knew about*
> *the Alto Library—and I invited him to go see the exhibit. The in-*
> *terview lasted about ½ hr . . .*
>
> *This was the first interview about my work I had had outside*
> *Albuquerque—and certainly the first by one who could not see*
> *me. I felt ill at ease talking about my painting in terms artists usu-*
> *ally use in interviews and I wonder what the outcome will be.*
> *Certainly the words fell upon him awkwardly; how they will be*
> *reflected in the written piece is hard to predict. I have showed my*
> *essay to several people—Dad and Margery [Overacher] in par-*
> *ticular—and they could not understand it. I think I cannot tell my*
> *thoughts clearly; even Zizi does not understand on a first telling—*
> *and one telling is all I usually get. I need to expand my essay . . .*
> *More than once I have been asked to explain the emotional impact*
> *of my works—but I am never aware that there is any . . . "*[22]

After spending several days in the Seattle area, they drove back to the Portland area to check in on family and friends. They drove to McMinnville to visit with Herman and Marge, then on to the coast for several days.

> *"Sun Apr 17—. . . Herman and I chatted about our things (we*
> *seem to be more and more involved in the philosophy of science*
> *subject) and Zizi and Marge chatted about theirs. And finally to*
> *bed. The house is very nicely finished now; it has taken Herman*
> *years, but finally it is nearly done—and so strong and practical.*
> *Herman calls himself a millwright not a carpenter!*

21. Ibid, 13 Apr 1988.

22. Unpublished journal *Spring Oregon Trip 1988* by Craig Hudson.

Mon Apr 18—Herman got us up by making a fire to warm the room. While Marge ad Zizi were making breakfast, H and I renewed our discussions and focused particularly on "God & the New Physics" by Davies[23](which I must get) and talked about the thermodynamic concepts—especially free energy and entropy. One has to wonder about how entropy can be integrated into religion because entropy changes in a direction which seems to be contrary to what religion would prefer . . . I must get Davies' book . . .

After breakfast, Herman and I and the dogs took a long walk out to the blueberry patch. This is the mark and symbol of his place . . . [Herman] is a man seeing the inevitability of change but not knowing how to go about it. This may be nearly the last year he can work so hard. But he feels deprived when he cannot. I'm sure he wants to die in his present house. Social Security is a great boon to Herman & Marge and even if he has to let his farm go to the weeds, he will be able to survive there . . .

We drove away from them seemingly happy but inwardly sad. This friendship that has lasted 50 years cannot go on forever and that is not a happy thought."[24]

Craig and Jeannine had a delightful surprise during a stay at the beach. They then headed back to family in Portland for several days; then back north to be on hand for the birth of a granddaughter.

"Thur Apr 22— . . . [at the Oregon beach house] I made clam chowder; Zizi braised lettuce; and we had cheese and wine to finish. And Zizi called my attention to the sun setting, an orange ball in a yellow-orange sky. As the last sliver of the disc dropped down, we both saw the green flash!![25] How many times we have watched for it but never saw it! . . .

Wed May 4— . . . We found a telephone message at the apartment that the Grants Pass exhibit had been wrapped and taken to Marge Overacher's house. All is well on that count; but there was no word about a sale. I was hoping one would sell.

Wed May 11—. . . Elianne's news from the doctor was not very encouraging: she is not yet ready to deliver and may not be for a week or more. Our timing is becoming more tight. We knew when

23. [Editor's Note] Craig is probably referring to *God and the New Physics* by Paul Davies published 1984, Simon and Schuster.

24. Unpublished journal *Spring Oregon Trip 1988* by Craig Hudson.

25. [Editor's Note] A green flash is a phenomenon in which the last bit of the sun's rays, as it is perceived to drop below the horizon, will briefly appear green.

we came up that she could be 2 weeks late—and apparently she will be (one week already)...[26]

Granddaughter, Olivia, finally decided to arrive on the thirteenth of May. Craig and Jeannine stayed on for a couple of days before heading south, through Portland to say their goodbyes, to Grants pass.

> "*Thurs May 19—Marge [Overacher] made us a big breakfast, filled our tank with gas (!) from her supply, and sent us off 2 hours late. That 2 hours forced us to stop at Fallon instead of Austin [Nevada]. So now we are not sure we can make it home Saturday...*
>
> *Fri May 20—We undertake today to drive to Green River [Utah].*
>
> *The country west of Fallon is quite rugged and beautiful; near Fallon it is green and fertile; then there are some salt flats; finally after the mountains are large grassy valleys miles across... Then we come to Eureka, a quite old town, with some business and agriculture around it. We had trouble deciding whether to proceed the fast way home or detour to Grand Canyon. We finally chose the fast way... and set off for Delta. Just outside Ely [Nevada] was a sign for Lehman Cave Nat'l Mon plus a new sign for a new Nat'l Park—the Great Basin Nat'l Park, about 12 miles SW of Baker. As we drove along, we came across a number of places that would be interesting to re-visit, places that offered many, many subjects for paintings...*
>
> *Sat May 21—We arose early for a quick start and drove out after gassing up. As we approached Moab, I took some pictures (actually Zizi took them) of the Orange Cliffs (I found the name on an old map) with the Mt Peale mountains in the background— still white with snow. These were views I had long wanted to paint ...*"[27]

The plan had been to be back in Albuquerque by mid-May because Craig had several exhibits to work on; then in mid-July they were to set off again driving to the Northwest for the exhibits at Mt Angel and Grants Pass. Those eight weeks turned out to be even more hectic. By the beginning of June Craig's health problems became an issue again.

> *(June 1988) "... I am again in the hospital. We had some pleasant times with the kids, a big coming home dinner, etc. then a couple of days later, I began to have hiccups. At first, I laughed it off, but after 20 hours of nearly continuous hiccupping, with only a*

---

26. Unpublished journal *Spring Oregon Trip 1988* by Craig Hudson.
27. Ibid.

few breaks (every 5 seconds—I counted them) we finally decided
something had to be done. All the usual cures had been tried, of
course, to no avail. So I was taken by Jeannine to a specialist for
gastro problem; but when he found that the exertion had elevated
my heart beat to 180/min he had me admitted directly to the hos-
pital as a cardiac patient. They have since reduced my heart rate
to a normal 68; but the hiccups have not really disappeared. They
stop for long times but always return; no one seems to be able to
offer much intelligent conversation on hiccups so far.

    This is certainly putting a crimp in my plans. I was supposed to
have 2 paintings finished for the Nat'l Parks Exhibition; only one
is done. Only 3 slides of paintings for the August showing in Silver
City are needed and fortunately they are ready. All I have to do is
send them in for the judging. But the painting for the State Fair
is only half done and is due in August—but we'll be gone most of
the time!

    Our plans are still the same for the return to Oregon. I have
every hope to be out of here in a day or so . . . I think we will be
able to make it with perhaps a few, only, omissions or errors."[28]

Craig's notes from the hospital describe the heart condition in more
detail. He wanted to limit the amount of drugs to his system, so that he
could remain clearheaded and focused for the remaining years of his life.

    ". . . there was a lengthy study of my heart structure done by echo
cardiogram. The results of this have been discussed by [the car-
diologist]: poor valves, enlarged main chamber. I asked him to
consider treating me conservatively meaning that I should have a
modest—no exercise—lifestyle for 10 years, so that I could com-
plete my painting program . . ."[29]

Hanging the exhibit at Mt Angel was done by some of the children. At
the end of June, Cyril and his wife, Sundee, flew to Seattle to connect with
Elianne. The three of them drove to Portland, picked up the paintings for
the *Natural Forces* exhibit from Rosie, and set up the exhibit at Mt Angel for
the July 1st opening.

    (13 June) "The unpleasant hospital experience is behind us . . . I
was there 5 days . . .

    By this time, I feel a little tired—or weak—but otherwise I am
fine . . .

28. Letter from Craig to 'Dad,' 29 May–3 June 1988.

29. From "A few notes about my Jun 88 illness" by Craig.

Now about the return trip. We have had to make some changes because it appears that the house is really going to be sold this time. We are once again seriously looking for a suitable apartment. Jeannine needs to maintain two desks (!), one for NYL and the other for her work with the French Boxcar Committee, which keeps growing slowly. And I need a studio . . .

At the moment, I am preparing my entry into the 2nd Nat'l Parks Exhibit which I must send in a few days. It is the 'Rain Forest' painting (Olympic Nat'l Park) that I told you about earlier. It's nice. Then there is the Silver City Show in September. All is ready for that entry except the mailing. It's a big year."[30]

(18 July) "The last 10 days have been pretty hectic. We managed to complete the sale of the house and the confusion of the move is over. We thought we had packed a great deal, but when the crew of movers came, it took 4 professionals 9½ hours to box, load and unload the household goods into our little apartment, pretty much helter-skelter. Jeannine had planned where to put the heavy pieces, so they went in first. Even now, a week later, only half the boxes are emptied.

We were supposed to leave yesterday; but on Friday when we took the Caravan thru the car wash, the windshield cracked (it was a hot day). The insurance people said get it replaced before the trip . . . but when [the replacement] came, it was cracked, too. So the windshield was only fixed this afternoon . . . We began to wonder if we could really leave."[31]

The trip to the Northwest happened without major incident including visits to family and friends as well as picking up Craig's paintings from the Mt Angel Exhibit. Craig notes in his journal that on the drive back they encountered car trouble and he had difficulties with his heart rate.

"19 Jul—We set out at about 6:30 AM. Packing had been quite rushed . . .

We were apprehensive, starting off with so little preparation. Things the day before had been hectic. So we stopped at the hotel in Las Vegas [New Mexico] for a lovely breakfast. That put us in good spirits . . .

Our plan this trip is: pick up the paintings; see Dad, Elianne, Marilynn, et al; visit some nat'l parks—and relax.

21 Jul—We arose again at 5:30 and got on the road by 6:30. We have a long drive to Bozeman[Montana] . . . to alleviate the heat, we stopped in an old fashioned place with ancient Idaho

30. Letter from Craig and Jeannine to 'Dad,' 13 June 1988.
31. Letter from Craig to 'Dad,' 18 July 1988.

potato sacks hung on the walls (with amazing pictures) for ice cream (Zizi) and the biggest root beer float for me I had ever seen, all for $1.50 . . .

23 Jul—We started off for Glacier Park with a light breakfast. There is a long tedious drive (40 miles, about) to the park entrance. We stopped and took a couple of pictures at the 'visitor center' and then started the long drive up. In truth, there is scarcely room for 2 RVs to pass and the dropoff is one of the most dramatic I have ever seen. Zizi drove (with my alto phobia, I would have been a nervous wreck). We stopped at a number of turnouts and I took photos, some of which will be very good. We arrived at length at the Logan Pass (only 6900 ft but very precipitous) and spent awhile looking around. Then we drove down the other side to St Mary [Montana], not so steeply situated but pretty steep anyway. We stopped at a picnic area on St Mary Lake and spent a lovely 2 hours in reasonable solitude, eating and sleeping. I picked up 7 or 8 flakes of stone of the several colors from the beach. The wind sighed in the cottonwoods and little waves lapped at the shore; lovely.

Later, we stopped at the St Mary's Visitor Center, much more modern, and better; went to St Mary's for coffee; and retraced our steps, seeing the wonderful scenery from the opposite point of view. And finally we ended the day with a nice meal at a fine little restaurant. We are planning our return via Spokane or Lewiston—probably the latter—to make an easy drive and to see some good country. The Lewiston route passes thru the Bitter Root Range, not far from the Salmon River of family fame[32].

24 Jul—[in Lewiston Idaho] . . . On evenings while waiting for Zizi, I read the Gideon Bible[33], thinking in terms of an archaeologist. It is rambling (in Genesis and Exodus) and repetitious with much material relevant only to the authors; but it does reveal much about the culture of the times, which Zizi and I enjoyed discussing.

25 Jul— . . . Zizi wanted to follow the Lewis and Clark Route so we left Lewiston, drove through Clarkston on the other side of the Snake [River] and then proceeded thru the rolling hills of the Palouse country toward Pasco [Washington], rather than aiming at Pendleton, roughly following the Snake. The idea was to cross the Snake as close as possible to its confluence with the Columbia [River]; and then to cross the Columbia. This we did in the vicinity

32. [Editor's Note] Craig references an unpublished manuscript 'Palmer History.'.

33. [Editor's Note] Gideon Bibles are Bibles placed in hotel rooms for use by any interested reader. .

of Richland [Washington] ... We were held up by road work at the little town of Irigon [Oregon] where we stopped for coffee. There was an enormous bar there made of a Douglas fir log sawed in half, inlayed with various artifacts, and covered with 20 coats of resin. Beautiful, if not very durable. The drive down the [Columbia] Gorge was very hot. We stopped at Celilo Park for lunch and dozed under the trees. Further down, the air was so clear Mt Hood stood out very clearly—but we were out of film ...

    27 Jul—We go to McMinnville [Oregon] to see H & M today ...

    Both Herman and Marge were as cuddly as could be and we loved them. Herman and I went out into his fields and picked cherries—they were dead ripe, never saw better. Huge, juicy, tasty. Later, we all went to bed and Zizi and I spent a comfortable night in their new bed near the stove. It became quite cool after the sun set.

    30 Jul—We prepare to take down the show ...

    Zizi planned a little picnic lunch ... We drove on to Silver Falls Park and had a delightful lunch on the grass under some trees. Then we looked over the old lodge, took some pictures, and drove back to the Abbey. I had been worried about keeping an appointment with [Brother] Cyril at 2 pm. But he was late. Zizi was annoyed at the lost Silver Falls time, and I paced. Eventually [Brother] Cyril came and we had a good chat ... Also he and a friend helped us pack the boxes into the car, and we left in good time ...

    In a way it is comforting to have the paintings back—old friends. But the exhibit had been successful. Half the cards had been taken. About 130 people signed the register, surely not all of the visitors. And the librarian said 500 on each night of the Bach Festival had seen the exhibit (2000–3000). One entry, in the register said 'should be in a book,' my sentiments exactly ...

    4 Aug—We said goodbye to Dad after taking some pictures. Then we drove to Grants Pass. On the way, we passed the blackened roadway (northbound) where the day before there had been a devastating 23 car pileup and fire—all because smoke from a run-a-way fire in a farmer's field swept over the highway, blinding. It was a real tragedy, but [field] burning is legal ...

    There was some difficulty with the car. It was very hot (later we learned 107°) and there were some steep hills and we used the air conditioner. The car was a little sluggish on hills (expected?) and when we stopped at the museum, it was a little difficult to start and would not idle. We got to the Overacher's and during the night it cooled ...

5 Aug—Car idles too fast. We stopped for gas and then at a Shell where a young mechanic loosened the idle all the way; it acts as if the automatic choke were on all the time. We drove out without trouble, however. Young man said not to worry. We drove over mountains easily—but rain has cooled off the air—and the car behaves well except for the idle. We check into [motel] at Redding and Zizi (Gods bless her!) searched out a garage to help tomorrow morning . . .

6 Aug— . . . I am worried about the car—can't help it—and it makes my heart go into the partial erratic state, giving me a feeling of weakness and nervousness. The situation feeds on itself. Zizi drove all day yesterday. I'd like to spare her some driving today if I can . . .

The car was checked this morning at the Chevron Station and the manager reported that the fast idle had been corrected by tightening two vac hoses and oiling the linkage . . . He also pointed out that one radiator hose needed to be replaced—I authorized it—that the radiator should be flushed—I authorized it—and that it was about time to change filter and oil of the transmission—I authorized it, too. These problems were not obviously urgent, but the service is appreciated . . .

We drove to Fallon, getting there at 7:30 pm. Zizi drove most of the way . . .

7 Aug—. . . We drove along, she driving, while talking about our exciting plans of what to do when we get back. In particular, we are short of lovemaking; but also the whole idea of the apartment stirs up Zizi's nesting instinct and she misses making bread— and I surely miss it too. Restaurant food has just about worn us out . . . Inevitably, we talked about finances and about Mamie's house . . . Well, even tho the overall picture is bleak, there were some chuckles as we drove along. This time, I did do a little driving. Rains began about noon and I got some pictures of marvelous clouds. We signed into the [motel] at Ely and after Zizi read to me for an hour (which I loved), we slept till dinner. Present plan is to [get a motel] at Green River & Farmington and get home about noon on 10th (Wed) . . .

This afternoon I tried every which way to calm my heart down to no avail. Zizi's reading was a help . . .

9 Aug—We pulled into Farmington before noon and were able to take the [motel] room . . . Zizi has driven almost all the way. I find driving tiresome and worrisome. There is reason to question long trips—tho Zizi can now drive steadily for 2 hours and 300 miles a day if fresh. We must plan more carefully unless my health and eyesight improve.

*Last night I reread Genesis 1 and 2 and found that the theory
that Moses' ideas of creation follow modern ideas except for time
scale is quite untenable. Agreed it is a clever myth—but no more
than that.*

*We slept until refreshed and then drove to Cuba for dinner, a
nice dinner at Bruno's . . . We came to the apartment and found
everything just as we had left it, and tumbled into bed. The air was
humid and warm but we slept til 6 am anyway. The noise of the
freeway is bad but we will get used to it . . .* "[34]

Craig and Jeannine finished the year settling into the new apartment
and getting back to work on their respective projects. The apartment was
quite a bit smaller than their house and, even with much of their belongings
in storage, it was a big adjustment. Craig had a painting accepted for an
exhibit in Silver City. He was not painting much at the moment, but he had
begun in earnest to organize the genealogy material.

*(Aug 15) "We are fairly well settled in the new apartment now.
Jeannine has done a marvelous job of organizing. If we look long
enough, we are sure to find what we want. Except, that is, my
paints and brushes. Somehow they have been mislaid and I cannot get back to work. For the moment, that is not serious: I have
so much paper-work to catch up on that work is not yet important.
All of those people and journals and societies (about 100) have to
be notified, since the blanket change of address only lasts a few
months. And all the accounts have to be brought current and
balanced!*

*One of my paintings was juried into a show in Silver City at
the end of the month, so we probably will have to drive there. It's a
good place to show, and in a beautiful countryside."*

*(Sept 12) "We are getting to be more comfortable in the
apartment.*

*Jeannine has her office set up in a corner and it seems to work
pretty well. People call her and she goes out to see them just as
before. Very few even visited her home office at Los Arboles, so
there is no change there. And she goes to pick up her mail at the
NYL office as before.*

*I have set up my easel in another corner of the same room.
It is crowded, so we share time. I have by now unpacked all my
painting supplies, but have not yet begun to paint—so many other
things to do. I went through all the genealogical file that I have and
divided it into three parts: Hudson ancestors, Palmer ancestors
and the Harvey-Bertha family. Then I wrote down the names of*

---

34. Unpublished Journal of *Oregon Trip Summer 1988* by Craig Hudson.

*all the people of which I had memories. My next project is to write
sketches of each of these people to put into the genealogy to make
it more interesting . . .*

*Since my last letter, Jeannine and I drove to Silver City to
take one of my paintings to the Grant County exhibit at Piños
Altos . . . It was an old mining town. The art gallery was the
abandoned church. My painting did not sell, but comments were
complimentary.*

*We have been giving thought to where we will move next.
Town houses are small separate houses with small yards and we
think this would be nice. Mamie's house is on a small lot; but the
house is too small for the 3 of us. She is beginning to need much
attention and we are thinking of remodeling her house to accommodate us and to build me a studio in the back. We found out that
it's do-able, but we're still in the talking stage."*[35]

The trip to Canyon de Chelly heralded a large family gathering including grandchildren. Elianne and Kelly came from Seattle with six month-old
daughter, Olivia. Marc and Isabel and year-old daughter, Aubrey joined
the group from Española. In addition to her work with New York Life, the
boxcar project was involving much of Jeannine's time. The autumn season
inspired Craig with his painting.

*(22 Nov) Our beautiful Indian Summer is definitely past and the
nip of winter is settling in. The sky is still brilliant blue but night
temperatures now drop well below freezing. Since there is a differential of 30 to 35 degrees, days are usually still warm, however.*

*I have recently painted a rather nice landscape of the Rio
Grande Bosque with the Sandia in the background, an autumn
scene; and I am now finishing a few of the cottonwood grove at
Canyon de Chelly with its yellow fall colors on the ground as well
as overhead . . .*

*The big news, I guess, is the recent flurry of activity for the
French boxcar. It appears that there will be a rather large grant
(perhaps $10,000) to assist in emplacing the new refurbished
car at the permanent site on the Fairground. There is nothing in
writing yet, but there are telephone calls and informal letters; the
situation looks good. I am encouraging Jeannine to go for a long
range plan for a French Pavilion to be constructed over a period
of time worth $100,000; she likes the idea but is frightened by the
work implications.*

*She is already on the French bicentennial committee for next
year which will consist of two major events: the 14th of July*

35. Letter from Craig and Jeannine to 'Dad,' 15 Aug 1988, 12 Sept 1988.

celebration and the November opening of the Boxcar site which is to be attended by French notables. She is afraid of committee work because she is so dedicated that she can't shirk and so people take advantage of her."[36]

Turbulent as this year was, it still ended with a family Christmas dinner. The family photo album documents Christmas 1988 at the apartment. Their first Christmas celebrated at the new apartment included Mamie and Marc, Cassandra, Cyril, and their spouses. Among many new things to get used to was the tiny size of Jeannine's new kitchen, so much smaller than at the Los Arboles house. Thus began a new tradition of everyone bringing part of the traditional Christmas Eve dinner to help out, each of the sibling striving to maintain Jeannine's culinary standards.

36. Letter from Craig and Jeannine to 'Dad,' 22 Nov 1988.

16

Remaining Years in a New Home

1989—1996

For the first four or five months of 1989 the Boxcar continued to be a main concern. Craig helped out by painting a representation of the finished boxcar. Craig's rapid heart rate continued to be an issue. There was talk of another trip to Oregon, but no exhibits were scheduled.

> *(20 Mar) "I was in the hospital again a couple of weeks ago to arrest my rapid heart rhythm but also to try to arrive at a balance of certain medications which would give a relatively long period of even rhythm . . .*
>
> *By this time, I have had enough diagnostics to know that there are two defects of my heart, both probably traceable to my bout of rheumatic fever years ago. One is valves that leak and other is the irregular beat. In a way, both have the same effect: to make me feel weak. But there is a difference: the valve problem shows up only under exercise, while the arrhythmia shows up at all times. Surgery can probably help the valves; medication may be able to help the arrhythmia. So the surgery has been put off indefinitely. I am waiting to see if the other problem can be treated.*
>
> *Nothing seems to be going very well with Jeannine's Boxcar project just now. The money she was promised has not come in and the committee members are slipping away to other things. She needs lots of moral support. I have painted a picture representing the recondi- tioned boxcar which will serve as a model. Left to do: clean the rusty*

metal; assemble the undercarriage and mount the wheels; replace some broken boards and paint the whole thing; design and build the 40 plaques as decorations; and locate the car in its permanent setting on the fairgrounds. I can help with the plaques but all the rest must be done by others, a daunting prospect . . .

I had hoped that we would have travel plans formulated by this time, but we haven't. In part, it is due to the uncertainly of my health, in part to Jeannine's workload, in part to an impending visit by Elianne and [daughter] Olivia, in part to some painting commitments that are pending. We think the visit may be in May-June, but I'll have to confirm later. At least, I don't think there will be any exhibits in Oregon this year."

(May 8) "At last we have got ourselves straightened out! . . .

We are arriving in Portland June 19 by plane and we leave July 5. Mamie is planning to come with us . . .

Jeannine is going to Phoenix next week to attend a French celebration of great importance to her: some French government leaders will be there and the Arizona boxcar committee is having a celebration. She will also pick up a check for her own group. I was expecting to go, but it is proving to be too expensive.

My state of health seems to have settled down to pretty stable. I'm not as strong as I used to be, but I can still do what I want to do. I do have irregularities from time to time and I have to rest during the day; but I am much better."[1]

(May 1989) "Jeannine has returned from her successful trip to Phoenix on behalf of the French Boxcar Committee and the Committee for the French Bicentennial. She was able to ride with the French Vice President in his car and, as she says, 'to shake the hand that shook the hand of President de Gaulle.' It was quite a time for her since she was put up in the luxurious Ritz-Carlton Hotel."[2]

Although the Boxcar project continued to dominate much of the focus in the coming months, the Oregon trip provided Craig and Jeannine a relaxing time with family and friends. Ultimately in October a pacemaker was put in to stabilize Craig's arrhythmia. Plans to remodel Mamie's house to also accommodate Craig and Jeannine were not successful. So Jeannine turned her attention to purchasing something that would accommodate all three of them. By the end of the year Craig and Jeannine were moved into a new home.

(Aug 1989) "We have nearly given up on Mamie's house. After all the bureaucratic delays, the final report was that we would not qualify for such a large loan. Still possible, but improbable.

1. Ibid, 20 March 1989, 8 May 1989.
2. Ibid, birthday card dated May 1989.

Jeannine's work on the French boxcar continues. It is scheduled to be in place by early September, but the shelter will not be ready; the money for it has not been raised yet. Some days she is very busy with it.

We went to the 14th of July celebration in Santa Fe. It was quite an affair, with perhaps 300 people attending, some of them French . . .

We also went to the Opera in Santa Fe to see Massenet's 'Cherubim'[3], a gentle story about the loves of a young man . . . "

(Sept 1989) *"Jeannine's big project, the French Boxcar, is drawing toward a close . . . the car has been cleaned and repaired and repainted and reassembled (with a great deal of volunteer work) out on the fairgrounds just in time for the fair. The NM Fair is located in the middle of Albuquerque, unlike fairs in other states. Therefore, it serves as a center for many other activities . . .*

Jeannine is meeting the French Consul from LA to see the boxcar today. He wants to understand the logistics of the big meetings he is planning at the site in Oct and Nov, when French people will be here.

Our plans to renovate Mamie's house are dead. Jeannine has found a place where the three of us can live and we are trying to buy it. So far, we have probably qualified, but changes will have to be made in some parts of it. The problems of moving our belongings and of selling Mamie's house and moving her loom big on our horizon just now. What to get rid of is a hard problem to solve—but it must be done."[4]

(Oct 1989) *"The doctor decided I needed a pacemaker after having me wear a portable EKG device for 24 hours. My heart beat actually stopped twice for 6 seconds during that time. So after a small operation, I now have a machine in my chest that forces beats when there are lapses . . . "[5]*

(Nov 1989) *"First about my new pacemaker . . . it does not bother me at all and it certainly improves my heart action. There are no more of those long pauses that were so disturbing; and people tell me that my color and appearance are much improved. Of course, the damage done to the heart valves by the disease is still there and may be worsening slowly; but for the present, my life is much improved; I can drive again. But I still take naps.*

Fortunately Jeannine is bearing up very well. She has been under considerable strain lately: preparing for the boxcar ceremony, carrying on her usual NYL activities and seeing me through all my

3. [Editor's Note] Jules Massenet, French composer .

4. Letter from Craig and Jeannine to 'Dad,' 8 Aug 1989, 20 Sept 1989.

5. Letter from Craig to 'Dad,' 19 Oct 1989.

problems. I don't complain much, but it is still a chore to arrange for my doctor visits, etc.

The big dedication ceremony for the boxcar takes place this Sunday, day after tomorrow. She (and her committee) will transfer ownership to the State of NM. The occasion will be celebrated by having a number of notables from France as well as 50 or so French veterans meeting their American counterparts (including a couple of generals and some Medal of Honor winners). Representatives of the Governor and Mayor (both being out of town) will be here to receive the document on behalf of the State. We think Richard de Roussy de Sales will be present, he being the only one around who actually rode one of the 40 & 8s with horses in WWI. There are pictures in your books in the basement. Richard is also a Legion of Honor winner, probably the only one in NM. The French Consul and his staff will be here from LA; Jeannine is being swamped with questions of protocol. The French press as well as the American press will be here. And our little Jeannine, with her tiny voice, will be mistress of ceremonies, which frightens her. She wrote a very nice poem for the occasion . . .

My Canyon de Chelly paintings (at least 19 of them) are on display at an exhibit at the 1st Unitarian Church here . . . It is a show very much like the one at Mt Angel 2 years ago. The comments so far have been very favorable; and indeed the show looks good. There are 4 new paintings being exhibited for the first time.

Our efforts to purchase a house (rather than renovate Mamie's) finally succeeded on Oct 31 when we closed. The house was about 1400 ft^2 plus a small studio for me. There is a large bedroom for Mamie and everything is on one floor since she cannot climb stairs. The house is known as a townhouse, although in earlier times it might have been called half of a duplex. We share a wall with some neighbors—who have been pretty quiet so far. There is very little space for yard and what there is has largely been planted to rugged shrubs with an automatic dribbler system which waters slowly without much attention. However, there is a small plat for some roses and a little space for beans and tomatoes. It should do about what we can handle."

(Dec 1989) *"We are finally in our new house and nearly unpacked. We have had to make a number of changes in order to get what we wanted, such as enlarging the patio, installing storage areas and converting half of the garage into a studio. The studio is not quite finished, but it looks great, so far. It will not be large, of course; however, I think it will be what I can use . . .*

Jeannine now has a small office all to herself in which she can conduct her NYL work. It is comfortable and convenient, with lots of shelves for storage and 2 filing cabinets to contain her records.

Mamie has a large bedroom and bath for her own use. She has not moved in yet, probably won't for 2 months."[6]

During December son Marc, who worked as a civil, structural and mechanical designer, was offered a job working on the Superconducting Super Collider (SSC) in Texas south of Dallas. He accepted the position and by January 1990 he and his family moved to Texas.

January and February for Craig and Jeannine were spent continuing the business of setting up the house and studio. On March 3, 1990 Craig's father died following an illness. Craig and Jeannine and Mamie flew to Portland for the funeral. Craig's sister, Marilyn, was executor and welcomed Craig's assistance and support. They also took time to drive to Seattle for the birth of grandson Tristan. At the beginning of April they returned to Albuquerque to continue settling in, adjusting to the new house and smaller garden, painting, working at New York Life, and family.

"Thank you so much for your pleasant card last March, and for the clipping of the H E H [Harvey Edwin Hudson] obit. We were in Portland for the funeral service, but did not try to visit. Dad was the last member of our family of that generation and there are many things to do to settle the estate.

The funeral had been planned before we arrived and it was, in my view, a dismal religious affair with hardly an adequate description of Dad's life. I prefer these services to be up beat with lovely music and warmhearted eulogy.

We have been in our new house about 6 months and it is adequate in every respect. It is a townhouse of about 1800 sq ft with small yards front and back. It is located at the edge of a golf course which overlooks the city toward the mountains. So we enjoy the pleasant morning sun streaming in onto the patio, the crimson coloring of the mountains at sunset, and the twinkling lights of the city at night climbing up the mountain slopes. The Sandias are nearly 11,000 ft high with flanks clothed in fir and pine forests, with bright emerald green patches of aspens at the top. The atmosphere is rarely clear enough to see all the beauty, but a trip up on the tram lays out below the woods, the watercourses, the rocks and occasional animals.

Speaking of animals, we have fun at breakfast counting the various species of birds that come to our feeder and watching the

6. Letter from Craig and Jeannine to 'Dad,' 10 Nov 1989, 11 Dec 1989.

rabbits and prairie dogs on the golf course. The wind lashed our
hummingbird feeder around so strongly that Jeannine tied it to the
fence. Now it is available to the finches who enjoy drinking from it.
The swallows swoop over the fairways in the evening, apparently
catching flying insects.

While our big house was ideal for serving elegant French din-
ners, this one is still adequate for the lesser festivities that we can
now manage. Neither of us is as strong as we were then, especially
me, and this house is in need of much less care. I love to see Jeannine
in her broad-brimmed hat and jaunty costume out in the bright
sun tending her plants. I have 6 tomato plants, all blooming but no
fruit set yet. She has all sorts of flowering things in pots. The yards
are mostly graveled with bushes here and there maintained by an
automatic drip system. We have a tiny hidden sculpture garden.

Jeannine has an office and I have a studio. There is also a large
bedroom set aside for Jeannine's mother who will move in when
her house sells. Jeannine works several hours a day and goes to
the NYL office once a day. I keep up my painting and read my
journals. I have just finished two paintings for the Nat'l Parks
Competition, one a view of St Mary Lake in Glacier and the other
a large sandstone monolith in Canyon de Chelly; and a physicist's
eye view of the Sombrero galaxy. Another, the Andromeda galaxy,
is on the easel. I recently sold a painting of Canyon de Chelly—it
does happen, but not often."[7]

By August 1990 Mamie's house had sold and she had moved into the
new house on El Tesoro Escondido with Craig and Jeannine. All the family
was around to help, support, and celebrate, including Elianne and family
from Washington and Marc and family from Texas. In October, Mamie,
Craig and Jeannine went to Canyon de Chelly on their own as each of the
children was occupied elsewhere. The year came to a close with the usual
gathering at Christmas with old friends and as many of the family members
as were in town.

---

7. Letter from Craig to 'Louise and Dick' [Godfrey], 30 May 1990.

Galaxy NGC 5194, painted 1990

Craig was very interested in Marc's new job with the SSC. Marc's recent visit had been the opportunity for good conversation and prompted continued correspondence on the subject.

> "In Science[8], there has been a running commentary about who is going to get the privilege of doing experiments on the SSC 8–10 years hence. In particular, who will get the job of building and operating the detectors. Three men's names have appeared: Ting (CERN), Trilling (FERMILAB) and Marx (GRUMANN). So far, Trilling is in, Ting is maybe and Marx is out, for now. But Marx's proposal was designed for SSC and was not a scaled up version, so he is not refused. The others are scaled up versions from the other two installations . . .
>
> Keep your eye on diamonds made of carbon-12. It is the material with the greatest thermal conductivity and would be valuable to remove heat from inside computers if it were available—as it will be in time. That is the carbon-12 isotope. Also, a novelty of carbon is the Buckminster fuller ball, or bucky ball, a cluster of 60 atoms of carbon (any isotope) arranged in a sphere having the unit shape of the geodesic dome. It is a spherically symmetric molecule in which all four of the carbon atom bonds are equally joined; a very strong structure which may have many applications. It is found naturally in soot and other carbon smokes in tiny quantities and can be made in carbon arcs."[9]

8. [Editor's Note] Craig is probably referring to *Science Magazine*.
9. Letter from Craig to 'Marc and [Isabel],' 10 Jan 1991.

In 1991 Craig and Jeannine and Mamie traveled in the spring and again in autumn. In spring they took a road trip to Texas to spend a few days visiting Marc and family in the Dallas/Fort Worth area. Along the way they visited an old friend, John Worrell and his wife (originally from Sandia days). The return trip began with a visit to friends in San Antonio, then a stop at Carlsbad Caverns National Park and White Sands National Monument before finally returning to Albuquerque.

In September the three of them drove to the Northwest, stopping to visit the Snake River at Farewell Bend State Park in Oregon, then on to Pendleton, the Bonneville Dam and the Columbia Gorge. Time was spent with old friends and family in Oregon, and Elianne and family in Washington. The return trip took them past the Grand Canyon and the meteor crater at Winslow, Arizona.

Other matters of interest for the year were helping Mamie to settle into a new house, Jeannine's work at New York Life, and Craig's painting (3 landscapes and a scientific).

In 1992 Craig and Jeannine worked on the garden (tomatoes, roses, zinnias), traveled in the spring and fall, and went to Canyon de Chelly. Craig painted four landscape paintings. In April the trio flew to New Orleans solely as tourists! Jeannine's album includes many notes about river cruises, city and plantations tours, a swamp tour, and lots of good food. In September they flew to the Northwest visiting family, friends and spending a few days at the beach.

> *"I have not been corresponding as much as I would like because I have been writing more detailed biographies than I had at first intended for the genealogy. I came into a number of old letters, news clips, etc. for the Hudson side and it has taken much time. I managed to trace back events to the point where the Hudsons & the Palmers got together originally from some comments Arthur made in a phone conversation. It was thru Molly who loved to dance and the Artisans (H S Hudson Pres) who put on dances at 28th & Clinton! Art was obliged to take dancing lessons. Also, Ruth & Lois and I had a conversation at Peach Cove, taped, which brought out a number of new facts from notes Anna had made.*
>
> *Your Mother's genealogy got me going on all of this, Louise; I had not intended to get deeply into biographical material, but now the characters are blooming; and some of the hardships and courage of the times are coming through also."*[10]

10. From Christmas card from Craig and Jeannine to 'Louise and Dick,' December 1992.

The year 1993 brought Jeannine the joy of another trip to France and the sadness of a difficult diagnosis. Craig worked on his scientific essays. Construction began on the Pavilion for the boxcar. The correspondence with cousin Louise developed into a friendly exchange of ideas and opinions as well as family news.

> (March 1993) "... at the end of April, Jeannine will fly to Paris, visit a few days, and then bring back her old friend Ann-Marie to stay with us for 3 weeks. Ann-Marie's daughter, coming from a stay in S.F., will pick her up and escort her back to Paris. So Jeannine has been making reservations and plans to show Ann-Marie everything here. A-M was J's baby-sitter when J was very young, and we don't know how she will do here: we are at 5000 ft and Santa Fe is at 7000 ft. It would really be a pity if the altitude bothered her. She has had no experience with elevations, but is in good health. So we are hoping the visit will be rewarding. And the trip to France will be good for Jeannine. This will be her first alone and she is looking forward to doing all sorts of things in Paris . . .
>
> What do you know about proteins from plants? I understand that animal digestion rearranges plant proteins but that animals cannot manufacture amino acids from sugars, starches and fats and therefore cannot manufacture proteins. So we depend on plant-eating animals (ungulates, etc) for a large part of our processed protein. Have plant banks devised a way to segregate seeds into the kinds of plant protein produced?
>
> I'm afraid I've run out of zip on the family history project, at least for the present. The Palmer branch needs editing, but I don't see any new material showing up. The Hudson branch is in rough draft except for my own story . . .
>
> We probably won't get to the NW this fall. Too much needs doing here . . . "
>
> (Sept 1993) "I agree with you that the Forest Products people are asking for more than is their due. It would be nice if a natural resource would be spared complete wipe-out. We are having a similar problem here in the SW with mining—uranium, coal, copper, molybdenum. Protect the industry in the short term, neglect the environment in the long term. In the mining industry, what often is left behind are large sterile areas of acid leaching. With the IBM, GM etc layoffs, the problem is a little different: direct impact on natural resources is not threatened. But we have made a tremendous investment in the training of these people, training in the wrong directions, as it turns out, so that now this valuable resource is also wasted. Health care is not the greatest challenge Clinton has.

Jeannine went to Paris, as expected, stayed 10 days . . . She stayed in the same retirement home as Ann-Marie, went out alone nearly every day and soaked up the atmosphere she has been remembering with so much pleasure. She saw some relatives and had visits with friends—altogether, she brought home enough photographs and materials to fill a whole album. After Ann-Marie was here, we four drove around the SW, showing her the sights. She loved it! . . .

Jeannine had been feeling a little strange for 2 months or so; her left side didn't work as well as her right and she was tired. After the trip noted above, we studied her situation for awhile, then went to a neurologist. Tests followed and then the diagnosis: incipient Parkinson's disease. So she is taking medication for it and the symptoms have receded, for how long, no one can tell. After a few days of depression, she has bounced back and appears to be her old self.

The French Boxcar project appears to be coming to a conclusion. The State Fair (in the middle of town) has accepted it. Money was raised (mostly Jeannine) and it has matured into a broad new stage covered by a flying canopy with two flagpoles showing the Blue-White & Red and exhibiting the two NM boxcars: one, the old original nearly wrecked; two, the one J. bought in France, had brought here and fixed up.

I have been very preoccupied with my Temperature Essay. It starts out with a section describing the meaning of temperature; then it describes the properties of the science of particles and fields and gravitation; then cosmology and the Big Bang; then stars and galaxies; then very high temperatures; then biological temperatures and the origin of life; then planets and the history of Man; and finally ultra-low temperatures. Everything flows smoothly by well-understood science except the Big Bang. There conservation of energy is discontinuous."

(Dec 1993) "I am pleased to be able to report that Jeannine's situation is not noticeably worsening so, as you said, the tiger is at bay for the moment. However many little things remind her of the tiger. We visited the glass shop of a scientific glass blower recently (a friend) and she tried to blow a Christmas tree ball under his guidance. Mostly it went well, but she was surprised to find it difficult to coordinate the left and right hands, necessary in that operation. . .sometimes she burns a finger in the kitchen, a lack of coordination—little things that remind her of how effective the medication is. Fortunately she is cheerful and bright, although she is learning to scale down her expectations. We used to entertain

about once a week; now she feels more comfortable with twice a month. But generally we keep up a good level of activity . . .

I have been working on my essay and now have it almost finished but the typing is going slowly. I add a final chapter that you will enjoy: the difference between reality (depends on temperature) and spirituality (independent of temperature) . . .

My latest painting is 'X-ray Star,' my contribution to a show in honor of the discovery of X-rays."[11]

In October 1993 Congress officially cut funding to the Superconducting Super Collider (SSC). Funding had never been assured on the project; funding had to be renewed each year. Although Marc and family found the climate and social surroundings challenging compared to their native state of New Mexico, Marc had enjoyed the work.

"So many people were unable to believe the result. It didn't make sense. But in a way, it is in the category of NAFTA[12]*: opinion is so sharply divided. Many bench scientists (i.e. people who work on one-man type projects) were opposing the SSC partly out of jealousy for funding and partly out of isolation from the field of particle physics. I'm sure they hope the SSC funding will be shifted into their fields; but it won't. It will fall to the drive to reduce the deficit.*

As I write, the battle for NAFTA is approaching its crisis. We here (Mother and our friends) are pro-NAFTA. But the unions are strongly opposed and if it passes next Wed, I think the unions will suffer more than just a political defeat."[13]

Grandson Nicholas was born in January 1994 to Marc and Isabel. In mid-May Craig, Jeannine and Mamie flew to the Northwest for family, friends and the Oregon coast. During this Oregon trip, an effort was made to get all the Palmer relatives together for a luncheon at a restaurant, reminiscent of the family gatherings of old at Peach Cove. The Fourteenth of July was celebrated for the first time at the French Pavilion at the State Fairgrounds. Later in the summer, Mamie became ill and was incapacitated for some time. The threesome was able to take an overnight trip to a favorite spot, Mesa Verde [Colorado]. Craig was no longer painting; he spent most of his time with his writing projects.

11. Letters from Craig and Jeannine to 'Louise and Dick,' 10 March 1993, 8 Sept 1993, 12 Dec 1993.

12. [Editor's Note] NAFTA, North American Free Trade Agreement, did pass and took effect January 1, 1994.

13. Letter from Craig to 'Marc and [Isabel],' 15 Nov 1993.

(July 1994) *"What a summer! No rain; 30 consecutive days of over 90° and 10 consecutive days of over 100 (peak 107). Our air conditioner is optimized for 90° and sometimes the house only cooled down to 80° at night . . . By now, however, clouds are beginning to build up in the west and there may be a break coming in the weather. We surely hope so; this is debilitating.*

We thank you for the nice note about the Cousins' Lunch . . .

I learned from Ed Palmer that his father John Henry Palmer was born in Dark and Bloody Ground, KY. But I could not find this location in any atlas and had to conclude that it wasn't a real place. However, a friend of mine from Kentucky said that he had heard of it but could not locate it; it was not dignified by a place name. The family record claimed it was in Howard County, which does not exist. This could be a corruption of either Hardin or Garrard, both of which exist. In the historical preliminaries of Carl Sandberg's 'Abraham Lincoln[14]*' there appears a quote by Chief Dragging Canoe of the Chickamauga Indians alluding to a county across the Cumberland Gap in Kentucky called Dark and Bloody Ground, an old Indian name for a particular battle field. This was about in 1790. John Henry was born in 1818, not so very much later. So I conclude that 'Howard' is a corruption of 'Garrard,' which is the closer of the two to the Cumberland Gap. There was a 1810 census of Garrard county which did not list the father Burton; but the 1820 census does. So I think our ancestor John Henry was born into Burton's family in Garrard County after the 1810 census . . .*

Chapter 12 [of the Essay on Temperature] is the essence of the essay; it is my concept of how the brain works, what we think of as 'free will,' where ethics come from, etc. It is based on my premise that reality is coincident with temperature which is well established in the first part of the essay."[15]

The year 1994 came to a close with the Craig spending most of his time writing, either on his essays or genealogy material. Painting was set aside for the time being. Jeannine was working to compile the documentation for the French Pavilion and boxcar project.

" . . . one of the big events of the year was our visit to the NW and the cousin's luncheon. We enjoyed that very much . . . While we were up there, we were able to have dinners with friends and to see our little family in Renton [Washington]. And we were at the beach for awhile, though that visit was somewhat marred by

14. Craig is probably referring to *Abe Lincoln Grows Up* by Carl Sandburg, 1928, Harcourt Brace & Company.

15. Letter from Craig and Jeannine to 'Louise and Dick,' 3 July 1994.

ill-health. We were so pleased to be able to get pictures of the cousins—the first ever, I think.

Growing old is a bitter-sweet experience. On the one hand, infirmities of the mind and body make everyday living such a tribulation. But on the other hand, the accumulation of years brings so many memories of good times and so many friends!

Madame Dumas, who was so vivacious during the NW trip, has become very forgetful and racked with pain—nearly bedridden. It's so sad for Jeannine to have to watch this deterioration in one she has always looked up to—indeed, the one who made it possible for J. and me to marry in the first place.

Jeannine's Parkinson's is developing slowly enough that she is not yet distressed by it; but the ugly signs are there and she dreads the future. We are trying to fill her days with pleasant things, not very easy with the demands of Mme. Dumas. Fortunately, my heart problems have pretty well stabilized, so that is no longer a threat. She has a major task to complete—composing the document to record the events of the last 10 years to establish the French Pavilion at the State Fair for which she was responsible. She is about half-done (it will consist of hundreds of pages of letters, photos and text) and is looking forward to the time when she can take up the other projects that have been on back burners.

As for myself, I have finally finished my 300 pp Essay on Temperature and have had the typed version reproduced and bound. It appears now that a second printing will be necessary. Hardly anyone understands it, but I have the satisfaction of having set down in one place all of the contemporary thought on the subject. That pleases me. Also, I have written my autobiography (up to the time of meeting Jeannine in Paris, at least). It seems silly to write such a detailed biography of a person of such modest accomplishments; but it really is a document of the times, so I feel it was worth it. And I have several other documents to finish: two on the subject of refraction of light in the atmosphere (about 400 pp each describing in detail all the studies that have been made through out the years on mirage, Fata Morgana, shadow bands, the Green Flash, etc); one of the phenomena of sound in all its ramifications (300 pp); and, if I can get to it, one on shock propagation (100 pp). these are mostly written but in sad need of editing. So my painting has been on hold for awhile.

There is a new building in town which I think may be a repository for wild seeds. I want to check it out, but have not yet had the chance. When the public finally realizes that most of our agricultural and livestock products are mutants that cannot survive

without the intersession of Man, I think there will be much more
interest in maintaining stocks of the wild things."[16]

Mamie had a short stay in the hospital at the beginning of 1995 but recuperated well at home and celebrated her 90th birthday in June with many friends present. In the spring a visit from Elianne and family from Washington brightened everyone's spirits. This year the third stage of the Boxcar project was underway. A kiosk was built to house the Merci Train information and some of the artifacts that arrived originally with the boxcar.

Craig and Jeannine had a tradition to light a candle on Christmas Eve to celebrate their Christmases together. As the years went by, they would exchange a large candle for ten small candles. This year, 1995, they lit a candle for their 48th Christmas together.

> (*Sept 1995*) "*These are duplicates of photos of my paintings taken in order to complete my record of drawings and paintings in album form. There are 236 of them dating from 1932 (still in grammar school) to 1993. The archive is nearly finished now. Of some interest: there is an exhibit of 8 of my science paintings at the UNM [Univ. of New Mexico] engineering complex—and just as I had thought my exhibiting days were over.*
>
> *Since 1993, date of my last painting, I have done a lot of writing: completed (maybe) the Palmer history and (maybe) the Hudson history and made a strong beginning on my own life story and marriage to Jeannine (all those betrothal letters were a great help). I got as far as J. coming to this country and our preparations to set up life at graduate school at U of O, so there is much left to do. But I also wrote the 300 page essay on temperature and edited my notes from years ago on the physics of vision. These latter two have been 'published' in the sense that they were bound and distributed. A third on sound is in the works. But now it is time to get back to painting.*
>
> *Jeannine is even today putting her last touches on the French Pavilion at the State Fair grounds. It has become the center for statewide activities of a cultural nature (almost no sports) so her two boxcars and the newly erected kiosk, all housed under a giant graceful canopy, are a very appropriate addition. The kiosk contains a small collection of the artifacts sent originally with the boxcar in 1949; most have been lost. The NM car (the one J. brought from France in 1987) now looks very much like the Oregon car in Astoria; the original one is there but not refurbished . . .*
>
> *Jeannine is now in the process of retiring from NYL, a process that is slow and careful. She can hardly wait to finally break the*

---

16. Letter from Craig to 'Louise and Dick,' 1 Dec 1994.

bond that has held her for so long. One of the factors, of course, is that her Parkinson's is slowly worsening—not showing but eroding her physical fitness. She has had to give up [her exercise class], a sad step.

Mamie has had a rejuvenation. In the last 4 months, she has not only shaken off the miseries that we thought were terminal; but she has also given up a number of her old self-imposed dietary restraints and now eats anything. Of course, one cannot really turn back the clock and at 90 she is still very frail. But her life (and ours) has much improved . . .

My health is not much worse than when I last saw you. My ailment, heart failure, cannot get better but at least (through doctors' interventions) it is worsening only slowly. At the present time, I am enrolled in a medical study to evaluate a new experimental medication to strengthen the heart. So far, after some weeks on the medication, I see no change and feel I am one of those on the placebo."

(Dec holiday card) "Mamie celebrated her 90th birthday. She is fading but is still active and in good spirits.

Jeannine does not let her Parkinson's hold her back . . .

Craig received his competition prize—a video disc player— from Kodak. His 'Beauty of Fluids exhibit is showing at UNM Engineering. Jeannine set it up.

Craig has now finished 'Temperature,' 'Vision' and 'Sound in the Atmosphere' essays. More to follow."[17]

In February 1996 Craig was hospitalized for a severe respiratory infection and continued heart problems. This had a very severe effect on Craig's health.

"I am pleased to be able to write this letter. February was a bad month.

The problem began simply enough. Jeannine took me to the Emergency room in the middle of the night (Feb 15) with difficulty breathing. It was diagnosed as bronchitis and I was hospitalized for antibiotic treatment.

A day later, I was moved to the cardiac intensive care unit. My weak heart was acting up. But treatment of the heart problem caused my kidneys to fail. Treatment of the kidneys worsened my heart, and so on—back and forth. One doctor said 'he isn't going to make it.'

But I did, although I came out of it weak as a kitten, unable to stand, hardly able to hold my head up. Through out it all, Jeannine had been standing by. Much of that time, I was only vaguely aware

17. Ibid, 7 Sept 1995, Dec holiday card 1995.

of what was going on. She filled me in later. Her motto is 'never fear, Jeannine is here,' for which I am grateful without bound. In due time, I was moved to the rehabilitation unit, a pleasant cheery place where the staff really tried to help. Even the food was good, though I could eat very little. And after a few more days, I came home but not before my doctor said frankly 'Your prognosis is not good.'

    So for the time being, I am trying to regain my strength (some what) and planning what is really important to do."[18]

When home, Craig continued his writing and reading. His mind was active and he had a desire to finish as many things as possible with his remaining days. His letters to Louise show that he continued to have an inquisitive mind.

(March 1996) "In the weeks following hospitalization I have been slowly recovering my strength, not that it will ever really return; but I am able to walk around freely, using the cane only to go outside.

    Two problems of old age are worth mentioning because I have never encountered them before. For a couple of years, the nerves in my lower legs have been dying, giving me a somewhat drunken gait and, of course, a certain numbness has set in. The cane is very comforting. The other has to do with the tiny sphincter at the end of the Eustachian tube where it enters the inner ear. It controls inner pressure on the eardrum and is normally closed. Mine are both open and the roar of my breathing and of my speaking make it difficult to hear. I guess these problems will be with me forever.

    But I have been able to have printed my third essay 'Sound in the Atmosphere.' It is long (450 p) and printing was expensive so only a few copies were made. They are part of my legacy in science to my children. The effort to give a better description to acoustics led to the development mathematical analysis some 200 years ago, so the essay is full of mathematics. But there are interesting parts, too—especially on natural sounds.

    I have been reading a most interesting little book (the most interesting books are always little) about language and its origins, by Derek Bickerton. The old theory was that the use of language caused the human brain to grow as large as it is, language being the only property that is truly human. Not so, says Bickeron. The large brain was characteristic of the Neanderthals who had no real language. No one knows what the selection was that led to their large brains. But as the Neanderthals died out, the CroMagnons came in and with them came language. Possibly because of a mutation of the throat that made speech possible. As Bickerton writes:

18. Letter from Craig to 'All' (this copy from Louise), 5 March 1996.

Neanterthals	Increase in brain size = no increase in intelligence
Cro Magnons	No increase in brain size = increase in intelligence
	Speech reorganizes the already large brain.
Bickerton also defines:	Proto language—a the sounds animal use
	Language—sounds that involve lexicon and syntax

Some animals have simple lexicons (vocabulary) but none have syntax (grammar) and cannot be made to develop it.

I have long thought that the human brain was evolving somehow. Bickerton argues that it is by complexity not size . . .

Jeannine's Parkinson's has not yet produced any of the dread symptoms and she is very active and enjoys a well-balanced life . . .

(April 1996) "Thank you for the Portland Punch[19]—truly an elixir of the Northwest. Unobtainable here, of course. Actually, the package came one day ahead of the letter. Perhaps the postal delivery, as opposed to the package delivery, is slowed by the glut of advertising. Once I complained to the postman about junk mail and how to stop it. He said 'don't try; it pays my salary.'

Indeed, our perception of age changes both by aging and by medical advances. When I had rheumatic fever at age 10, the doctor said to Mother, 'expect him to live to about 20.' But that age came and went, as did many others, and finally the combinations of good genes and improved medical practice got me on the way to 80. And on good days, I feel like 60 . . .

Jeannine's Parkinson's disease is progressing ever so slowly. She is very active in a support group and can see firsthand where time is taking her; but she refuses to bow to the changes and keeps a life full of activities, family, friends, and—more and more now that NYL is leaving the picture—of things she has always wanted to do—like poetry.

Our daughter Elianne and family spent 10 days here (from Seattle) and we greatly enjoyed it. On one day, all four children and spouses and grandchildren were able to come together for a huge party. We have pictures as well as memories and it will become a major section of Jeannine's album. But this time, that album has run into many volumes and seems to grow almost too fast for her to keep up with. She also has a little black book of the

---

19. [Editor's Notes] Portland Punch, a blend of loganberry and raspberry juices, is a fruit drink that dates from the early 1960s. All of Craig's children remember drinking it on summer vacations in Oregon. .

dinners served to guests (going all the way back to 1952), which
includes one memorable occasion including Henry Kissinger! And
the cookbook! A lifetime of testing French recipes has resulted in a
volume for posterity.

I have brought my biography up to Dec 1952. What a year
that was! Full of activities and decisions, the greatest one being the
move from Oregon to New Mexico. It was difficult to do but as the
years rolled by, clearly it was a good decision.

Now I shall put the biography aside for a few weeks and finish
my 4th essay: Earth's Atmosphere. It has long been a subject of
interest and is so near completion. The number 3 essay 'Sound in
the Atmosphere,' recently completed, really depends on essay #4;
but it just worked out that this succession was easier—like Mozart
mis-numbering some of his works.

While the children were here, little Olivia (about 8) wanted to
paint. So I got out the colors, the brushes, the turpentine and an
old canvas of an astronomical scene. And she painted a beauti-
ful big star in one corner. Do you remember Van Gogh's 'Starry
Night'? Very much like that. But the real news is that once the
smell of the paint got in my nose, I had a strong desire to paint
again myself—so I will have to save time for it."[20]

In the autumn, on a suggestion that Craig's heart might have less difficulty functioning at sea level instead of at 5000 feet altitude, Craig and
Jeannine made a trip by train to San Diego to visit with Craig's sister and her
family. The strain became too much, however, and Craig was again hospitalized in San Diego. Craig stated that he wanted to be at home for his last days.
Jeannine, with the help of Elianne who had come from Seattle, flew Craig
home to Albuquerque. Craig died at home of congestive heart failure on
December 2, 1996.

> *"My accomplishments as I see them*
>   *Raising a fine family*
>   *Having lovely Jeannine for all these years*
>   *Writing the histories of the family*
>   *Writing my Essays*
>   *Leaving a collection of beloved paintings*
>   *Making furniture (I loved woodworking)*
>   *Designing our Family House"*[21]

20. Letters from Craig and Jeannine to 'Louise and Dick,' 30 March 1996, 23 April
1996.

21. Craig's unpublished notes, 8 September 1996.

A memorial was held for Craig in February. It included good food, good wine, good music, good friends and family. Many friends, who could not attend, sent letters and messages to Craig's family. Herman Johansen was one of those:

> *"In Memorial:*
> *Bereaved wife, sons and daughters, relatives and many friends of Craig C. Hudson:*
> *He was born June 29, 1918 and died on December 2, 1996 at the age of 78. We are gathered here to mourn and to celebrate a life now gone from us but this releases to us all a flood of memories of all our past experiences and emotions.*
> *Craig Hudson was a man of many aspects: devoted family man, dedicated scientist and scholar, artist of note, outdoorsman, gourmet, and judge of good wine. He was a friend to many. He was also a prolific writer and his last days were marked by his urgency to complete a series of essays on several abstruse topics in physics: essay on temperature, the seeing sense, the Earth's atmosphere, sound in the atmosphere, astronomical refractions, and his last essay, refraction with dispersion, left unfinished by the swift progress of his illness. You will surely agree that this is a remarkable accomplishment of writing for a dying man. His family received copies of these essays and I was also privileged to receive them . . .*
> *Craig Hudson was highly trained in physics and mathematics and applied this knowledge for the many years he worked at Sandia. He also displayed a great talent for organizing symposia and meetings with many scientists of note attending, thus promoting a free exchange of ideas which was a hallmark of Craig Hudson's character. Craig Hudson was an artist of special ability. His lifetime work as a painter in oils ranged from portraits to landscapes to depictions of scientific phenomenon in painting. In his last days he had resolved to switch to watercolor as being a new challenge. Sadly he never made it.*
> *I may lay claim to being one of Craig's oldest friends. We first met at a stormy, wet outing in the mountains in Oregon in the fall of 1939, a college sponsored event which was a disaster. But somehow Craig had managed to find an abandoned tent and frame in the woods and invited me in with him. The first of many times when he offered me support and encouragement . . .*
> *Over those years we corresponded regularly and exchanged occasional visits. Always there were the long and detailed talks on a great variety of topics. You name it! There was nothing in science, politics, religion, sex, war, ethics, art, music, medicine that we did*

not examine. Sometimes we stopped only from exhaustion from talking so much . . .

After the receipt of Craig's essay on the Earth's atmosphere, I read it through then I wrote him that I missed any mention of the Coriolis Effect. In a letter and a phone conversation, he explained that the Coriolis was not truly a force it was an effect and it was a rather a trivial one at that. I knew this and was just pulling his chain to let him know that I had appreciated his great and very solid effort and contribution.

So to the very last he was teacher, confidant, patient explainer, and careful designer of and illustrator of ideas, concepts and theories. He was also a consummate critic and observer. He completely enjoyed, we might even say, he worshiped his wife and family and most certainly they loved and respected him and this love of family extended to his forbears as well so that he compiled an extensive genealogy to add to the rich heritage of his own.

I regret that age, infirmity and distance did not allow me to attend this final solemn tribute to a great and good friend. All of us are the poorer for his death but vastly enriched to have known him when he lived."[22]

Elianne and Craig, 1985

22. from Transcript of audio recording by Herman Johansen, February 1997.

Craig at his easel, 1987

Proud grandparents, 1988

Craig on Sandia Peak, 1995

Appendix
Catalog of Craig's Paintings

* Indicates paintings that are reproduced in this edition. See *List of Illustrations* for page numbers.

1932 Mediterranean Village (oil)

1933 Apple Orchard (oil)
Maple Tree (watercolor)

1934 Italian Girl (oil)

1935 Becalmed (watercolor)
Pink Lady (oil)
Oregon (oil)

1936 Le Corsaire (oil)
Desert Mirage (gouache)

1938 H. S. Hudson (oil)*

1939 Wyoming Buffalo (gouache)
Yellowstone Spring (gouache)

1940 Camp Kettle (watercolor)

1941 Still Life with a Mushroom (oil)*
Jar of Poppies (oil)
Still Life (oil)

1942 Bombers (watercolor and pencil)
Rain (watercolor)
Kloo Hills (watercolor)
Canyon Bridge II (watercolor)
Canyon Campsite (watercolor)
Cloud Shadows (watercolor)
Yukon Hills (watercolor)
St. Elias Mountains I
(watercolor)

St. Elias Mountains II
(watercolor)
Axmen at Work (gouache)*
A Tall Tale (watercolor)
Swamp Pond (gouache)
Fall Colors (watercolor)
St. Elias Mountains VI
(watercolor)
Yukon Tragedy (oil)
Grim Leader (watercolor)

1943 St. Elias Mountains VII (oil)
Florida Scene (pastel)
Beach Watch (pastel)
Cliff Anet – looking at artist
(pastel)*
Cliff Anet – eyes averted
(pastel)
Mrs Isaacson (pastel)*

1946 Mount Adams (pastel)
Camp Cook (oil)*

1947 Bison (oil)

1948 New Wife (oil)*
Dezedeash Valley (oil)*

1949 Mountain Stream (oil)

1954 Lady Bathing (oil)*
Forest Glen (oil)

1957 Midnight Watch (watercolor)
A Bull Run at Hendaye (pen and ink)
Jemez Canyon (watercolor)
Nuclear Fireball (watercolor)

1958 Prehistoric Bull (oil)
Abstract Galaxy I (oil)
Vision of Venice (oil)
Summer Flowers (oil)

1959 Mary Ellen (oil)

1960 Oregon Coast I (oil)

1963 Voluptuous Bosom (oil)

1964 Forest Glade (oil)
New House (oil)

1965 Oregon Coast II (oil)
Gentle Beach (oil)
Pseudo Geometry (oil)
Elianne (oil)
Cyril (oil)
Opera Lovers (oil)

1966 Youth (oil)

1982 Pueblo Bonito (oil)
Shock I, subsonic (oil)
Shocks II, supersonic (oil)
Excitons (oil)
Krafla (oil)
Water Strike (oil)
La Soufrière (oil)
Columbia Glacier (oil)
Sahara Loneliness (oil)
Convalute Bedding (oil)
Continental Fragment (oil)
Deep Sea Phillipsite (oil)
St Helens Topography (oil)
St Helens Erupts (oil)*
Spirit Lake Primeval (oil)
In Search of Pain (oil)
Heart Muscle (oil)
Nucleus Exploding (oil)
Uranium Fission (oil)
Cell Parasite (oil)
Plant Crystals (oil)
Orion Nebula (oil)
Fire on Io (oil)
NGC 4603 (oil)

Aurora's Crown (oil)
Baby Diamonds (oil)

1983 October (oil)
Canyon de Chelly (oil)
Black Canyon I (oil)
Betatakin Sunset (oil)
Rio Grande Canyon/Gorge (oil)
Sandia Granite (oil)
Limestone Blossoms (oil)
Still Dunes (oil)
Chaco Sunset (oil)
San Juan Canyon (oil)
Deep Pool (oil)
Mesa Fault (oil)
White Sands (oil)
Canyon Bottom (oil)
Chinle Mud (oil)
Rock Salt (oil)
Quartz Grain (oil)
Chert (oil)
Gypsum Chrystals (oil)
Morning Glories (oil)
Buttercup (oil)
Pasque Flower (oil)
Shooting Star (oil)
Entrance to Le Combel (oil)
Magdalenian Man (oil)
Horse at Lascaux (oil)
Horse at Niaux (oil)
Hunt at Lascaux (oil)

1984 Bull at Lascaux (oil)
Aurocks Gambol – Lascaux (oil)*
Black Ibex – Niaux (oil)
Rhinoceros – at Rouffignac (oil)
Feline of Les Trois Frères (oil)
Mammoth at Pech Merle (oil)
Horse at Commarque (oil)
Venus de La Magdelaine (oil)
Trillium (oil)
Blood Root (oil)
Iceland Poppy (oil)
Swertia (oil)
Penstemon (oil)
Methadone Molecule (oil)
Slow Flow (oil)
Wall Drag (oil)
Tornado (oil)

Comber (oil)
Solar Gas (oil)

1985 Liquid Sheet (oil)
The Wake (oil)
Galaxy I (II) (oil)
Thermals (oil)*
Randomness (oil)
Benard Cells (oil)
Karman Street (oil)*
Shocks III (oil)
Anvil Cloud (oil)
Roll Clouds (oil)
Boundary Mixing (oil)
Shedding Eddy (oil)
Swirl (oil)
Vortex Rings (oil)
Bubble Burst (oil)
Black Hole (oil)
Lightning Cloud (oil)
Galactic Center (oil)
Earth Storm I (oil)
Earth Storm II (oil)

1986 Sand Bars (oil)
Morning Light (oil)
Old Trail (oil)
High Noon (oil)
White House in Moonlight (oil)
Cool Shade (oil)*
Summer Canyon (oil)
White House 1984 (oil)
Desert Varnish (oil)
White House 1149 (oil)
Indian Pink Spigelia (oil)

1987 Fissure (oil)
Mesa Top (oil)
Waves of Stove (oil)
Trail Head (oil)
Spider Rock (oil)*
Tsegi (oil)
Inner Glow (oil)
Cyril's Arch (oil)
Cleft (oil)
Marc – Arriving Storm (oil)

Black Canyon II (oil)
Blue Settee (oil)
Jeannine at La Pasada (oil)
Jeannine – Wrapped in Silk (oil)
Dream (oil)
Ladies Chatting (oil)

1988 Cassandra – Wedding Day (oil)
Mountain Storm (oil)
Mysterious Mountain (oil)
High Sandias (oil)
Hunters Point (oil)
Jackson Lake (oil)
Rain Forest – Olympic (oil)
Forest Trail – Redwood (oil)
Nevada Rainstorm (oil)
Albuquerque Bosque (oil)
Cottonwood Grove (oil)

1989 Crumbling Mesa (oil)
French Boxcar (oil)
5 O'Clock Shadows (oil)
Sunset, Moonrise (oil)
Shocks IV (oil)
Shocks V (oil)
Unstructured Molecule (oil)
Summer in the Rockies (oil)

1990 Galaxy (III), Sombrero (oil)
Lookout (oil)
Galaxy (IV), NGC 5194–5 (oil)*
Galaxy (V), Andromeda (oil)
Star Genesis (oil)
Shoshone Falls (oil)*

1991 Glacier Valley (oil)
Glacier Peaks (oil)
Glacier Lake (oil)

1992 Olympic Mountains – Glacier (oil)
Mt Rainier (oil)
Yellowstone – Lower Falls (oil)
Quarai (oil)
Grand Canyon Overlook – Side canyon (oil)

1993 X-ray Star (unfinished) (oil)

Bibliography

Albuquerque Civic Symphony. http://web.archive.org/web/20090318045338/http://www.nmso.org/About/history.php

Albuquerque Historical Society. *Statehood Economy 1945-now*. http://www.albuqhistsoc.org/SecondSite/pkfiles/pk186postwareconom.htm, 2008

Albuquerque Mountain Club. http://nmmountainclub.org/who-we-are

Arcadian Flooring. *History of Terrazzo*. http://arcadianflooring.com/history.html, 2014

Auel, Jean M. *Valley of the Horses*, 1984.

Bennett Sr., Earl. *Merci Train*. http://www.mercitrain.org/, 2014

Conley, Manuel A. *What Ever Happened to Those Forty And Eights?*. France Magazine (No. 9), Fall 1987

Cummings, Robert. *Guarneri Quartet Biography*. http://www.allmusic.com/artist/guarneri-quartet-mn0001588714/biography, 2015.

Decker, Doug. *Tillamook Burn*. Oregon Encyclopedia, http://www.oregonencyclopedia.org/articles/tillamook_burn/#.VF8OEWertQM, 2014

Encyclopedia Britannica. *Cancan*. http://www.britannica.com/EBchecked/topic/92194/cancan, 2012

Forman-Brunell, Miriam (Annotated). Children and Youth in History, Item #330. http://chnm.gmu.edu/cyh/primary-sources/330, 2014

Hastings Museum. *History of Kool-Aid*. http://hastingsmuseum.org/exhibits/kool-aid/the-history-of-kool-aid, 2012

Hillman, Bill. *History of Tarzan*. http://www.tarzan.org/history_of_tarzan_part1.html

Hudson, Craig C., *Experimental Evidence of a Twinkling Layer in the Earth's Atmosphere*, Nature Magazine, Vol. 207, 247—249 (17 July 1965) http://www.nature.com/nature/journal/v207/n4994/abs/207247a0.html

Kramer, Ronald. *Pioneer Mikes: A History of Radio and Television in Oregon*. Western States Museum of Broadcasting and JPR Foundation, 2008

Life on the Home Front. *Bombs Fall on Oregon: Japanese Attacks on the State*. http://arcweb.sos.state.or.us/pages/exhibits/ww2/threat/bombs.htm, 2008

Mitchell, L. A. *A Scientific Eye for Art*. IMPACT / Albuquerque Journal Magazine, 8 Feb 1983

Olsen, N. H., & Bice, R. A. *The Albuquerque Archaeological Society: The First Twenty-five Years, 1966–1991*. The Albuquerque Archaeological Society, 1995

Portland's Rose Gardens & Rose Garden Store. http://www.rosegardenstore.org/rosefestivalhistory.cfm

Prats, Elia J. *Dekum Building*. http://www.hmdb.org/marker.asp?marker=1155, 2007

Random House, Inc. *Larousse Gastronomique.* http://www.randomhouse.com/book/34555/larousse-gastronomique-by-librairie-larousse/9780307464910/#aboutthebook, 2012

Remley, David A. *Crooked Road: The Story of the Alaska Highway,* 1976

Time Magazine. *Education: Husky Reed. Vol. XXXIV No. 23* 2012. http://content.time.com/time/magazine/article/0,9171,762975,00.html

Time Magazine. *Astronomy: The Twinkle Belt.* (30 July 1965) http://www.time.com/time/magazine/article/0,9171,834064,00.html

Wikipedia. *Manilkara Chicle.* http://en.wikipedia.org/wiki/Manilkara_chicle, 2014

Index

Note: Painting titles refer to Craig's paintings unless other name is given. Page numbers with "n" refer to information only found in a footnote.

www.ingramcontent.com/pod-product-compliance
Lightning Source LLC
Chambersburg PA
CBHW071837270326
41929CB00013B/2027